Praise for

COACH, Third Edition

I was thrilled to learn about this updated version of *COACH*, and equally enthusiastic once I reviewed its contents. *COACH* is the quintessential planning tool for teachers and IEP team members.

—Colleen A. Thoma, Ph.D.
Professor, Department of Special Education & Disability Policy,
Virginia Commonwealth University, School of Education

A powerful and gentle tool for helping parents and educators focus on what is most important in the lives of individuals with disabilities, providing the framework for designing and implementing dynamic quality-of-life supports.

—Joanne M. Cafiero, Ph.D.
private autism and augmentative communication consultant

The most thoughtful, systematic approach to planning for the inclusive education of students with intensive support needs available today.

—Michael L. Wehmeyer Ph.D.
Professor, Department of Special Education, University of Kansas

This revised edition of *COACH* does it all, assisting teams to create and implement a high-quality program that addresses both accessing and making progress in the general education curriculum and meeting individual student needs.

—Terri Vandercook, Ph.D.
Chair, Special Education and Gifted Education Department,
University of St. Thomas, Minneapolis

The principles of *COACH* support full inclusion and family–school collaboration. . . . This is an outstanding text and one I recommend highly for teacher preparation programs, school districts, and community agencies!

—Katrina Arndt, Ph.D.
Assistant Professor, Inclusive Education Department,
St. John Fisher College, Rochester, New York

There is no better tool for planning rich, appropriate educational programs for learners who have intensive support needs. Rooted in just principles and current research, *COACH* honors the wisdom of families, while effectively guiding teams to translate vision into practice.

—Roberta Schnorr, Ph.D.
Professor, The State University of New York at Oswego

An essential tool . . . presents amazing practice strategies for supporting collaboration between and among school and family. A must have for building successful outcomes for kids!

—Christi Kasa, Ph.D.
Associate Professor, College of Education,
University of Colorado, Colorado Springs

COACH 3

Choosing Outcomes & Accommodations for Children

THIRD EDITION

COACH 3

Choosing Outcomes & Accommodations for Children

THIRD EDITION

A Guide to Educational Planning for Students with Disabilities

by

Michael F. Giangreco, Ph.D.
University of Vermont
Burlington

Chigee J. Cloninger, Ph.D.
University of Vermont
Burlington

and

Virginia S. Iverson, M.Ed.
Vermont State I-Team
Hinesburg

·P·A·U·L·H·
BROOKES
PUBLISHING Cº ®

Baltimore • London • Sydney

KH

Paul H. Brookes Publishing Co.
Post Office Box 10624
Baltimore, Maryland 21285-0624

www.brookespublishing.com

All royalties from the sale of this book will be donated to nonprofit agencies that address human needs.

Typeset by Integrated Publishing Solutions, Grand Rapids, Michigan.
Manufactured in the United States of America by
Versa Press, Inc., East Peoria, Illinois.

The individuals described in this book are composites or real people whose situations are masked and are based on the authors' experiences. In all instances, names and identifying details have been changed to protect confidentiality.

Library of Congress Cataloging-in-Publication Data

Giangreco, Michael F., 1956–
     Choosing outcomes and accommodations for children (COACH) : a guide to educational planning for students with disabilities / by Michael F. Giangreco, Chigee J. Cloninger, and Virginia Salce Iverson. – 3rd ed.
        p.   cm.
     Includes bibliographical references and index.
     ISBN-13: 978-1-59857-187-5 (pbk. with cd)
     ISBN-10: 1-59857-187-7
     1. Children with disabilities—Education—United States.   2. Mainstreaming in education—United States.   3. Home and school—United States.   4. Quality of life—United States.   5. Inclusive education—United States.   I. Cloninger, Chigee J., 1946–   II. Iverson, Virginia Salce, 1951–   III. Title.
LC4031.G5 2011
371.9–dc22   2011004782

British Library Cataloguing in Publication data are available from the British Library.

2015   2014   2013   2012   2011

10   9   8   7   6   5   4   3   2   1

3/6/10

Contents

†Fillable forms are available on the accompanying CD-ROM.

CD-ROM Contents

[†] Fillable forms
** CD-ROM only

About the Authors

Michael F. Giangreco, Ph.D., Professor, Department of Education and Center on Disability and Community Inclusion, University of Vermont, 208 Colchester Avenue, Mann Hall 301A, Burlington, Vermont 05405-1757

Michael F. Giangreco has devoted the past 35 years to working with children and adults with disabilities, their families, and service providers in a variety of capacities, including as a special education teacher, community residence counselor, school administrator, educational consultant, university teacher, and researcher. Dr. Giangreco received his bachelor's degree from Buffalo State College, graduate degrees from the University of Vermont (M.Ed.) and University of Virginia (Ed.S.), and his doctoral degree from Syracuse University (Ph.D.). His work focuses on various aspects of education for students with disabilities within general education classrooms, such as curriculum planning and adaptation, related services decision making and coordination, and special education service delivery issues. Dr. Giangreco is the author of numerous professional publications on these topics and has created a compilation of more than 300 cartoons depicting educational issues and research findings, *Absurdities and Realities of Special Education: The Complete Digital Set* (Corwin Press, 2007).

Chigee J. Cloninger, Ph.D., Research Associate Professor Emeritus, Department of Education and Center on Disability and Community Inclusion, University of Vermont, 208 Colchester Avenue, Mann Hall 301A, Burlington, Vermont 05405-1757

Chigee Cloninger has been a teacher of children and adults with and without disabilities for many years. Even in leadership or research positions, teaching—in the sense of bringing about change—has been a key component to Dr. Cloninger's work. She is past Executive Director of the Center on Disability and Community Inclusion (Vermont University Center for Excellence in Developmental Disabilities Education, Research, and Service), and past Coordinator of the Vermont State I-Team, a statewide training and technical assistance team providing intensive special education supports to children and youth with disabilities, educational personnel, and families. She also is a former director of the Vermont State Project for Children and Youth with Deafblindness and a faculty member in the Intensive Special Education graduate program at the University of Vermont. A national presenter on issues pertaining to students with intensive educational needs, Dr. Cloninger is interested in creative problem-solving approaches, communication, and learning processes for individualized education and leadership.

Virginia S. Iverson, M.Ed., Educational Consultant, Vermont State I-Team, 3364 Silver Street, Hinesburg, Vermont 05461

Virginia S. Iverson has worked in the field of education for more than 35 years as a teacher assistant, an educator, an administrator, and a consultant. In addition to teaching fifth grade, she has been a special education teacher across the continuum of placements, including institutions, special schools and classes, and inclusive classrooms from preschool through high school. Ms. Iverson also teaches courses at the university level and presents nationally on issues related to inclusive education. She is an educational consultant for the Vermont State I-Team for Intensive Special Education, for which she provides consultation, training, and technical assistance to teams of educators, parents, and related services providers on behalf of students with intensive special education needs. Ms. Iverson is primarily interested in blending systematic instruction with inclusive educational practices for students with severe disabilities.

Contributors

Timothy J. Fox, M.Ed.
Coordinator, Vermont State I-Team
Center on Disability and Community
   Inclusion
University of Vermont
Burlington, Vermont

Victoria Graf, M.Ed., C.A.S.
Principal, Jericho Elementary School
Jericho, Vermont

Jacqui Farmer Kearns, Ed.D.
Co-Principal Investigator, National
   Alternate Assessment Center
Associate Director, Inclusive Large-Scale
   Standards and Assessment Project
Human Development Institute
University of Kentucky
Lexington, Kentucky

Harold L. Kleinert, Ed.D.
Professor, Department of Rehabilitation
   Sciences
Executive Director, Human Development
   Institute
Co-Principal Investigator, National
   Alternate Assessment Center
University of Kentucky
Lexington, Kentucky

Jesse C. Suter, Ph.D.
Research Assistant Professor, Department
   of Education and Center on Disability and
   Community Inclusion
University of Vermont
Burlington, Vermont

What's New in the Third Edition of COACH?

This is the ninth version of COACH since 1985. Although this is the third edition with Paul H. Brookes Publishing Co. since 1992, there were six earlier versions (1985–1990) distributed through the National Clearinghouse of Rehabilitation Training Materials. This history of revision is a reflection of our understanding that what constitutes exemplary practices is always changing and being refined, while some key aspects of good practice are timeless (e.g., involving families, connecting curriculum content to valued life outcomes, identifying focus and breadth of curricular content). We offer you the ideas contained in this book as our current thinking at the time of writing and with the recognition that future change is inevitable and desirable. In this edition of COACH we have made a variety of updates and improvements to COACH while retaining key elements of COACH and its organization so that it is readily recognizable to previous users of the tool. Here are some of the key changes:

- The principles upon which COACH is based are updated, reflecting a contemporary emphasis on access to the general education curriculum while retaining the COACH emphasis on also addressing family-selected priority learning outcomes typically not included in the general education curriculum.

- The descriptions and directions for the steps of COACH are reorganized into separate sections. Now all of the descriptions are found in Section I (Introduction to COACH) of the manual, while all of the directions are found in Section III (Directions for Completing COACH Steps). This was done to facilitate first learning about COACH and then having all of the instructions handy without pages of description in between.

- A CD-ROM is included with the manual, providing printable and fillable PDF versions of all forms included in Appendixes B–D as well as printable examples and supplemental materials.

- COACH Student Record Forms and accompanying processes are updated and streamlined. Examples include the following:
  - The Preparation Checklist is updated and shortened.
  - The Steps of COACH are reduced from 10 to 6, while retaining steps from the previous edition as supportive materials referred to in Section IV (Implementing COACH-Generated Plans) with revised and new forms available in Appendix D.

- Step 1.1 (Valued Life Outcomes) questions are updated and the culminating substep is changed from a ranking to a rating task in an effort to acknowledge the potential importance of each valued life outcome.

- Step 1.2 (Selecting Curriculum Areas to Explore During the Family Interview) is organized onto a single page with a facing reference page that includes all of the learning outcomes listed in COACH. This eliminates former page turning and reduces confusion that some users experienced in earlier versions when Step 1.2 was embedded on each learning outcome area listing along with Steps 1.3 and 1.4.

- In Step 1.3 (Rating Learning Outcomes in Selected Curriculum Areas), the curriculum area previously referred to as "Selected Academics" is split into two new areas: 1) Access Academics (e.g., Reacts to objects, activities, and/or interactions; Explores surroundings and objects; Imitates skills used in daily life) and 2) Applied Academics (e.g., Reads [decodes] words/phrases; Uses writing/drawing tools; Uses money; Uses schedule or calendar).

- Also in Step 1.3, the curriculum area previously referred to as "Home" is no longer present because families or teachers rarely identified it as a priority area. A few important learning outcomes from the Home area are retained by shifting them to other curriculum areas. For example, the learning outcomes 1) Selects appropriate clothing to wear and 2) Cares for personal hygiene were added to the Personal Management curriculum area.

- The total number of listed learning outcomes in Step 1.3 is reduced from 91 to 83. This change reflects not only the elimination of infrequently selected learning outcomes, but also includes the addition of some new learning outcomes. For example, in the Communication area, the following items are added: 1) Displays consistent communication mode(s) (e.g., gesture, points, vocalizes, facial expression, uses AAC) and 2) Recognizes if misunderstood and uses another way (e.g., uses "repair strategy," perseveres); other learning outcomes have been added and others have been reworded.

- In Step 1.4 (Prioritizing Learning Outcomes in Selected Curriculum Areas), the number of learning outcomes ranked to move forward to Step 1.5 (Cross-Prioritization) is reduced from five to four because learning outcomes ranked fifth in Step 1.4 rarely were listed among the top priorities selected in Step 1.5.

- Step 1.5 (Cross-Prioritization) is slightly updated for clarity, and the number of overall ranked priorities has been reduced from eight to six.

- Although conceptually the same, the form associated with Step 2.2 (Additional Learning Outcomes from General Education) is substantially updated to improve clarity and includes definitional components of multilevel curriculum and curriculum overlapping.

- The Step 4 (Annual Goals) form is updated.

- Appendix E is added to provide COACH users with a contemporary explanation about the relationship between COACH and alternate assessment, co-authored by Harold L. Kleinert and Jacqui Farmer Kearns of the National Alternate Assessment Center at University of Kentucky.

- Appendix F is added to provide COACH users with suggested roles for various team members in inclusive classrooms, including 1) teachers, 2) special educators, 3) paraprofessionals, 4) related services providers, 5) administrators, and 6) students and parents, that would be congruent with implementing a COACH-generated educational program in an inclusive classroom.

- Appendix G provides an updated example of a completed set of COACH Student Record forms for a kindergarten student with sensory and intellectual disabilities. Appendix H offers an example for a high school student with Down syndrome; both examples are found on the accompanying CD-ROM only.

Although there have been many changes in the manual and forms, current users of COACH will readily recognize the core elements, and processes are maintained and improved. For new users of COACH, we simply hope that this latest edition helps your teams plan high-quality educational programs for your students.

COACH 3

Choosing Outcomes
& Accommodations
for Children

THIRD EDITION

X

Section I

Introduction to COACH

WHAT IS COACH?

COACH (Choosing Outcomes and Accommodations for CHildren) is a planning tool designed to help teams determine the components of individually appropriate educational programs for students with intensive special educational needs. COACH also offers initial suggestions for implementing and evaluating students' educational programs in typical classrooms settings and activities. When using COACH, team members (e.g., family, school personnel) join together to prepare an individually appropriate educational program using a set of field-tested steps that turn ideas about inclusive education into action plans. By making a front-end expenditure of time, teams can reap quality benefits (and potentially save time) throughout the school year by identifying a shared focus around the student's educational program and by contributing to constructive relationships among team members.

COACH is divided into two major parts that include six steps (see Figure 1). Part A (Determining a Student's Educational Program) includes the *Preparation Checklist* followed by Step 1, the *Family Interview*, which determines family-selected learning priorities; Step 2, *Additional Learning Outcomes*, which selects a broader set of learning outcomes in addition to those selected by the family; and Step 3, *General Supports*, which determines what needs to be done with or for the student. A complete set of blank forms for Part A is available for duplication in Appendix B and on the accompanying CD-ROM.

Part B (Translating the Family-Identified Priorities into Goals and Objectives) includes Step 4, writing *Annual Goals* based on the family-selected priority learning outcomes; Step 5, writing *Short-Term Objectives* to correspond with each annual goal, and Step 6, a *Program-at-a-Glance* for summarizing a student's educational program components (family-selected priorities, additional learning outcomes, and general supports) into a brief list that can be available to team members. A complete set of blank forms for Part B are available for duplication in Appendix C and on the accompanying CD-ROM.

Each of the steps is described in more detail later in this introduction. Section II answers commonly asked questions about COACH. Directions corresponding to each COACH step are found in Section III, including an example for an elementary school student. Two additional examples, for a kindergarten student and a high school student, are available on the accompanying CD-ROM.

This manual also includes additional strategies for implementing COACH-generated plans (e.g., scheduling matrix, formats for planning and adapting instruction, formats for evaluating the affect of learning outcomes and supports on valued life outcomes) (see Section IV

Steps of COACH

Part A: Determining a student's educational program

Preparation Checklist

Step 1: Family Interview

> Purpose: To determine family-selected learning priorities for the student through a series of questions asked by an interviewer

Step 2: Additional Learning Outcomes

> Purpose: To determine learning outcomes beyond family priorities
>
> > 2.1: Select additional learning outcomes from COACH to ensure important items from the Family Interview that were not selected as priorities are not forgotten.
> >
> > 2.2: Identify additional learning outcomes from the general education curriculum to 1) ensure access to the general education curriculum, 2) ensure team members have a shared understanding about what general education content the student will pursue, 3) determine a starting place for the general education teacher (e.g., sample learning outcomes).

Step 3: General Supports

> Purpose: To determine what supports need to be provided to or for the student

Part B: Translating the family-identified priorities into goals and objectives

Step 4: Annual Goals

> Purpose: To ensure that the family's priorities are reflected as IEP goals

Step 5: Short-Term Objectives

> Purpose: To develop short-term objectives to achieve annual goals

Step 6: Program-at-a-Glance

> Purpose: To provide a concise summary of the educational program

---

Use COACH-generated information to assist in completing the IEP
(e.g., inform present levels of performance, make related services decisions,
document accommodations, finalize placement decision).

Figure 1. Steps of COACH.

and Appendix D). Blank forms associated with each of these additional strategies referred to in Section IV are available in Appendix D and on the accompanying CD-ROM. Although COACH is not designed specifically for use in alternate assessment, it has long been associated with it. In Appendix E, Harold L. Kleinert and Jacqui Farmer Kearns of the National Alternate Assessment Center discuss the relationship between COACH and alternate assessment. Appendix F provides additional material for implementing COACH-generated plans by articulating potential roles of team members developed with the input of experienced general and special education professionals working in inclusive schools.

COACH is a tool that provides an organized process to assist teams in making complex decisions culminating in an individualized, workable educational plan (learning outcomes and supports) for a particular student to be implemented in inclusive settings. It assists in clarifying the student's participation in general education curriculum and classes. By using COACH you will develop a unified plan whereby team members agree on a shared set of educational goals, rather than having separate goals for different professional disciplines. COACH provides a constructive forum for professionals and parents to listen to each other and clarify expectations. This increases meaningful family involvement in educational planning, particularly identifying priority learning outcomes that will be targets of instruction. When used as intended, COACH encourages parents and professionals to think about educational planning in new ways, in part by considering how their choices about educational curriculum can influence broader life experiences and opportunities for a student with disabilities. COACH is much more than asking questions and filling in forms; it is a tool, that when used properly, can enhance working relationships between professionals and families by establishing or extending mutual regard for each person's respective contributions to the team and sharing in decision making. COACH can be an important piece in planning an appropriate and quality education when used in conjunction with other exemplary practices in inclusive environments. Because COACH is designed to be used in a thoughtful and individualized manner, not in a rote or completely standardized way, we trust that you will apply your own knowledge and experiences to make it better each time you use it.

PRINCIPLES FORMING THE BASIS OF COACH

This section describes six guiding principles on which COACH is based.

1. All students are capable of learning and deserve a meaningful curriculum.
2. Quality instruction requires ongoing access to inclusive environments.
3. Pursuing valued life outcomes informs the selection of curricular content.
4. Family involvement is a cornerstone of educational planning.
5. Collaborative teamwork is essential to quality education.
6. Coordination of services ensures that necessary supports are appropriately provided.

Becoming aware of these foundational principles assists teams in determining whether or not they wish to use COACH. It can also help team members develop a common framework for their work together. Although COACH offers explicit instructions for its use, it also requires skillful adaptation to adjust to the varied circumstances in which it is used. Our research and common sense tell us that if you adapt COACH in ways that match its underlying principles, then you are more likely to have positive outcomes. Conversely, if you adapt COACH in ways that do not match its underlying principles, then you are less likely to have positive outcomes (Giangreco, 1996a; Giangreco, Edelman, Dennis, & Cloninger, 1995). By understanding the principles on which COACH is based, team members put themselves in the best position to get the most out of COACH.

PRINCIPLE 1 All Students Are Capable of Learning and Deserve a Meaningful Curriculum

COACH is rooted in a foundational premise that team members approach every student, regardless of perceived level of ability or current level of functioning, as an individual capable of learning. Even individuals who need lifelong supports share a fundamental human trait—"the capacity to learn" (Snell, 2003, p. 2210). Some may think this is an unnecessary point to make, but unfortunately attitudes about each person's abilities (or perceived inabilities) to learn continue to threaten the civil and educational rights of too many individuals with developmental disabilities and endanger opportunities to explore and encourage their potential.

In the early 1980s, the special education field was actively debating whether *all* students were capable of learning, particularly those considered to have the most severe intellectual disabilities. Although some scholars of that era questioned the educability of children with the most severe disabilities and whether we should attempt to educate them or just care for them (Kauffman & Krouse, 1981), an alternative viewpoint articulated the benefits to students, the field, and our society when we approach every student as capable of learning and make the effort to teach every student, regardless of the perceived severity of his or her disability (Baer, 1981). Leaders in the field who viewed individuals with severe disabilities as capable of learning advocated for selecting curriculum based on the criterion of ultimate functioning (Brown, Nietupski, & Hamre-Nietupski, 1976), namely by identifying and teaching an individually determined set of skills a person needed to participate as independently as possible in typical adult environments (e.g., home, vocational, community); this included the option for partial participation (Baumgart et al., 1982).

By the mid-1980s, this movement had spawned Donnellan's *criterion of the least dangerous assumption* in which she asserted, "in the absence of conclusive educational data, educational decisions should be based on assumptions which, if incorrect, will have the least dangerous effect on the student" (1984, p. 142). She described this conceptualization across a number of dimensions, persuasively arguing that certain practices are inherently less dangerous for students than their counterpoints.

- More frequent opportunities to interact with peers and others without disabilities is less dangerous than restricting access to primarily peers and others who have similar disabilities.

- Access to individually determined, heterogeneous educational placements and grouping (e.g., typical schools and classrooms) is less dangerous than automatic placement in homogeneous groupings (e.g., all students with autism grouped together in a special education class).

- Use of natural materials, cues, and consequences is less dangerous than relying on artificial or contrived materials, cues, and consequences.

- Instructional arrangements that include variation (e.g., large group, small group, individual) delivered by a combination of people who are more or less familiar to the student is less dangerous than instructional arrangements that rely primarily or exclusively on one-to-one instructional arrangements always delivered by familiar people.

- Use of chronologically age-appropriate curricular content is less dangerous than using chronologically age-inappropriate curricular content.

In terms of an instructional stance, Donnellan explained, "Generally, the criterion of the least dangerous assumption holds that there is less danger to students if teachers assume instructional failure is due to instructional inadequacy rather than student deficits" (1984, p. 147).

By the late 1980s, the federal *zero reject* principle embedded in IDEA, affirming that *all* school-age children, regardless of the severity of disability, are entitled to a free appropriate public education (FAPE), was tested and affirmed in a U.S. Court of Appeals case of a student with severe multiple disabilities who had been denied admission to his local public school because school officials deemed him too severely disabled to benefit from education (*Timothy W. v. Rochester School District*, 1989). The Court affirmed that education is defined broadly, to include not only traditional academic skills, but also basic functional life skills. At that time, the dominant curricular model for students considered to have severe disabilities might be characterized as a life skills approach, with minimal attention devoted to general education curricular content.

By the 2000s, the discussion in the education field had shifted away from discussing whether all students *could* learn to *what* they could learn and should have access to. This has meant moving beyond an exclusive or primary focus on a life skills curriculum and operating by the least dangerous assumption by approaching each student with a presumption of competence (Jorgensen, McSheehan, & Sonnenmeier, 2010), in part, by ensuring that all students have access to the general education curriculum (Browder & Spooner, 2006; Dymond, Renzaglia, Gilson, & Slagor, 2007; Ford, Davern, & Schnorr, 2001; Wehmeyer, 2006). This shift does not eliminate the option for a student's educational program to include some high-priority life skills typically not part of the general education curriculum. Rather, it extends earlier curricular models by retaining the appropriate aspects of earlier models (e.g., relevant life skills) while adding access to individually determined general education curriculum content available to students without disabilities. This individualized and balanced approach to identifying meaningful curriculum creates opportunities for students to exceed our expectations and surprise us with their capabilities. The ceiling for student learning should never be capped by disability labels, our own expectations, or historical patterns of educational achievement for students with similar characteristics. Students with developmental disabilities continually exceed expectations when given full access to inclusive environments, quality curriculum, effective instruction, and necessary supports (Giangreco, 2009; Vianello & LanFranchi, 2009).

Erin McKenzie (2008), a 2004 high school graduate, provides a shining example of exceeding expectations. Erin had Down syndrome accompanied by intellectual disabilities, but that is not what defined her. She was a personable, active, engaged high school student with a network of close friends and ongoing access to general education curriculum in supported general education classrooms. During a short speech to the audience at her graduation, she shared what she loved most about high school. Reading from her prepared text, she spoke positively about her relationships with her friends, some of the challenges of high school, her enjoyment of cocurricular activities such as drama club and choir, and her love of Shakespeare. In earlier times (and in too many places still today), students with intensive special education support needs were inappropriately denied access to the general education curriculum. For Erin, theatre, especially Shakespeare, genuinely interested her. Luckily for her, she had parents who persistently advocated for her inclusion in general education classes and access to general education curriculum. She was also fortunate to have some special and general education teachers willing to challenge themselves and historical expectations about what students with intellectual disabilities could learn and what was important. Anyone who knew Erin knows that being part of general education English classes in high school was important to her. For another student, the curriculum content that captures his or her attention or imagination will be something else—ancient Egypt, rainforest habitat, astronomy, the lives of the presidents, painting, or politics. The possibilities are endless.

We are writing about Erin in the past tense because she unexpectedly died just a couple of months after she graduated, which raises another important point about blending the best or earlier approaches (e.g., functional life skills) and more contemporary approaches (e.g., access to general education curriculum). Applications of earlier approaches often overemphasized preparation for future environments (e.g., home, school, community), such as spending disproportionate amounts of time in community-based instruction while peers without disabilities are at school. Although preparing for the future beyond school and providing community-based options (e.g., service learning) are important components of the educational program for all students, being *at* school is where most students are during the day until they are 17 or 18 years old—this is their natural environment. So, as we appropriately prepare students for the future, it is vital we do not forget about the here and now.

The design of COACH Step 1 (Family Interview) and Step 2 (Additional Learning Outcomes) helps teams identify an individually determined set of learning outcomes for a student that include 1) a small set of the highest priority learning outcomes from a family-centered perspective and 2) a broader set of additional learning outcomes. These two sets of learning outcomes come from combining the general education curriculum as well as the learning outcomes listed in COACH, many of which are not typically included in the general education curriculum. Ultimately, all students, including those with disabilities, deserve not only access to functional curriculum content designed to improve their ongoing participation in a variety of inclusive environments, but also to rich and interesting curriculum content reflected in age-appropriate general education curriculum (Doyle & Giangreco, 2009).

PRINCIPLE 2 Quality Instruction Requires Ongoing Access to Inclusive Environments

Ensuring that students with disabilities receive quality instruction requires ongoing access to general education classrooms and other inclusive environments. General education classrooms are where you find 1) teachers who are highly qualified across the range of general education curriculum content areas; 2) materials, equipment, and other resources to match the range of general education curricula; 3) high expectations for learning and behavior; 4) classmates who are potential friends and sources of natural support as well as models of communication and behavior; 5) opportunities for students with disabilities to be valued members of the school community; and 6) opportunities for students without disabilities and teachers to learn and grow from the diversity offered by the presence of a class member with a disability. Providing special education services within inclusive environments is readily available when it is recognized that every positive aspect of special education is portable (e.g., people with specialized skills, adaptive equipment, instructional methods). This reinforces the notion that special education is a service, not a place (e.g., resource room, special class, special school) (Gartner & Lipsky, 2007; Taylor, 1988).

As a field, we already know how to place students with disabilities in general education classes in ways that are not adequately supported; unfortunately, this still happens all too often. It is a main reason some parents are constantly advocating for more appropriate supports in general education classes and why others prefer the shelter of special classes, fearing that general education will not change quickly or sufficiently enough to meet their child's educational needs. What some people refer to as "dumping" a student with a disability in a classroom without adequate planning and support is certainly not inclusive education. Fragmented, partial, disjointed, or low-quality efforts are too often inaccurately labeled as inclusive education (Davern et al., 1997). As our colleague Michael Hock likes to say about misguided efforts to implement inclusive education, "Doing it wrong doesn't make it wrong!" (Giangreco, 1998, p. 28).

At the same time, we have known for decades how to separate students with disabilities and provide them with intensive, research-based instruction either individually or in small, homogeneous groups. There is a great deal of evidence that such approaches can be effective in gaining skills, but at what cost? When we separate students in the name of providing quality instruction, based solely on the goal of achieving certain skills, too often we fail to consider the broader impact of these decisions on a student's valued life outcomes. When we justify educational segregation in the name of instruction, we are in danger of having students go through an entire school career and possibly learn many skills, only to graduate to a life that few of us would consider desirable. Although opportunities and outcomes are slowly improving for students with severe disabilities, postschool outcomes for students with disabilities leave much to be desired. When students with disabilities who have extensive or pervasive support needs leave school, it not uncommon for their world to become smaller at a time when the lives of their peers without disabilities are getter bigger. Too many of these students are at a higher risk of being unemployed, poor, unhealthy, lonely, lacking in adequate supports, and isolated (Certo et al., 2008; Giangreco & Snell, 1996; Johnson, McGrew, Bloomberg, Bruininks, & Lin, 1996). Yet, as educators, we point to our students' progress on their annual goals or other assessment measures, pleased that they learned the skills we targeted as important. Our point here is that either approach—inadequately supported placement in a general education classroom or rationalizing the segregation of a student in order to receive quality instruction—are neither good for students nor good for advancing our practices. Quality instruction and inclusive education should not be an either–or proposition. The challenge is to advance opportunities for students by figuring out how to apply the best available evidence about instruction in the context of inclusive settings, routines, and activities.

Conceptualizing Education for Students with Disabilities in General Education Classes

One of the most common and potentially challenging aspects of planning for the inclusion of a student with significant disabilities in general education is getting it to make sense to all the team members. People often ask, "How can a student with severe disabilities be included in a general education class when the content being taught is different from what this student needs?" This is a legitimate question to ask and demonstrates a desire to ensure the integrity of each student's education.

It is often incorrectly assumed that grade-level placement is synonymous with curricular content. In other words, all fifth-grade students must do the same fifth-grade work. Rather, grade-level placement and individual curricular content should be independent of each other (Giangreco, Cloninger, Dennis, & Edelman, 2002; U.S. Department of Justice, 2002). For example, students in the same fifth-grade class can be functioning below or above the designated fifth-grade level and still receive appropriate quality education if their individual learning needs are addressed. Even in classes where there are no students with labeled disabilities, it is a myth that all students in a particular grade function at the same level in all academic areas or socially. Purposeful heterogeneous grouping of students can be desirable and beneficial as students learn from each other in a diverse classroom community. As we explore ways of including students with significant disabilities, we are learning approaches that benefit all students. Inclusive education, although prompted by the presence of students with disabilities, is about educational access, equity, and quality for all students; it is not exclusively a disability issue.

The following sections will define the term *inclusive education*, provide a framework for conceptualizing inclusive options, and describe two ways of approaching curricular and instructional planning when a student's learning goals differ significantly from his or her classmates (i.e., multilevel curriculum and instruction, curriculum overlapping).

Elements of Inclusive Education

There is no single, agreed-on definition of inclusive education, although there are some generally accepted elements and related practices (Jackson, Ryndak, & Billingsly, 2000). The elements of inclusive education listed demonstrate it is more than mere physical presence in general education classes or other inclusive environments. At its heart, inclusive education is rooted in an interrelated set of values from which we make decisions and a corresponding set of practices designed to support equitable and appropriate education (Doyle, 2008; Giangreco, 2011). Inclusive education exists when each of the following elements occurs on an ongoing, daily basis (Giangreco, Carter, Doyle, & Suter, 2010):

1. All students are welcome in general education. The first placement options considered are the general education classes the students would attend if they did not have a disability.

2. Disability is recognized as a form of human diversity. As such, students with disabilities are accepted as individuals and not denied access based on disability.

3. Appropriate supports are available, regardless of disability label or severity. Given their portability, supports are provided in typical environments, rather than sending students to specialized settings to receive needed supports.

4. Students are educated in classes reflecting the naturally occurring proportion of students with and without disabilities. Therefore, the percentage of students without disabilities in each class would be substantially higher than those with disabilities.

5. Students, irrespective of their developmental or performance levels, are educated with peers in the same-age groupings available to those without disability labels rather than with younger students. Students with disabilities need not function at or near the same academic level as their classmates (although some do) to benefit from a chronologically age-appropriate inclusive placement.

6. Students with and without disabilities participate in shared educational experiences while pursuing individually appropriate learning outcomes with necessary supports. Educational experiences are designed to enhance valued life outcomes that seek an individualized balance between the academic–functional and the social–personal aspects of schooling.

We will know that inclusive education has really become embedded in our educational culture when the term becomes obsolete; when designations such as the inclusion school, inclusion classroom, and inclusion student are no longer used as part of our educational vocabulary. To paraphrase Biklen and Knoll (1987, p. 21), inclusive education survives as an issue only so long as some of our students continue to be excluded.

Inclusive Education Options

Student participation can be broadly characterized along two dimensions within general education classes, activities, and routines: 1) the program—what is taught (e.g., curriculum content, annual goals, additional learning outcomes) and 2) the supports—what is provided to assist the student in gaining access to and achieving his or her educational program (e.g., materials, teaching strategies, personnel) (Giangreco & Putnam, 1991). There are four basic options in this approach for including students in general class activities using the learning outcomes you will generate from COACH (see Figure 2). It is important to recognize that these four options should be considered fluid rather than static. Individual students may gain access to some or all of these options throughout the course of a school day or even within a single lesson or activity, flowing back and forth between options as needed.

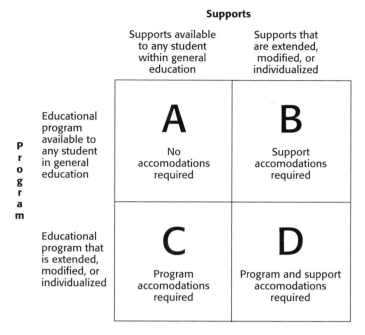

Figure 2. Inclusive options within general education environments. (From Giangreco, M.F., & Putnam, J. [1991]. Supporting the education of students with severe disabilities in regular education environments. In L.H. Meyer, C. Peck, & L. Brown [Eds.], *Critical issues in the lives of people with severe disabilities* [p. 247]. Baltimore: Paul H. Brookes Publishing Co.; adapted by permission.)

Option A exists when a student is pursuing the general education program that is readily available to any student and can pursue that program given the supports typically available to all students. The availability of supports varies, so what is typically available in one school may not be in another.

As general education becomes increasingly accessible, specialized accommodations become typical, which is consistent with the principles of universal design for learning (Dalton & Gordon, 2007; Rose, Meyer, & Hitchcock, 2005). Many students, even those with severe disabilities, have portions of the school day or parts of activities in which they require no accommodations. Educational team members need to identify these opportunities and expand on them. All too often, with the most benevolent of intentions, support is provided to students even when they do not need it (Giangreco, Edelman, Luiselli, & MacFarland, 1997). By relying more on natural supports (Nisbet, 1992) and providing supports that are "only as special as necessary" (Giangreco, 1996b, p. 37), students can be provided with the appropriate and socially valued opportunities to receive their education.

Option B exists for students who require extended, modified, or otherwise individualized supports while gaining access to and pursuing the general educational program. For example, a student who is deaf may require an interpreter, a student who is blind may require reading materials in braille, or a student with motor difficulties may require a tape recorder to "take notes" in order to participate in the general education program.

Option C exists when a student requires extension, modification, or individualization to the content of his or her educational program, but does not require specialized supports. For example, a teacher may adjust the amount of production (e.g., 5 new spelling words instead of 10), the level of content (e.g., asking questions at the student's level), or the type of content (e.g., selecting a different subject content) without the student needing unusual or specialized supports to gain access to the modified program content. Like Option A, this option encourages educational teams to consider the use of natural supports.

Option D exists at times when a student needs extension, modification, or individualization of both the educational program and the supports to gain access to and participate in class activities. This option, although necessary for some students, should be considered only after trying Options A, B, and C. When using this option, it is crucial to be aware that few, if any, students require this on a full-time basis. Look for opportunities to educate students using other options that allow them the most normalized opportunities.

When using Options C or D, there are a couple of ways to think about adjusting a student's educational program (see Figure 3). First, *multilevel curriculum and instruction* refers to teaching a diverse group of learners within a shared activity in which students have different individually appropriate learning outcomes within the same curriculum area (e.g., social studies) (Campbell, Campbell, Collicott, Perner, & Stone, 1988; Giangreco, 2007). Multilevel curriculum and instruction is consistent with the principles of differentiated instruction (Kronberg, 2007; Tomlinson, 2001, 2003) and takes it a step further. Although differentiated instruction encourages teachers to differentiate materials, activities, assessment, and other aspects of their teaching to create multiple pathways for learning and offer students a variety of ways to demonstrate what they have learned, most examples are based on students pursuing substantively the same learning outcomes.

When using multilevel curriculum and instruction, all of the principles of differentiated instruction can be applied, but are extended to substantively different learning outcomes within the same curriculum area. Although one student may be learning at a basic knowledge or comprehension level, another student may be working on an application or synthesis level. For example, second-grade students are playing a small-group social studies board game devised by their teacher to learn about their neighborhood, town, and state. The teacher has prepared a set of 10 game cards for each student that target individual learning outcomes. For one student, the game cards require applying knowledge about the roles of community helpers (e.g., police, fire fighters, store clerks, postal workers) by moving game pieces to respond to scenarios on cards (e.g., move your player to the place where you might go if you wanted to send a

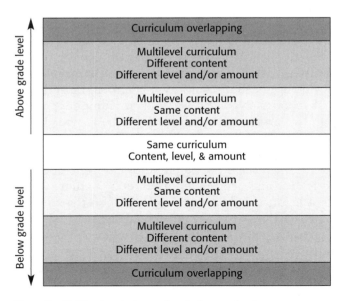

Figure 3. Multilevel curriculum and curriculum overlapping.

card to your grandmother for her birthday). For another student, it is learning to answer questions about where she lives (e.g., street address, telephone number, neighbors). A third student is using map skills such as north, south, east, and west to respond to questions (e.g., If you started at the bookstore, went 2 blocks north and 1 block east, then where would you be?). In this example, all the students have social studies learning outcomes that have been individually selected to match their level of functioning and needs. In all cases, using commonly available, age-appropriate technology or student-specific assistive technology should be considered. For example, some of these mapping and neighborhood outcomes might be addressed using tools such as MapQuest, Google Maps, and Smartphone or iPad applications.

Multilevel curriculum can include variations across subject content, level of learning outcomes pursued, or both. For example, the subject content in a seventh-grade social studies class focuses on American history from the American Revolution through the Civil War. The team for Joseph, a student with disabilities, decided that the subject content should be the same for him, but the level of learning outcomes needed to be adapted. In other words, his studies would focus on American history, but be adapted to an appropriate level (e.g., historical people, places, and events). Joseph's math class is studying algebra. His team decided that the subject content for Joseph needed to be different, basic computation (e.g., adding, subtracting), and the level and quantity of the learning outcomes needed to be adjusted. In both classes, Joseph is working on learning outcomes within the same curriculum area as his classmates.

Curriculum overlapping refers to teaching a diverse group of students within a shared activity in which students have different, individually appropriate learning outcomes that come from two or more curriculum areas (e.g., a student is pursuing communication learning outcomes in a science activity, whereas other students have science learning outcomes). For example, in a high school biology class, lab teams of three students each are assembling a model of a human heart. Two of the students have goals related to the identification, anatomy, and physiology of the human heart. The third student, Marta, who has severe disabilities, participates in helping to assemble the model heart but is working on communication and social skills (e.g., developing a consistent pointing response, taking turns, following instructions, maintaining socially acceptable behavior). By participating in the activity with her classmates, Marta is being exposed to general education curriculum content even though her targeted learning outcomes (those planned for and being assessed) are early communication and social skills. As her pointing responses develop over time, giving her a consistent way to respond, science learning outcomes can also be targeted. It is important to recognize that curriculum overlapping need not be an exclusive option; it can be used concurrently with multilevel curriculum and instruction. In such cases, Marta can have some nonscience learning outcomes (curriculum overlapping) and some modified science learning outcomes (multilevel). In fact, using curriculum overlapping exclusively, without some multilevel learning outcomes, is quite rare.

Curriculum overlapping can also address other general education curriculum areas. For example, it was mentioned previously that Joseph, a seventh-grade student with disabilities, was participating in social studies and math via multilevel curriculum. His team agreed that his participation in French class would be through curriculum overlapping. In French class he would be exposed to French words, language, and culture, but he would not be assessed on competencies in French. The team agreed that participation in French class provided opportunities to pursue learning outcomes identified from his seventh-grade English class pertaining to listening, speaking, reading, writing, and spelling. For example, his spelling words from English class could be duplicated in French and he could practice reading and writing both sets, use them in sentences, and read them orally. As he learns, the team should continually reassess what the most appropriate learning outcomes should be for Joseph as targets of instruction. Curriculum overlapping occurs when learning outcomes from two or more curriculum areas are overlapped within the same activity. Opportunities for both curriculum overlapping and multilevel curriculum and instruction are abundant in classrooms where participation in learning is active and creative.

Pursuing Valued Life Outcomes Informs the Selection of Curricular Content

A basic premise of COACH is that students' lives should be better because they attend our schools. COACH pursues a better life for students by relying on a set of valued life outcomes, based on information collected from parents who have children with severe disabilities, to inform the selection of curricular content. These valued life outcomes are designed to facilitate student independence and interdependence, as well as pursue personal growth by expanding access, creating new opportunities, developing individual abilities, and providing ways to contribute to one's community (Giangreco, Cloninger, Dennis, & Edelman, 1993; Giangreco, Cloninger, Mueller, Yuan, & Ashworth, 1991; Giangreco et al., 1995). The valued life outcomes in COACH include

- Safety and health (physical and emotional)
- A home, now and in the future
- Meaningful relationships
- Control and choice (suited to the student's age and culture)
- Meaningful activities in various and valued places

These valued life outcomes will hold different meanings to different families depending on a variety of factors, such as where they live, their family configuration, and their cultural beliefs and practices. Valued life outcomes are equally applicable, whether or not a student has a disability (Dennis, Williams, Giangreco, & Cloninger, 1993). Although each family will pursue valued life outcomes for their child in unique ways, COACH is one of the few planning approaches that explicitly links selection of curriculum to individually determined valued life outcomes. By selecting curriculum based on valued life outcomes, we are encouraging people to look beyond splintered skills and provide a curricular focus that has meaning to the family. Without an emphasis on valued life outcomes, students with disabilities are at risk of completing their education without a coherent set of meaningful outcomes.

Although there may be some general agreement about what constitutes valued life outcomes, how to best assess, plan for, and pursue these outcomes through education remains debatable. One approach suggests that increasing independence in performing daily living skills will lead to valued life outcomes. Although this may be true in some situations, there is no guarantee that skill development necessarily leads to improvement in a person's valued life outcomes. For instance, teaching banking skills to a student who will have little opportunity or need to use them may have no affect on that individual. But for a young adult with a job, learning to use an automated teller machine may offer him or her more choice, control, and independence. Alternately, a student's valued life outcomes can be improved when people without disabilities provide necessary supports by applying inclusionary knowledge, skills, and attitudes—this does not require the person with a disability to necessarily develop his or her skills (although that is always desirable).

COACH is based on the assumption that the pursuit of valued life outcomes is through a combination of 1) having students learn relevant skills and 2) providing students with necessary supports. This assumption is consistent with the expectation that all students can learn (see Principle 1). At the same time, it does not presume that people with disabilities need to become less disabled in order to be valued and have a good quality of life. By approaching our students as individuals with unique characteristics and focusing on their attributes rather than perceived deficits, we can advance valued life outcomes for students by facilitating their learning as well as our own.

COACH encourages families to clarify their vision for the student's current and future valued life outcomes. Having the family establish this individualized vision of what they value sets a meaningful context for educational planning. The following sections describe each of the five valued life outcomes included in COACH. Each family will attach a different meaning to each valued life outcome based on their own circumstances and beliefs. Although each child shares some characteristics with all other children and shares other characteristics with some other children, each child also has characteristics uniquely his or her own (Speight, Myers, Cox, & Highlen, 1991). Thus, individualization is required to ensure that educational planning yields meaningful outcomes. These descriptions show how some families have interpreted the valued life outcomes and do not imply that a family using COACH must match any of the examples. It is also crucial to remember that valued life outcomes are pursued by developing skills of the student and providing supports from those who interact with the student.

Safety and Health (Physical and Emotional)

Personal safety and health are foundational outcomes. Like all valued life outcomes, safety and health can be enhanced by the supports we provide for people as well as skill development on the part of the person. The range of how families interpret this valued outcome is vast. One family may be concerned that their child needs to drink more liquids by mouth to avoid the need for tube feeding. Another is concerned about their inquisitive child being burned by a hot stove or bolting across a parking lot. A third may be concerned that their overly trusting and friendly teenager will be a target of "stranger danger."

Frequently, safety and health issues overlap other valued life outcomes or are embedded within them. For example, learning pedestrian skills may address 1) access to new activities and places, 2) safety to avoid being hit by a car, and 3) expanded personal choices. Learning to respond to an emergency alarm improves safety and may increase a person's access to certain types of living arrangements. We can affect people's personal health and wellness through the foods they eat, the care we take to ensure that their specialized equipment is properly fitted, or the fitness activities we teach them.

Safety and health frequently must be balanced with personal control and choice. With new choices come new physical and emotional risks to safety, ranging from the pain of a broken leg to the pain of a broken heart. The balance between safety and health and control and choice should be determined individually by each family and include the student. Research on COACH indicates that the valued life outcome pertaining to safety and health was situationally important to families (Giangreco et al., 1995). Although all families are generally concerned about their children's safety and health, typically these issues were a major concern only to families in situations in which the child had chronic health problems or where there was an imminent safety threat (e.g., busy streets, gang violence).

A Home, Now and in the Future

Home means a place of belonging, security, safety, privacy, and where you can feel free to be yourself. Like health and safety, our research on COACH indicates that having a home, now and in the future, is situationally important to families (Giangreco et al., 1995). Identifying "home" as an important valued life outcome has tended to be of concern primarily in circumstances in which the family perceived it as an imminent need. One such situation occurs with older students, in which making the transition to community living is an option for them. For example, Gina had a wonderful home growing up with her parents, brother, and sister. Both

Gina and her parents hope that as a young adult she will be able to live in an apartment with a friend as a roommate. Gina's experiences living on her own can be enhanced by learning certain skills, such as responding to emergency alarms, using public transportation, and being able to make purchases. Because the valued life outcome of having a home can also be realized through supports provided to people with disabilities, Gina's opportunity to live in her own apartment need not be predicated on her skill development. Supports can be provided (e.g., personnel) so that living in an apartment with a roommate becomes a reality regardless of her skill development (Taylor, 2006). Families may pursue community living options for their children out of concern regarding who will advocate for them after they are gone and out of fear their children will be institutionalized.

In other cases in which an imminent need was perceived related to having a home, families questioned their capacity to cope with their child's behaviors or characteristics (e.g., lack of sleeping through the night, aggressive or destructive behaviors, high physical care needs). In these types of situations, the balance of having the student learn new skills and receive supports can come in to play. For example, a teenager who routinely destroys parts of the family's home needs to learn new skills to address his or her needs more constructively and being able to raise this child at home may be facilitated by supports provided to the family (e.g., respite care, counseling). Another teenager who has severe physical disabilities, and who has grown to a mature adult size, may be able to live at home easier and more enjoyably if he or she learns certain skills (e.g., assisting in personal care) or by receiving needed supports (e.g., adaptive equipment). These types of issues are critical for some families and not for others.

Meaningful Relationships

When we think about the most important things in life, relationships with other people are at, or near, the top of the list. We all need other people in our lives. For most people the range of relationships we have is quite diverse, including immediate or extended family relationships, friendships, relationships that revolve around specific interests (e.g., music, sports, hobbies), relationships with co-workers, acquaintances, and others. By developing various types of relationships with others, we experience an important range of human emotions such as love, kinship, and companionship. By interacting with others, we learn from them and also learn more about ourselves. People with disabilities deserve access to the same range of relationships available to people without disabilities. This is most likely to occur when people with disabilities have opportunities to live, work, play, and go to school with people without disabilities, but also are not restricted from interacting with others who have disabilities. Too many people with disabilities have not been given the opportunities to develop a full range and network of relationships that sometimes puts undue pressure on the smaller existing network of family and friends. Being with other people in a variety of ways is, in part, the essence of the human experience, regardless of our varied characteristics.

Control and Choice (Suited to the Student's Age and Culture)

Some people with disabilities have less personal choice and control than people without disabilities who are the same age. For example, it is not unusual to observe a youngster with severe physical or intellectual disabilities who has little or no control over important, or even mundane, aspects of his daily life. Someone else may decide what he eats, what he wears, where he goes, how long he stays, whom he will see, when he will get out of his wheelchair, what he will play with, where he will work, or whether he will work at all. Such lack of control may lead to passivity, whereby the person becomes resigned to his plight, lacking the will to challenge others' control over aspects of life many people without disabilities take for granted. For others, lack of choice and appropriate control may result in challenging behaviors, such as aggression.

What is considered an appropriate level of choice and control varies in different cultures depending on factors such as age, sex, and religious beliefs (Harry, 2008). In some cultures, giving children age-appropriate choice and control is considered highly desirable. In other cultures, it is the parents who are expected to remain in control; child choice and control may be viewed in some cultures as disrespectful or rebellious (Dennis & Giangreco, 1996). A common theme that cuts across cultures is that children are given increasing choice and control, along with corresponding responsibilities, as they are prepared for adulthood. Because people with disabilities are sometimes viewed as "eternal children" (Wolfensberger, 1975), at times they are not afforded the same types of choices and levels of control made available to their peers without disabilities. This perpetuates an unproductive cycle of limited expectations and opportunities for people with disabilities. Providing people with disabilities chronologically age-appropriate levels of choice and control is consistent with Donnellan's (1984) criterion of the least dangerous assumption. If we are not sure about the motivations or intentions of an individual, then we are safer to err on the side of providing opportunities for choice and control rather than summarily denying those choices and control.

Meaningful Activities in Various and Valued Places

Having a variety of activities to do and places to do them is part of what separates a boring existence from an interesting life, even when the person's level of participation is partial (Ferguson & Baumgart, 1991). *Meaningful activities* refer to activities that are valued both by society and the individual. An individual can demonstrate he or she values an activity by showing a preference or interest in the activity on an ongoing basis, highlighting the importance of actively teaching choice making. Activities may be intrinsically valued by the person, as in the fun of swimming, or may have some secondary value to the person, as in earning money in exchange for work. Parents of children with severe disabilities tell us their children's lives are improved by participating in meaningful activities in places frequented by people without disabilities (e.g., school, extracurricular activities, work, community recreation facilities, friends' homes) (Giangreco, Cloninger et al., 1993; Giangreco et al., 1995).

PRINCIPLE 4   Family Involvement Is a Cornerstone of Educational Planning

One aim of COACH is to assist families in becoming better consumers of education and related services, as well as partners in the educational process. We use the term *families* with the recognition that it means many things, such as two-parent families, single-parent families, blended families with step-children, adoptive families, and multigenerational families. This emphasis on consumerism and partnership is based on the following five tenets.

Families Know Certain Aspects of Their Children Better than Anyone Else

Although school personnel get to know their students well throughout a 6-hour school day, this is only a fraction of the students' entire day. The rest of the day, as well as weekends, holidays, and school vacations, present a more complete picture of a student's life. Parents, brothers, sisters, and others are present for much of the student's nonschool time. Nonschool time provides key information that has educational implications, such as the nature of the student's interests, motivations, habits, fears, routines, pressures, needs, and health. By listening to families, educators can gain a more complete understanding of the student's life outside school.

Families Have the Greatest Vested Interest in Seeing Their Children Learn

In our professional eagerness to help children learn, we sometimes convey a message to parents that teachers care more about their children than they do. Of course, this is rarely the case. It can be dangerous to make assumptions about a parent's intentions based on certain behaviors. Parents may withdraw from the educational process (e.g., choose not to attend educational meetings) for any number of reasons. As a parent reported in one study, "It doesn't matter what I say because they [professionals] are going to do what they want anyway" (Giangreco, Cloninger, et al., 1993, p. 20). COACH addresses this problem by providing a forum and a process for families to share their ideas and encourages professionals to listen.

Families Should Be Approached in Culturally Sensitive Ways

Approaching families in culturally sensitive ways is becoming increasingly important as professionals are working with more children and families who have varied cultural backgrounds (Hanson & Lynch, 2003; Harry & Klingner, 2005; Lynch & Hansen, 2004). As Beth Harry eloquently stated

> For me, this is the essence of culturally sensitive practice; not that professionals need to know particular details of all cultural groups; this being in fact impossible and tends to lead to stereotyping, but rather that they are open to different belief systems, and capable of listening in a nonjudgmental way to concerns that may surprise or even shock them. Next, they must be able to collaborate with families in such a way as to respect their cultural framework, while simultaneously honoring their own. (Dennis & Giangreco, 1996, pp. 110–111)

Based on feedback from special educators from various cultural groups, Dennis and Giangreco (1996) suggested the following principles and guidelines to facilitate family interviewing in culturally sensitive ways:

- Appreciate the uniqueness of each family.
- Be aware of the influence of your role as a professional.
- Acknowledge your own cultural biases.
- Seek new understandings and knowledge of cultures.
- Develop an awareness of cultural norms.
- Learn with families.
- Seek help from cultural interpreters before the interview.
- Ascertain literacy and language status of family members.
- Involve family members in planning interviews (e.g., time, place).
- Preview the interview with family members (e.g., Appendix A).
- Adapt the time frame to meet the needs of the family.
- Carefully examine the nature of the questions you ask.

The Family Is Likely to Be the Only Group of Adults Involved with a Child's Educational Program Throughout His or Her Entire School Career

Over the course of a school career, a student with special education needs will encounter so many professionals that it will be difficult for the family to remember all of their names. Some of these professionals will work with the child for a number of years, others a year or less. Eventually, even the most caring and competent among them will depart because they are professionals who are paid to be part of the student's life. All of these professionals, however, will bring with them unique skills and ideas that can have a positive effect on the student and family. Although such diversity of ideas and personal energy can be helpful and invigorating if it is well coordinated, the varying input of professionals could prove harmful if it is so territorial or chaotic it does not contribute to developing a cohesive plan or direction. Professionals are encouraged to build on an ever-evolving, family-centered vision for the student, rather than reinventing a student's educational program each year as team membership changes. Throughout the student's school career, the family is most likely to be the only human constant. COACH is designed to assist families in clarifying and articulating their own vision for themselves and their children.

Families Have the Ability to Positively Influence the Quality of Educational Services Provided in Their Community

Historically, families have been responsible for improving access to educational and community-based opportunities for their children with disabilities (Zuna, Turnbull, & Turnbull, 2011). In the 1950s and 1960s, when schooling was unavailable to many children with disabilities, parents created schools. Families were a driving force behind the passage of the Education for All Handicapped Children Act of 1975 (PL 94-142), which first mandated FAPE for all children. Families were influential in the subsequent reauthorizations of IDEA and its amendments. Active parent groups and advocacy groups that include many families continue to be influential in improving education for students with disabilities. Undoubtedly, families will continue to play a vital role in improving educational services for all children.

Families Must Live with the Outcomes of Decisions Made by Educational Teams, All Day, Every Day

People should be involved in making decisions that will affect their lives. When families do not do what professionals have prescribed, this may indicate that the family was inadequately involved in the decision-making process. As professionals, when we make decisions we must constantly remind ourselves they are likely to affect other people besides the child and have an effect outside the school. COACH encourages families to be part of the process of deciding what their children's educational program will look like because they know what the child and family need, what is most important to them, and what they can handle. In our experience, when given the opportunity to participate in educational planning using COACH, families are invaluable in determining appropriate educational experiences and do an excellent job of pinpointing priorities.

PRINCIPLE 5 Collaborative Teamwork Is Essential to Quality Education

COACH is predicated on family members and school professionals working together as a team. Teams typically include the student, parents, the classroom teacher and assistant(s), special educators, related services providers, and others (e.g., principal, bus driver) as needed. The nature of each member's participation should be individually determined. Teamwork requires having two or more members, distributing labor agreed to by the team, sharing resources, effectively communicating, ongoing interactions, and consensus decision making. Ironically, you can have all these important teamwork characteristics and still not have a team. For these aspects of teamwork to be effective they must be applied within "an ever-evolving shared framework, which consists of a set of beliefs, values, or assumptions about education, children, families, and professionals to which team members agree" (Giangreco, 1996b, p. 4). Second, teamwork needs to be applied to a set of shared student goals agreed to by the team. By establishing common student goals, teams can avoid the problem of each member having his or her own separate goals. When team members establish common student goals, they pull in the same direction for the student, rather than pulling in different directions.

Teams should include those who will be most directly affected, rather than everyone who might be affected. Sometimes teams become so large that planning and decision making is unnecessarily complicated. Teams can reduce the number of people involved in regular team meetings by designating a core team consisting of people who have the most ongoing involvement with the student, an extended team that includes the core team plus those members who have less frequent involvement with the student, and situational teams consisting of individually determined combinations of team members to address specific issues or concerns. In other words, everyone does not need to be involved in everything. Everyone's time is used more efficiently by clarifying who are core members, extended members, or situational resources to the team.

PRINCIPLE 6   Coordination of Services Ensures Necessary Supports Are Appropriately Provided

A common question asked about COACH planning is, "Where are the therapy goals?" The short answer is, "There aren't any therapy goals in COACH." This does not mean some students do not need support services or support services are unimportant. On the contrary, some students can only gain access to and participate in their educational program given appropriate supports provided through the skills of service providers such as physical therapists, occupational therapists, speech-language pathologists (SLPs), orientation and mobility specialists, and others. It is equally important that these services be coordinated to be supportive of the student's education.

Support services are provided if they are needed for the student to gain access to or participate in his or her educational program—within the context of school. They should not be parallel services. All too often, each professional establishes his or her own set of goals based on the orientation of his or her discipline, leading teams down a path likely to be educationally fragmented and disjointed (Giangreco, Edelman, & Dennis, 1991). To provide effective education, support services need to be coordinated in ways that account for the interrelationships that exist among the disciplines to avoid unnecessary and undesirable service gaps, overlaps, and contradictions (Giangreco, 2000). An underlying precept of support services within the COACH framework is students with disabilities do not go to school to get therapy/support services— they go to school to get an education and receive therapy/support services necessary to get that education (Giangreco, Prelock, Reid, Dennis, & Edelman, 2000).

Encouraging the development of shared educational goals that are discipline-free is one way COACH addresses these issues. Discipline-free goals are based on learning outcomes free of the orientations of the various professional disciplines (e.g., physical therapy [PT], occupational therapy [OT], speech-language pathology). Discipline-free goals typically do not use professional jargon; this differs from goals that are discipline-specific and use professional jargon. For example, the goal, "Maria will point to symbols on her communication board to request people, toys, food, and getting out of her wheelchair at school and at home," is discipline-free when we know that it was selected as a priority learning outcome during the Family Interview in COACH. This goal includes a functional, observable behavior as well as a context in which the behavior will occur.

The following are negative examples of individualized education program (IEP) goals that are discipline-specific, not discipline-free (Giangreco, Dennis, Edelman, & Cloninger, 1994):

The student will improve postural stability and increase antigravity of head, trunk, and extremities.

The student will produce three bilabial speech sounds: /b/, /m/, and /p/.

The student will initiate correction to midline when displaced laterally while prone or sitting astride a horse or bolster.

These examples are stated as: 1) nonfunctional subskills, 2) were selected by specialists based on the orientation of their disciplines, 3) are jargon filled, and 4) do not include a context for use.

Once a student's educational program has been determined (i.e., discipline-free annual goals, additional learning outcomes from an educational perspective, general supports), it then becomes appropriate for team members to ask, "In what ways are support services required to assist the student in gaining access to or participating in his or her educational program?" (Giangreco, 2001).

Making decisions about which support services are needed, what function they need to serve, how they should be provided (e.g., directly, indirectly), how frequently they are needed, and a variety of other questions are beyond the scope of COACH but are addressed in related literature (Giangreco, 1996b; 2000; McWilliam, 1996; Orelove, Sobsey & Silberman, 2004).

DESCRIPTION OF COACH PART A (STEPS 1–3): DETERMINING A STUDENT'S EDUCATIONAL PROGRAM

Part A consists of three steps designed to assist teams in determining the primary content of a student's educational program—the "what" (rather than the how) of the educational program. Determining the educational program content is vital in providing a quality education because a team must know where they are headed if they have any hope of getting there. Too often, students' educational programs lack sufficient direction and substance leading toward individual meaningful outcomes, referred to in COACH as *valued life outcomes*, such as having meaningful relationships with others and participating in meaningful activities in varied and valued places.

The Family Interview (Step 1) is at the heart of the educational program (see Figure 4). It culminates in the family selecting a small set of the highest learning priorities that will serve as the focus of the team's work throughout the year. Additional Learning Outcomes (Step 2) represent a slightly larger, though reasonably sized, set of learning outcomes from COACH and the general education curriculum that are targets of instruction. This is designed to ensure that students have a sufficiently broad educational program and access to general education (Spooner & Browder, 2006; Wehmeyer & Agran, 2006). Whereas Steps 1 and 2 emphasize selecting targeted learning outcomes that seek skill development and applying those skills in natural contexts, General Supports (Step 3) are used to identify supports to be provided to or for students with disabilities. General supports are not learning outcomes for the student, but rather learning outcomes for the team members because they require skill development and application by team members in natural contexts. Each of these three steps is described in further detail in the following subsections. Ultimately, the steps in Part A are designed to help teams clarify the team's vision for the student's educational program so they have a shared understanding to effectively collaborate around a set of relevant and individually determined program components.

Cover Page and Preparation Checklist

As you begin the COACH process, you will notice that the cover page of the Student Record form (Appendix B) includes spaces to list basic demographic information about the student (e.g., name, date of birth, planning year, educational placement), but does not list any diagnostic or categorical disability-related information because it is not relevant to completing COACH. COACH will draw out descriptive information about a student's educational needs without the use of disability or categorical labels.

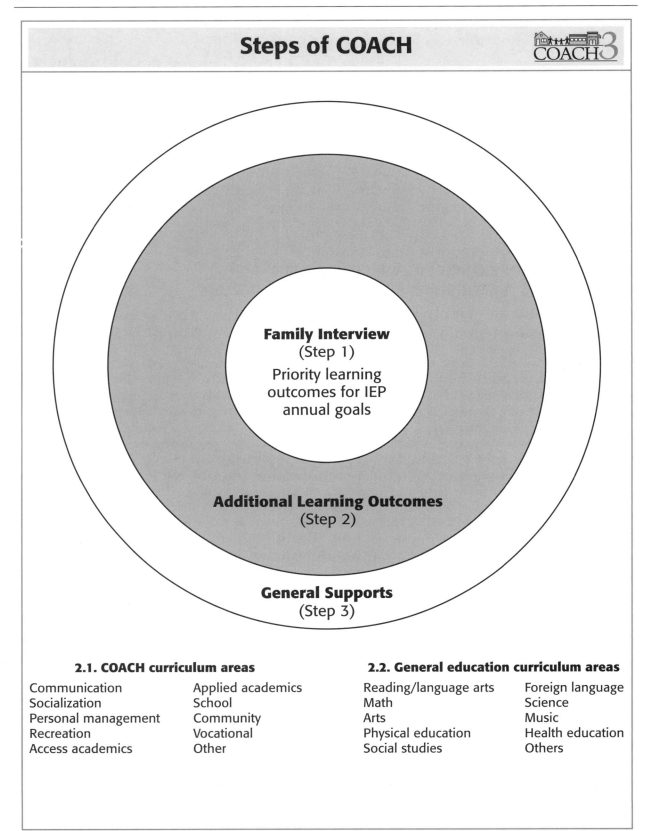

Steps of COACH

Family Interview
(Step 1)

Priority learning
outcomes for IEP
annual goals

Additional Learning Outcomes
(Step 2)

General Supports
(Step 3)

2.1. COACH curriculum areas

Communication	Applied academics
Socialization	School
Personal management	Community
Recreation	Vocational
Access academics	Other

2.2. General education curriculum areas

Reading/language arts	Foreign language
Math	Science
Arts	Music
Physical education	Health education
Social studies	Others

Figure 4. Relationship between COACH Steps 1, 2, and 3.

The Preparation Checklist is a series of six preparatory steps designed to facilitate the productive use of COACH and ensure accountability for completion (see Figure 5). The checklist includes some logistical steps pertaining to the Family Interview (e.g., arranging time and place, preparing forms) as well as substeps related to knowledge and awareness meant to facilitate understanding of COACH and use of all its steps.

Earlier research on COACH indicated that some people attempt to use COACH without understanding its underlying assumptions or directions (Giangreco et al., 1995); in other words, they were not adequately prepared. Anecdotally, we find lack of adequate preparation to be an ongoing concern. Not surprisingly, lack of adequate preparation is likely to result in less favorable outcomes. We also have found that some teams use Step 1, but then do not go on to Steps 2 and 3. The purposeful design of COACH necessitates completion of at least Steps 1, 2, and 3 for favorable results—the team is prompted to record their plan to complete at least those steps using the Preparation Checklist.

The remaining steps in Part B (e.g., writing Annual Goals and Short-Term Objectives) and Strategies to Implement the COACH-Generated Plans (see Section IV) are important components, though they are not unique to COACH. Although we offer suggested ways to approach these and other educational planning tasks (e.g., Program-at-a-Glance, Scheduling Matrix, Evaluation of Impact), we realize that there are a variety of ways and excellent resources you can access to accomplish these same tasks (Bateman & Linden, 2006; Downing, 2008; Janney & Snell, 2011; Peterson & Hittie, 2010; Snell & Brown, 2011).

Although COACH includes explicit directions for use, it is not a standardized process, so understanding the underlying principles is essential. The potential value of COACH is maximized when skillful facilitators thoughtfully individualize the process (e.g., adjust their language to match the situation). This requires a foundational understanding of its underlying principles to ensure that any modifications are consistent with, and not contradictory to, those guiding principles. As indicated in Item 2 on the Preparation Checklist, a lay-language summary of COACH is found in Appendix A to help familiarize team members with COACH.

The Family Interview

The Family Interview is the initial step in Part A; it is facilitated face to face with the family (typically one or two parents and the student, when appropriate) and purposely selected school personnel (typically a special educator and a classroom teacher). Using the Family Interview, a facilitator guides the family through a process designed to assist them in selecting a small set of the most important learning outcomes from the family's perspective for the student to pursue during the school year. The Family Interview also provides excellent opportunities for professionals to learn about the student and family. Too many attempts at parent–professional collaboration are unsuccessful (Blue-Banning, Summers, Frankland, Nelson, & Beegle, 2004), in part, because they are dominated by professionals telling parents what they think is important based on their assessment and observations of the students with insufficient family input (Soodak & Erwin, 2000). COACH reverses this all too common practice during the Family Interview by giving professionals the roles of asking questions and listening in order to better understand the family's perspective. Each of the substeps of the Family Interview is described in the following subsections with particular emphasis on their purpose and unique features.

Introducing the Family Interview

By introducing the Family Interview, the participants will understand what will happen during the interview. This orientation should simply be a reminder to participants, not an initial orientation to COACH because that should have occurred prior to the Family Interview. Introducing the Family Interview includes six categories of information to share with the family prior to asking them questions (see Figure 6). Occasionally we hear about parents who are unknow-

Preparation Checklist

Before proceeding with COACH (Part A), ensure that all items below are completed. Check (✓) inside the ○ when completed.

○ 1. All professional team members understand the COACH process and at least one member has the skills to facilitate all parts of COACH.

○ 2. The family understands the COACH process and makes an informed decision to complete COACH with professional team members to develop their child's educational program. (See Appendix A and/or Sections I and II.)

○ 3. All professional team members agree to accept and act on the educational priorities identified by the family during the Family Interview.

○ 4. Mutually agreeable times and locations for the Steps 1, 2, and 3 are arranged so that at least the family, facilitator, special educator, and general educator can attend.

Family member(s): _____

_____

Facilitator: _____

Special educator: _____

General educator(s): _____

_____

Others: _____

Step 1:

Date: _____ Start time: _____ End time: _____ Location: _____

Step 2:

Date: _____ Start time: _____ End time: _____ Location: _____

Step 3:

Date: _____ Start time: _____ End time _____ Location: _____

○ 5. A Student Record booklet or a copy of the COACH forms is ready for use.

○ 6. Plans are made to complete Step 4 (Annual Goals), Step 5 (Short-Term Objectives), and Step 6 (Program-at-a-Glance).

Figure 5. Preparation Checklist.

Introducing the Family Interview

To be read to person(s) being interviewed.

Welcome and the Importance of Family Involvement

Thank you for agreeing to meet with us to use COACH to help plan for your child's IEP. We are glad you are here to help us understand your family's perspectives about his or her educational needs and priorities.

Purpose of the Family Interview

The purpose of the COACH Family Interview is for all of us to gain a better understanding of what you think is important for [student's name] so the educational team can develop and implement an appropriate IEP.

Curriculum Content Included in the Family Interview

COACH includes nine categories of curriculum with corresponding learning outcomes that typically are not included in the general education curriculum. These learning outcomes are not designed to replace the general education curriculum—they are meant to augment or extend it. That is why it is so important to complete later steps of COACH where we will ensure that [student's name] has appropriate access to the general education curriculum available to his or her classmates without disabilities.

Interview Activities and Time Frame

It will take about 60–90 minutes to complete the interview. I will ask you a series of questions, listen carefully to your responses, and record them. The questions start broadly in order to consider many possibilities. As we proceed, the questions are designed to help you focus in on what you think are the most important learning outcomes for [student's name] to work on this year. Because the interview includes so many questions, we will be asking you to share brief answers. If there is anything you do not want to answer, then feel free to say so.

Outcomes of the Family Interview

By the end of the COACH Family Interview, you will have a selected a small set (e.g., 5–7) of learning outcomes that you think are the most important for [student's name] to work on in the coming year and should be listed on the IEP as annual goals.

Next Steps

After the interview is completed, we will share your selections with the other team members who were not present today. The priorities you identified to be included in the IEP will be worded as annual goals with short-term objectives or benchmarks for your review. Next, we need to complete Steps 2.1 and 2.2 of COACH to identify the additional learning outcomes and Step 3.0 to identify the general supports that will be part of [student's name] overall educational plan. Do you have any questions before we get started?

Figure 6. Introduce the family interview.

ingly invited to a COACH meeting without adequate team preparation and are asked questions from COACH without the benefit of beginning with an introduction. These seemingly small but important actions (i.e., Preparation Checklist, Introducing the Family Interview), in conjunction with the helpful hints offered in each step of the directions (e.g., considering where participants are seated during the interview), can make the difference to ensure successful facilitation of COACH.

Step 1.1: Valued Life Outcomes

Valued life outcomes set a context for the rest of COACH. COACH has built on and modified the longstanding environmental/ecological approach to curriculum selection first popularized by L. Brown and his colleagues (Brown et al., 1976, 1979) in which selecting curricular content is based on the skills needed to function in current and future environments (e.g., home, school, community, workplace). In COACH, although considering environments in which skills will be used is still important (especially when crafting the annual goals and short-term objectives), selecting priority learning outcomes are primarily referenced to the current and desired future status of five valued life outcomes. These were identified by interviewing parents of children with disabilities about indicators they believe do or would make for a "good life" for their children (Giangreco, Cloninger et al., 1991). In other words, we want students lives to be better as a result of attending school; in part, this is pursued by learning skills that contribute to valued life outcomes, such as those listed in Table 1.

After reviewing the list of valued life outcomes and understanding they are to be interpreted broadly and from the family's perspective, parents are asked a series of questions to gather information about the current and desired future status of valued life outcomes for their child. For each valued life outcome area, the family is first asked, "Are you interested in answering questions on this topic?" This is done to respect the cultural and individual differences among families, giving them the opportunity to simply decline answering questions about any topics they consider unnecessary or too personal, without requiring an explanation.

Questions pertaining to valued life outcomes purposely have been written in a broad manner so families can attach their own meanings to them. Figure 7 shows an excerpt from this step that first asks about the current status and then asks about the future.

At the end of Step 1.1, the family is asked to rate each of the valued life outcome areas to indicate their level of concern/importance about the area, with an emphasis on this year (see Figure 8). This convergent step provides valuable information to school personnel to assist them in planning an appropriate educational program responsive to the needs identified by the family.

Step 1.2: Selecting Curriculum Areas to Be Explored During the Family Interview

This step offers families the opportunity to consider all nine curriculum areas included in COACH and then make a decision about which subset of areas (up to four) should be explored in greater depth during the Family Interview because they represent the four most important areas within COACH for the student this year from the family perspective (see Figure 9). This substep helps parents become familiar with the curriculum areas and corresponding lists of learning outcomes included in COACH, given the understanding they are designed to extend

Table 1. Valued life outcomes

Safety and health (physical and emotional)
A home—now and in the future
Meaningful relationships
Control over personal choices (suited to the student's age and culture)
Meaningful activities in various and valued places

Meaningful Relationships

"Are you interested in answering questions on this topic?"
Mark (✓): ○ Yes or ○ No

5. Who are the people (e.g., family, neighbors, friends) that [student's name] spends the most time with during a typical week?

_____

_____

_____

_____

6. How, if at all, would you like to see [student's name] relationships change or expand in the near future (e.g., more time with same-age peers)?

_____

_____

_____

_____

Figure 7. Excerpt from Valued Life Outcomes: Meaningful Relationships.

or supplement learning outcomes included in the general education curriculum, not replace them.

Although some overlap exists with early grade academic curricula, for the most part, the learning outcomes listed in COACH are those typically not explicitly listed in the general education curriculum, yet remain important for many students with disabilities. In addition, the lists of learning outcomes have purposely been limited to a relatively small set of the most frequently identified priorities by families based on 25 years of field testing dating back to the earliest versions of COACH designed for school use (Giangreco, 1985).

We are not suggesting that the learning outcomes listed in COACH are necessarily more important than general education curricula; in our experience, both sets of learning outcomes are important. The COACH curriculum areas do not attempt to duplicate the general education curricular areas, which are already documented in other ways in schools. Therefore, more extensive academic content is not included in Step 1 of COACH because areas such as math, language arts, social studies, science, art, music, and physical education are already included in the general education curriculum, which is considered in COACH Step 2.2 (Additional Learning Outcomes from General Education).

In Step 1.2, the family is oriented to the contents of the curriculum areas by sharing the lists of learning outcomes from the nine curriculum areas using the reference information on the second page of Step 1.2, which lists all the possible COACH learning outcomes from which the family may choose; these same learning outcomes also appear in Step 1.3 (learning outcome lists). Six of the curriculum areas include lists of learning outcomes typically used by students across many environments, referred to as *cross-environmental*. These curriculum areas include 1) communication, 2) socialization, 3) personal management, 4) recreation, 5) access academics, and 6) applied academics. Learning outcomes within these listings (e.g.,

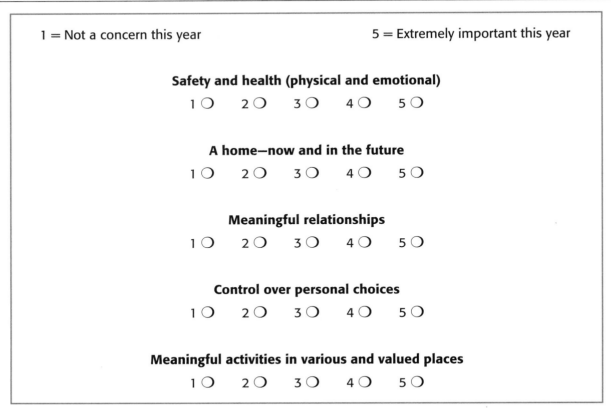

Figure 8. Excerpt from Valued Life Outcomes: Ratings.

making requests, following instructions, commenting, offering assistance to others, drinking/ eating, reading words) are used within many activities and functional routines across settings such as home, school, work, and a variety of community locations—in other words, cross-environmentally.

Motor (i.e., gross, fine), cognition, and sensory skills are three other areas of development that cross environments, yet are not listed as separate curriculum areas in COACH because they represent subskills embedded in all learning outcomes listed in COACH. Subskills are ultimately useful only when they are embedded in the context of functional learning outcomes or routines. For example, the motor skill of grasping and the cognitive skill of means/ends only become useful when they are combined to produce a meaningful outcome, such as feeding oneself, playing with a toy, or using a vending machine to get a drink. The purposeful omission of motor, cognition, and sensory skills is not meant to diminish their importance, but rather to encourage team members to embed these important subskills and consider how they might be combined and incorporated into functional learning outcomes and routines that contribute to valued life outcomes (Rainforth, Giangreco, & Dennis, 1989).

The three remaining curriculum areas—school, community, and vocational—list learning outcomes typically used primarily or exclusively in these specific environments and, therefore, are referred to as *environment-specific*. For example, doing a classroom job and managing school-related belongings are done in school. Making purchases and using public transportation are done primarily in the community. Interacting appropriately with co-workers and using a time clock/sign in primarily are done at work. In each of these examples, the learning outcomes are associated with a specific environment where they are primarily used.

Step 1.2

Selecting Curriculum Areas to Explore During the Family Interview

Consider all nine COACH curriculum areas and select up to four areas to address *now* in the Family Interview. For those remaining areas, indicate whether to address *later* or *skip* for this year. Only one box will be marked (✓) for each area.

Curriculum areas	**Now** Address in Family Interview	**Later** Address in Step 2.1	**Skip** for this year
Communication			
Socialization			
Personal management			
Recreation			
Access academics			
Applied academics			
School			
Community Consider for transition-age students (14–21 years)			
Vocational Consider for transition-age students (14–21 years at community worksites)			

Figure 9.   Selecting curriculum areas to be explored during the Family Interview.

Once familiarized with the curriculum areas and the learning outcome lists, the facilitator asks the parents to choose one of three options for each of the nine curriculum areas. Their choices include whether to address the curriculum area 1) now (during the Family Interview) if they believe the listing includes potential priorities for their child this year, 2) later (during Step 2.1) for somewhat less important (though not unimportant) curriculum areas than those to be explored in the Family Interview, or 3) skip for this year.

When a family selects the skip option, it usually indicates one of four possibilities. First, if the student is already doing well enough on the learning outcomes listed in the curriculum area, then they are presently not of great concern to the family. For example, when considering the curriculum area access academics, a family may recognize these early learning skills (e.g., directs and sustains attention, explores surroundings and objects, imitates) as those their child already possesses to a substantial degree and therefore can be skipped.

Second, in a small number of cases, the contents of a curriculum area may overlap substantially with general education curriculum to be addressed in the classroom. The most common example of this would be the overlap between the COACH curriculum area applied academics and the general education curriculum within primary grades (e.g., K–2). So the parent of a kindergarten student may decide to skip that area in COACH, knowing that the contents (and more) are included in the general education kindergarten or primary grades curriculum. Those same applied academic learning outcomes are included in COACH because they may be relevant for older students in cases in which they are not typically part of the general education curriculum in higher grades.

Third, in some cases, parents communicate that they perceive the listed learning outcomes to be significantly beyond the student's current functioning level to be a priority focus for this year. For example, if a parent looks at the access academics curriculum area and recognizes his or her child needs to acquire or improve these types of foundational learning outcomes (e.g., reacting to interactions, directing attention, discriminating, imitating), then he or she may feel that the types of learning outcomes in the area of applied academics (e.g., writing, reading, using money) may be beyond what makes sense as instructional targets for this year. It is important to never put limits on what students are capable of learning, even when decisions to skip a curriculum area are made to ensure that instructional targets are at an appropriate level of difficulty. Therefore, even in cases in which content from the applied academics area is not targeted by the family for review during the family interview or Step 2.1 (Additional Learning Outcomes from COACH), such academic curricula still should be considered in Step 2.2 (Additional Learning Outcomes from General Education). In other words, even if a parent does not select reading as one of his or her top priority curriculum areas to review during the family interview (for whatever reason), the school still has a responsibility to teach literacy and other academic content to all students as part of ensuring access to the general education curriculum.

Fourth, parents may decide to skip a curriculum if they believe the listed learning outcomes are not sufficiently important this year, even though they may be important in the future. For example, the community and vocational listings are geared toward older students and are not recommended as potential areas of focus for elementary and middle school age students. Although community-based and vocational preparation are vital for students with disabilities (McDonnell & McGuire, 2007), being in school during the school day is the natural environment for elementary, middle school, and even most high school age students. Because students with more intensive special education needs frequently take advantage of their right to receive a public education through age 21, there is plenty of time to work on community and vocational skills during the 17- to 21-year-old time frame in integrated community sites. Community-based and vocational experiences prior to the time when most other students without disabilities are graduating should correspond to options available for and with their classmates who do not have disabilities, such as field trips for younger children, experiential and service learning options for students as they get older, and inclusive technical or vocational education for high school students.

After considering all nine curriculum areas in COACH, parents are to asked to be convergent by limiting their selection of curriculum areas to be addressed now (during the Family Interview) to a maximum of four (they may choose fewer than four). Our field testing has indicated that when families select more than four curricular areas to review in depth during the Family Interview (as was the practice in earlier versions of COACH), learning outcomes from all of those areas do not make it to their final list of selected priorities. So, capping the number of areas to review assists families in focusing on their priorities and makes the remaining parts of the Family Interview easier and less time consuming.

Some parents find it challenging to narrow the selection down to four curriculum areas because they want to be comprehensive in their review of potential priorities or are concerned that eliminating some areas may allow some important learning outcomes to "fall through cracks" and be lost from the student's educational program. COACH is designed to address this concern through Step 2.1 (Additional Learning Outcomes from COACH) and Step 2.2 (Additional Learning Outcomes from General Education). The facilitator can reduce parents' potential anxiety about missing something valuable in the listings by explaining the additional learning outcomes during the introduction to the Family Interview. When parents understand they will have an opportunity to revisit curriculum areas during Step 2.1, they are more comfortable limiting their selection of curriculum areas to four. Conversely, if they are not familiar with Step 2.1, they may request that every area be reviewed during the Family Interview in an effort to be comprehensive.

Ultimately, capping the number of reviewed curriculum areas to four is designed to facilitate the selection of the highest priorities from the family's perspective, whereas the option to revisit the areas later (during Step 2.1) ensures that other potentially important learning outcomes are not missed. The four curriculum areas selected by the family are the only ones addressed in the remainder of the Family Interview.

Step 1.3: Rating Learning Outcomes in Selected Curriculum Areas

Step 1.3 provides lists for each of the nine curriculum areas and corresponding learning outcomes considered in the Family Interview. A blank form is also available to add any curriculum areas and learning outcomes that are potential priorities but do not logically fit into one of the existing COACH listings.

The learning outcomes listed in Step 1.3 are observable, functional behaviors carefully selected based on field-testing over many years. Learning outcomes purposely have been worded in broad terms so families can interpret them differently. These broadly stated learning outcomes are made up of clusters of skills that, when grouped together, facilitate student participation, at least partially, in typical settings and with people who do not have disabilities. An effective facilitator of COACH will individualize the language of the learning outcomes to match each situation.

At the culmination of the Family Interview (Step 1.5: Cross-Prioritization), a priority learning outcome is selected by the family, and the meaning attached to it will be further clarified when the priority is translated into an Annual Goal (Step 4) and Short-Term Objectives (Step 5). This broad, interpretative approach assists families with the process of sorting and selecting priorities by avoiding the review of hundreds of variations and subskills. For example, some checklists include more than 50 subskills pertaining to dressing—COACH includes one: dresses/undresses (personal management, Item 31). In using the more extensive listing, a parent could assess or consider all 50 items, yet still not have identified which are priorities. It is conceivable that none of the dressing items will be priorities for a particular student or that only a couple of items are important this year. Therefore, reviewing the entire subset represents a significant waste of time (assuming your purpose is to develop an individualized education program [IEP]). If dressing is not a priority concern, then you will either not address it at all, or you will spend only the time to address it as a single item (dresses/undresses). If, however, dressing ends up being selected as a priority concern, then it will be identified, clarified, and explored in more detail as needed. For example, if the concern is putting on shoes or dressing after using the bathroom, then this level of specificity would come to the forefront in Steps 4 and 5.

In Step 1.3, the family is presented with each learning outcome and asked how their child currently does with that particular learning outcome using the following scoring key: 1) early/emerging skill, 2) partial skill, or 3) skillful (see Figure 10). These scoring codes are purposely written in a positive way to encourage all participants to think about what the student can do, rather than what he or she cannot do. Occasionally people ask, "Shouldn't there be a score for no skill?" The absence of a no skill option in COACH is purposeful. Every student has some early skills or behaviors for any learning outcome listed in COACH. Not only does it serve little useful purpose to indicate a student has no skill, it also can create a negative experience for families, particularly those whose children have the most severe or multiple disabilities. Imagine what it might be like to repeat 40 times, "My child has no skill," or worse yet, if the scale were numeric to repeat "zero" many times. In our estimation, no one benefits by designating a student's skill as zero or nonexistent.

This scoring system is meant to provide a gross indication of functioning level as perceived by the family and may not necessarily be consistent with the opinions of other team members. This scoring approach frequently leads to parents providing additional descriptive information about their child and may prompt follow-up questions by the facilitator. Although such an exchange can be very informative, be aware that extended discussion on every item may interfere with completing the Family Interview in a timely manner and might interfere with achieving its intended purpose—namely, the family selecting priority learning outcomes. Rather than spending a great deal of time discussing items unlikely to be priorities, COACH suggests first identifying the priorities, then more in-depth discussions and planning focused on those priorities can occur when developing the goals and objectives and planning for instruction.

Another aspect of Step 1.3 is to ask the following question for each learning outcome rated as early/emerging skill, partial skill, or skillful: "Does the learning outcome need work this year?" This is one of the unique features distinguishing the COACH Family Interview from other checklists of functional or developmental skills. Regardless of various scoring approaches, most tests, assessments, and checklists infer assumptions based on the score or rating. Typically, a low score presumes a student needs work, whereas a high score often presumes a student does not need work. We think these are inappropriate presumptions to make.

In the COACH Family Interview, the score and whether the item needs work this year are related but independent of each other. Just because a learning outcome has the lowest rating in COACH (i.e., early/emerging) does not necessarily mean that it needs work this year. It simply may be a low priority, may be too far beyond the student's current level to be appropriate this year, may be more important when the student is older, or may be focusing too much on perceived weaknesses rather than on student strengths. Traditional assessment approaches place a great deal of emphasis on identifying what students do poorly and then selecting those perceived deficiencies as learning priorities. The Family Interview encourages consumers to consider a variety of criteria in selecting priorities and not to automatically make something a learning priority just because it has a low score.

Conversely, just because a learning outcome has the highest score (i.e., skillful) does not necessarily mean that it does not need work this year. This allows the option to build on student strengths or to acknowledge a student has a particular skill, but he or she may need to display it in more appropriate ways. For example, a parent may rate his or her child as skillful at expressing rejection/refusal (communication, Item 6) because the child's meaning is clearly un-

Socialization

Complete only if **Now** was selected in Step 1.2.

Learning outcomes	STEP 1.3 Mark score	STEP 1.3 Needs work this year?	STEP 1.4 Rank up to four priorities
14. Responds to the presence and interactions of others (e.g., family, peers, adults)	E P S ○ ○ ○	N Y ○ ○	
15. Initiates social interactions (e.g., approaches others, joins group)	E P S ○ ○ ○	N Y ○ ○	
16. Sustains social interactions (e.g., explores objects with others, takes turns, provides mutual attention)	E P S ○ ○ ○	N Y ○ ○	
17. Ends social interactions	E P S ○ ○ ○	N Y ○ ○	
18. Distinguishes and interacts differently with friends/family, acquaintances, and strangers	E P S ○ ○ ○	N Y ○ ○	
19. Maintains prosocial behaviors when alone and with others	E P S ○ ○ ○	N Y ○ ○	
20. Accepts assistance from others	E P S ○ ○ ○	N Y ○ ○	
21. Offers assistance to others	E P S ○ ○ ○	N Y ○ ○	
22. Makes transitions between routine activities	E P S ○ ○ ○	N Y ○ ○	
23. Adjusts to unexpected changes in routine	E P S ○ ○ ○	N Y ○ ○	
24. Shares with others	E P S ○ ○ ○	N Y ○ ○	
25. Advocates for self (e.g., directs personal care, selects projects/classes, asks for help if needed, makes decisions available to peers)	E P S ○ ○ ○	N Y ○ ○	

Comments:

Scoring key (use scores for Step 1.3 alone or in combination):
E = Early/emerging skill (1%–25%); P = Partial skill (25%–80%); S = Skillful (80%–100%).

Figure 10. Excerpt from Rating Learning Outcomes in Selected Curriculum Areas: Socialization.

derstood by all who encounter his or her refusals, even though the way the refusal is expressed is considered undesirable (e.g., tantrum). Yet, at the same time, the parent may respond "yes" to the question, "Does your child need work on that skill this year?" to work on more socially desirable ways to express refusal. In another example, a parent may rate his or her child's ability to "make requests of others" as skillful because the child has an effective way to make a request using an augmentative and alternative communication (AAC) device. Yet, at the same time, the parent may respond "yes" to the question, "Does your child need work on that skill this year?" to build on a perceived student strength by expanding the number and types of requests the student can make using the AAC device. So, in the Family Interview, a learning outcome can be scored at any of the three rating levels and the decision as to whether the item needs work this year is an independent one. By the time Step 1.3 has been completed, the set of potential priorities has been further narrowed to only those reviewed items that were marked "yes."

Step 1.4: Prioritizing Learning Outcomes in Selected Curriculum Areas

Prioritizing allows the family to consider which of the learning outcomes are their top priorities within each curriculum area reviewed. This step narrows each list from all the learning outcomes that need work this year to those the family considers priorities within the lists they reviewed. The family is asked to rank a maximum of the top four priorities. In doing so, they consider a variety of criteria in determining their priorities, such as the strengths and interests of their child, immediacy of the need, frequency of use, practicality, future use, and its potential affect on valued life outcomes. In some situations, the family may identify fewer than four priorities within a learning outcome listing. The ranked priorities are transferred to Step 1.5 (Cross-Prioritization) so they may be viewed on a single page.

Step 1.5: Cross-Prioritization

Cross-prioritization provides an opportunity for the family to select and rank overall priority learning outcomes for their child. This is accomplished by considering the priorities they have selected within the curriculum areas they have reviewed and ranked in the previous parts of the Family Interview. Using the same criteria as in Step 1.4, the family ranks a maximum of their top six overall priorities (see Figure 11). The result is a short, individualized set of priority learning outcomes to work on during the coming year.

Cross-prioritization provides another opportunity to reconsider each remaining learning outcome in relation to the others the family identified as priorities within and across curriculum areas. It is not uncommon for an item that was ranked as a second or third priority to move up in the overall ranking. This phenomenon lends credibility to the fact that people sometimes adjust their decisions when presented with multiple opportunities, at a slightly different time, and with different sets of choices. When using COACH, each step provides another chance to reconsider the potential priorities, so by the time the cross-prioritization is completed, both the family and the other team members are confident the selections truly represent important priorities for the student from the perspective of the family.

The learning outcomes listed in COACH are purposely stated broadly so they can be individually interpreted by families. Therefore, it is important for the facilitator and other team members to be sure they understand the intent behind the selection of each priority. This is done by reviewing each ranked priority and having the facilitator offer his or her understanding of the meaning behind the family's selection by indicating which valued life outcomes the priority is designed to support. For example, if the priority was "initiates social interactions," then the facilitator might say, "My understanding is that you selected that priority because you are interested in your child establishing more friendships with classmates. Is that accurate?"

Then the parents would have the opportunity to verify the accuracy of the facilitator's statement, clarify it, or restate it. In most cases, we find that facilitators do understand the meaning behind the family's priority selections. This aspect of Step 1.5 sends a clear and important message to the family that the facilitator has been listening intently to them and wants to understand their perspectives. Occasionally, the facilitator has misunderstood the meaning behind the selection of a priority; this substep provides the opportunity to clarify the meaning and also sends another important message to the family that the facilitator recognizes that communication is sometimes misunderstood and that he or she is open to clarification.

Finally, just because a family selects a particular learning outcome as an overall priority does not necessarily mean that it needs to be documented on the IEP as an annual goal and short-term objective. Some overall priorities do end up as IEP goals and objectives. Other overall priorities end up being part of the student's additional learning outcomes or as a home responsibility. For example, a family selecting "participates in small and large groups" as a priority for their child recognizes that this is an ongoing part of classroom routine and expresses comfort listing this learning outcome on the additional learning outcomes from COACH (Step 2.1) list. Even though the item is not listed as an IEP goal, it still provides the school team with important information about the family's perspective; namely, that they value having their child work in groups with other children rather than being isolated with a teaching assistant. In a different example, a parent identifies "brushes/flosses teeth" as a priority because of ongoing dental health concerns for his or her child. Though this is a priority from the perspective of the family, and they do want the child to brush after lunch at school, they do not wish this to be a focus of their child's instruction while in school and prefer to take the responsibility for this at home. By the end of the Family Interview, the family will have selected a small set of discipline-free, priority learning outcomes that will be restated as IEP goals and objectives.

Additional Learning Outcomes

After completing the Family Interview (Step 1), the assembled team members complete the Additional Learning Outcomes (Step 2). This step recognizes that selecting priorities from the Family Interview, although important in providing a focus to a student's educational program, are insufficient to comprise a complete educational program. All students deserve a broad-based curriculum, including appropriately adapted access to general education curriculum. This is especially important for students with intensive special educational needs who historically have had their access to rich and interesting curriculum artificially restricted based on inappropriately presumed levels of capability.

Determining the additional learning outcomes requires a subset of team members who know the student and who have knowledge of the general education curriculum. This step is divided into two substeps: Additional Learning Outcomes from COACH (Step 2.1) and Additional Learning Outcomes from General Education (Step 2.2). Although these two subsets are presented sequentially in the same order as they appeared in earlier editions, we do not mean to imply that the one completed first is necessarily more important. In fact, as you will find in the directions related to Step 2, we encourage each team to make a conscious decision about which of these two substeps to complete first. Completing Step 2.1 before Step 2.2 may help retain a conceptual and practical flow by allowing the team to make all their decisions about the learning outcomes listed in COACH before shifting their attention to general education learning outcomes. Completing Step 2.1 first may also ensure that the facilitator's promise to parents to revisit potentially important, yet deferred, COACH learning outcomes until Step 2.1 is addressed. A potential hazard of completing Step 2.1 first is the number of selected learning outcomes becomes too numerous, leaving insufficient room for general education learning outcomes.

Cross-Prioritization

COACH 3

Transfer priority learning outcomes in their ranked order from each COACH curriculum area reviewed with the family in Step 1.4.

	Communication	Socialization	Personal management	Recreation	Access academics
1					
2					
3					
4					
	Applied academics	School	Community	Vocational	Other
1					
2					
3					
4					

Cross-Prioritization

COACH 3

Rank	Overall priority learning outcomes (Word priorities to explicitly clarify what the student will be expected to learn)	Indicate which valued life outcomes the priority is meant to support					Check (✓) only one box for each priority		
		Safety/health	Home	Relationships	Control/choices	Activities	IEP goal	Additional learning outcomes	Home
1									
2									
3									
4									
5									
6									

Next step: The interviewer explains Steps 2.1, 2.2, and 3 and the relationship of the Family Interview to the next steps.

Figure 11. Cross-prioritization.

Some teams prefer to move directly from the Family Interview to considering the general education curriculum in Step 2.2 to send a strong philosophical message about the importance of ensuring access to the general education curriculum. Completing Step 2.2 first helps ensure sufficient emphasis and time are devoted to general education learning outcomes that can further contribute to making the least dangerous assumptions about student potential. Because COACH is not standardized, this sequence within Step 2 can be determined by each individual team.

After completing both substeps in Step 2, the team must review the final selection of targeted learning outcomes to ensure that the combined set can be reasonably addressed given available time. Too often, teams are tempted to select too many learning outcomes in Step 2, rendering it so large it is unhelpful. Remember, the goal of these two substeps is not to identify every possible learning outcome the student will be exposed to or may learn. Rather, it is designed to help teams develop a shared understanding of which learning outcomes should be targeted for instruction while providing the team with a balance of focus and breadth in curricular content. Information generated from both steps can be attached to the IEP as an addendum to document team decisions about the student's educational program, but need not conform to any particular format, thus providing teams with flexible ways to document their decisions.

Step 2.1: Additional Learning Outcomes from COACH

Step 2.1 ensures that important selections made during the Family Interview, but not slated for inclusion as IEP goals, as well as learning outcome areas tabled in Step 1.2 (Selecting Curriculum Areas to Explore during the Family Interview) are revisited. This is a safety-valve step so learning outcomes from COACH not selected as priorities during the Family Interview are not forgotten. Step 2.1 presents all the learning outcomes listed in COACH in a checklist format (see Figure 12).

Step 2.2: Additional Learning Outcomes from General Education

Step 2.2 ensures that students with disabilities are provided with the same opportunities as their classmates to pursue a broad-based educational program and to be exposed to a variety of educational content (e.g., language arts, math, science, social studies, art, music, health, physical education). The set of general education learning outcomes selected for the student should be individualized and at an appropriate level. Far too often, students with disabilities are excluded unnecessarily from general education class activities because they are functioning at a different level than their classmates. This is frequently accompanied by disagreement among team members about the curricular expectations for the student in various subject areas. Step 2.2 draws on the earlier discussion of multilevel curriculum and curriculum overlapping by asking team members to consider the student's primary type of participation in general education classes (i.e., same, multilevel curriculum, curriculum overlapping) (see Figure 13). Even when a primary type of participation is identified (e.g., multilevel curriculum; same content, different level), there are frequently opportunities for secondary types of participation (e.g., curriculum overlapping) within the same class session or activity. When instruction is active, the opportunities to pursue multiple learning outcomes and types of participation within a single lesson or activity are numerous (Giangreco, 2007). When Step 2.2 is completed, team members have reached a general agreement about the learning expectations for a student in the various general education curriculum areas and identified examples of learning outcomes for the classroom teachers to provide a starting point for instruction, recognizing teachers should be afforded the opportunity to get to know the student and adjust accordingly.

Step 2.1

Additional Learning Outcomes from COACH

Select and mark (✓) only those additional learning outcomes to be targeted for instruction (limit to reasonable number). See manual for directions.

Date: _____ Participants: _____

_____

Communication

____ 1. Displays consistent communication mode

____ 2. Expresses continuation or "more"

____ 3. Makes selection when given options

____ 4. Makes request of others

____ 5. Signals desire/need for attention

____ 6. Expresses rejection/refusal

____ 7. Sustains communication with others

____ 8. Recognizes when misunderstood and uses another way

____ 9. Expresses greetings and farewells

____ 10. Follows instructions

____ 11. Answers questions

____ 12. Comments/describes

____ 13. Asks questions of others

Socialization

____ 14. Responds to the presence and interactions of others

____ 15. Initiates social interactions

____ 16. Sustains social interactions

____ 17. Ends social interactions

____ 18. Distinguishes and interacts differently with friends/family, acquaintances, and strangers

____ 19. Maintains safe and healthy behaviors when alone and with others

____ 20. Accepts assistance from others

____ 21. Offers assistance to others

____ 22. Makes transitions between routine activities

____ 23. Adjusts to unexpected changes in routine

____ 24. Shares with others

____ 25. Advocates for self

Personal Management

____ 26. Gives permission and/or directs others to provide personal care support

____ 27. Drinks and eats

____ 28. Feeds self

____ 29. Cares for bowel and bladder needs

____ 30. Selects appropriate clothing to wear

____ 31. Dresses/undresses

____ 32. Cares for personal hygiene

____ 33. Is mobile between locations

____ 34. Manages personal belongings

____ 35. Gives self-identification information

____ 36. Uses telephone

____ 37. Responds to emergency alarm

____ 38. Recognizes and avoids potentially dangerous situations

____ 39. Maintains safe and healthy behaviors

Recreation

____ 40. Engages in spectator events with others

____ 41. Engages in recreation activities on his or her own

____ 42. Engages in recreation activities with others

Figure 12.   Excerpt from Additional Learning Outcomes from COACH.

General Supports

COACH also provides a simple method for documenting general supports that need to be provided to or for a student (see Figure 14). The general supports serve to allow access to, or participation in, the education program. Unlike learning outcomes, which seek observable change in student behavior, general supports identify what other people need to do to assist the student. General supports are broad based and often are cross-situational, rather than highly specific to a particular lesson, activity, or instructional routine. Elements referred to in COACH as *general supports* may be known by other terms in some locales (e.g., accommodations, management needs). General supports typically fall into five categories.

1. Personal needs (e.g., feeding, dressing, giving medication)

2. Physical needs (e.g., therapeutic positioning, managing specialized equipment, environmental modifications)

3. Teaching others about the student (e.g., teaching classmates about a student's AAC system, teaching staff health emergency procedures, teaching staff positive behavior supports and crisis intervention protocols)

4. Sensory needs (e.g., providing books in braille, providing access to large-print materials, maintaining charged batteries in a hearing aid)

5. Providing access and opportunities (e.g., arranging community vocational experiences, providing literacy materials in a student's native language, providing access to general education class activities)

Classroom teachers, special educators, related services personnel, teacher assistants, family members, and others might provide general supports. Peers may appropriately provide some general supports. For example, a small group of students who were in class with the student with disabilities the previous school year can explain to their new classmates how the student with disabilities communicates and how they might interpret some of his or her unique sounds and movements (e.g., an "ahhh" sound with eyes up means *yes* or an affirmation). Caution should be exercised when involving peers in assisting with the provision of general supports to ensure that such involvement is considered mutually beneficial, appropriate, and respectful.

Some general supports can be appropriately addressed within the general education classroom when doing so is status neutral or, preferably, status enhancing. In other words, providing general supports in typical settings should have a neutral or positive affect on how other people perceive the student with disabilities. Conversely, some general supports should be provided in private (e.g., dressing, health procedures). These private places need not be exclusively for students with disabilities, but places available for the same purposes for students who do not have disabilities (e.g., an accessible lavatory). It is critical to not subject students with disabilities to status-diminishing experiences. In other words, we should not do things to or for students that might cause personal embarrassment, lack of personal dignity, or otherwise cause them to be perceived negatively—this should be true for any student, whether or not they have a disability label. By the time the team has completed Step 3 they will have selected a set of general supports that need to be done to or for the student to facilitate access and participation in school.

HOW AND WHY COACH WORKS

COACH has been successfully used to plan educational programs for students with disabilities since the 1980s, in part, because it relies on combining several time-tested approaches to effective educational planning (e.g., using collaborative teamwork, involving families in meaning-

Additional Learning
Outcomes from General Education

COACH3

General education curriculum areas (provide brief description)	Indicate primary participation option	Provide example Starting points if multilevel or curriculum overlapping
✓		
Language arts:	○ Same (grade-level expectation) ○ Multilevel (same content) ○ Multilevel (different content) ○ Curriculum overlapping	
Math:	○ Same (grade-level expectation) ○ Multilevel (same content) ○ Multilevel (different content) ○ Curriculum overlapping	
Science:	○ Same (grade-level expectation) ○ Multilevel (same content) ○ Multilevel (different content) ○ Curriculum overlapping	
Social studies:	○ Same (grade-level expectation) ○ Multilevel (same content) ○ Multilevel (different content) ○ Curriculum overlapping	

Figure 13. Excerpt from Additional Learning Outcomes from General Education.

(continued)

Step 3

General Supports

COACH 3

Select and mark (✓) all necessary general supports. See manual for directions.

Participants: _____

Personal Needs

_____ 1. Needs to be fed food and drinks

_____ 2. Needs to be dressed

_____ 3. Needs assistance with bowel and bladder management

_____ 4. Needs assistance with personal hygiene

_____ 5. Needs to be given medication

_____ 6. Needs suctioning and/or postural drainage

_____ _____

_____ _____

_____ _____

_____ _____

_____ _____

_____ _____

_____ _____

Physical Needs

_____ 7. Needs to be physically repositioned at regular intervals

_____ 8. Needs to have environmental barriers modified to allow access

_____ 9. Needs to have physical equipment managed (e.g., wheelchair, braces, orthotics)

_____ 10. Needs specialized transportation accommodations

_____ 11. Needs to be moved and positioned in specialized ways

_____ 12. Needs to be physically moved from place to place

_____ _____

_____ _____

_____ _____

_____ _____

_____ _____

Teaching Others About the Student

_____ 13. Teach staff and classmates about the student's AAC system and other communicative behaviors

_____ 14. Teach staff and students how to communicate with the student

_____ 15. Teach staff seizure management procedures

_____ 16. Teach staff emergency procedures (e.g., medical, evacuation)

_____ 17. Teach staff preventive behavior management procedures

_____ 18. Teach staff behavioral crisis intervention procedures

_____ 19. Teach peers and adults to ask the student to repeat or communicate in another way if not understood

_____ _____

_____ _____

_____ _____

_____ _____

Figure 14. Excerpt from General Supports.

ful ways, ensuring both focus and breadth in curriculum selection) and has incorporated feedback from field-testing in its revisions. Although COACH shares these types of similarities with other planning and assessment approaches, it also has some unique features distinguishing it from other tools. This section briefly describes a few key aspects of COACH that make it unique and contribute to its effectiveness.

Developing a relevant educational program for a student with disabilities can be a challenge or, in one sense, a problem to be solved. Professionals with good intentions often seek input from families, but fail to provide them with methods for making important decisions. Using open-ended questions such as, "What would you like to see on Jaime's IEP this year?" or "What are your priorities for Bella?" might work for some families. But all too often, open-ended approaches result in parents deferring to professionals or making selections that do not necessarily represent their top priorities. This may occur because families are faced with trying to make priority selections of hundreds of potential options without any strategies to help them organize and sort this vast array of possibilities. Using problem-solving methods facilitates meaningful selections.

COACH relies on selected elements of the *Osborn-Parnes Creative Problem-Solving Process* (CPS) (Osborn, 1993; Parnes, 1988, 1997), an approach with a long history of documented effectiveness (Parnes, 1992). Aspects of CPS are imbedded in COACH to help families select the most important learning outcomes to be included in their child's educational plan. Once a problem or challenge has been identified, CPS offers these basic steps.

- Visionizing or objective finding (identifying a general challenge)
- Fact-finding (gathering information)
- Problem-finding (clarifying the problem)
- Idea-finding (brainstorming a quantity of ideas)
- Solution-finding (selecting the best ideas based on criteria)
- Acceptance-finding (making a plan, refining it, and taking action)

Although COACH does not employ a classic application of the CPS process, it retains many of its key features. The following sections describe how three key concepts of CPS are embedded in COACH.

Fact-Finding and Deferring Judgment

COACH establishes a pattern within steps whereby at certain times participants are asked various types of fact-finding questions that encourage them to defer judgment and share information without making a judgment about it. At other times within the same step, they are asked to actively engage their judgment. Consciously deferring judgment initially allows the family to consider ideas that might be lost or discarded if judged prematurely.

Alternating Between Divergent and Convergent Steps

Alternating use of divergent and convergent thinking within steps is an overarching characteristic of CPS that meshes closely with fact-finding and deferring judgment. The divergent aspects encourage problem solvers to explore information and ideas broadly by extending in different directions from a common point (the problem to be solved). Convergent aspects encourage analysis of the divergent data to focus on a smaller set of options moving toward ultimate selections. COACH alternates between divergent and convergent thinking within each of its steps and substeps. For example, Step 1.1 begins by asking fact-finding questions that encourage participants to think divergently about the current and future status of valued life outcomes. Step 1.1 culminates convergently by asking the family to make some judgments about the valued life outcome categories by rating their importance for the student this year. In Step 1.2, the family is asked to defer judgment and divergently consider all nine curriculum areas in COACH, then be convergent by narrowing down to the four areas they deem to be most important to examine during the Family Interview. Steps 1–3 include divergent fact-finding with deferred judgment followed by an element that requires participants to engage judgment and be convergent as they focus in on the desired elements of the students educational program.

The divergent and convergent aspect of COACH steps are purposely separated because generating ideas and attempting to evaluate them at the same time can inhibit informed decision making. Firestien (1989) likened this to driving a car with your feet on the brake and the gas pedal at the same time; such an approach is unlikely to get anyone very far. Effective problem solvers actively defer judgment during divergent/fact-finding and purposefully engage judgment when it is time to be convergent.

Multiple Opportunities and Various Perspectives

COACH also helps families select priorities by providing multiple opportunities to consider the large number of curricular possibilities from various perspectives, in increasingly smaller and different sets, multiple times, prior to the final selection. In more traditional approaches, such as asking, "What would you like to see on Miguel's IEP this year?" parents have a single chance to respond. By the time a particular learning outcome has been selected as a priority to be included in the IEP (Part A, Step 1.5), it has been considered by the family from six to nine different times, in different sets of items in Steps 1.1–1.5 (see Figure 15). This increases the likelihood that the family will select learning outcomes that are truly relevant for their child.

DESCRIPTION OF COACH PART B (STEPS 4–6): TRANSLATING THE FAMILY-IDENTIFIED PRIORITIES INTO GOALS AND OBJECTIVES

Part B consists of three steps that assist teams in translating the family-identified priorities into 1) Annual Goals, 2) Short-Term Objectives, and 3) Program-at-a-Glance, in which the annual goals and earlier components of COACH (additional learning outcomes, general supports) are summarized in a short, easily accessible format.

Annual Goals

Step 4 provides a process for developing annual goals based on the family-selected priorities (from Step 1.5) that include an observable behavior judged to be attainable within a year and the contexts in which the observable behavior will be used (e.g., school, home, community, with peers who do not have disabilities, with co-workers in the breakroom at a job site) (see Figure 16). Identifying the context encourages team members to plan for instruction in natural environments and naturally occurring situations in which the student is expected to function. Documenting the context within annual goal statements also can provide justification for access to general education classes and other age-appropriate places frequented by people without disabilities (e.g., community worksites for older students).

Translating a family-selected priority into an annual goal statement requires a thorough understanding of a student's present level of performance related to the identified priority. This understanding may come from existing assessment information or may require collecting ad-

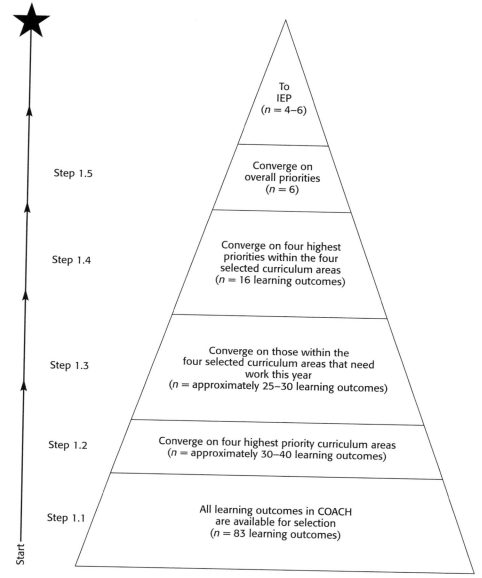

Star (top)

Step 1.5

Step 1.4

Step 1.3

Step 1.2

Step 1.1

Start

To
IEP
($n = 4$–6)

Converge on
overall priorities
($n = 6$)

Converge on four highest
priorities within the four
selected curriculum areas
($n = 16$ learning outcomes)

Converge on those within the
four selected curriculum areas that need
work this year
($n =$ approximately 25–30 learning outcomes)

Converge on four highest priority curriculum areas
($n =$ approximately 30–40 learning outcomes)

All learning outcomes in COACH
are available for selection
($n = 83$ learning outcomes)

Figure 15.   How COACH helps parents converge on their highest priorities.

ditional assessment information specific to the priority (Brown & Snell, 2011). Because COACH learning outcomes are stated quite broadly and are purposely open to wide interpretation, their translation into annual goals begins to clarify the meaning of the priority for the student. At times, the wording of a learning outcome from COACH will fit nicely into an annual goal statement. At other times, the wording will need to be adjusted to more closely reflect what the team feels is attainable in a year, while always keeping in mind how any modified language is leading toward the family-selected priority.

Because annual goals are designed to serve as a road map of the educational program, they should be stated in ways that offer direction to the team implementing the plan. For example, stating the mode of responding (e.g., speaking, pointing, eye gazing, writing, drawing) helps clarify an annual goal because it adds to the observable aspect of the priority. This becomes par-

---

| Goal _____ | **Annual Goals** | COACH3 |

1. Priority learning outcome from Step 1.5: _____

2. Present level of performance based on current assessment of the priority learning outcome:

   _____

3. What are the natural, age-appropriate contexts (places and activities) in which the student will be expected to use the skill/behavior this year?_____

   _____

4. What aspect of the priority learning outcomes should be reflected in the annual goal? Check all those to be addressed this year.

   __ Decreasing extra   __ Acquiring core skills   __ Quality of performance
      cues/supports   __ Expand repertoire   __ Tempo, rate, or fluency
   __ Respond to natural supports   __ Extend or reduce duration   __ Retention over time
   __ Generalization across   __ Other   __ Other
      settings, people,   __ Other
      materials/cues

5. What is the specific observable, measurable skill/behavior the team wants the student to learn this year? _____

   _____

6. Final annual goal (include contexts and skill/behavior): _____

   _____

Figure 16. Excerpt from Annual Goals.

ticularly important when developing an educational plan that spans parts of 2 different school years, corresponding with placement or staff changes, or both. When these types of changes occur and annual goals are not clearly written, there is a danger that the receiving team may misunderstand the intention behind the goal selection.

Clarifying which aspect of the behavior is the focus of instruction is another helpful component to include in an annual goal. For example, if a goal was written, "In community stores, Tommy will improve his ability to make purchases," one might assume that the focus of this goal was the acquisition of core skills associated with purchasing (e.g., locating merchandise, paying for it). Although such core skills may be the intent for one student, other students with the same goal may have a different focus related to purchasing. For example, one student may need to learn problem-solving strategies for what to do when he or she cannot find an item; another may need to expand his or her repertoire of purchasing to extend beyond prepackaged items to include fresh produce, bulk, or deli purchases—each of which require different skills. COACH encourages the team to consider which specific aspects are relevant for a student, including core skills and other aspects of learning outcomes such as 1) decreasing extra cues and supports; 2) responding to natural cues; 3) generalizing across setting, people, materials, and cues; 4) extending or reducing duration; 5) improving quality of performance; 6) increasing tempo, rate, or fluency; 7) improving retention over time; or 8) identifying other aspects of a learning outcome that is important for a student (Brown, Evans, Weed, & Owen, 1987; Brown, Lehr, & Snell, 2011; Brown & Snell, 2011). Clarifying the intent of the annual goal and writing it as an observable behavior provides direction for further refinement during the development of short-term objectives (Step 5).

Annual goals generated using COACH are designed to provide a relevant, individualized focus to a student's education and avoid some of the common problems historically associated with educational planning (Giangreco et al., 1994). Here are some of these common problems with potential alternatives:

- **Problem 1:** Goals are vague and use broad categories of behavior (e.g., "Jose will improve communication."). What communications skills are being referred to? This goal does not tell us.

  COACH alternative: Individualized learning outcomes (e.g., "Jose will initiate the use of 15 new manual signs during first-grade activities.").

- **Problem 2:** Rhetoric without substance (e.g., "Gina will enlarge her circle of friends."). What will Gina learn to help her enlarge her circle friends? This goal does not tell us.

  COACH alternative: Family-selected priorities based on valued life outcomes (e.g., "Gina will initiate and maintain social interactions [e.g., greetings, conversation] with classmates during cocurricular activities.").

- **Problem 3:** When IEPs are unnecessarily long it renders them less usable, making it difficult to fulfill the promises they infer, and making it difficult to figure out which goals are the priorities.

  COACH alternative: Develop a Program-at-a-Glance, which is short, useful, and distinguishes priority learning outcomes from additional learning outcomes.

- **Problem 4:** Goals that are written as behaviors for the staff rather than for the students (e.g., "Mary Ann's hearing aids will be checked daily by the speech-language pathologist [SLP].").

  COACH alternative: Goals for students are distinguished from general supports provided by staff (e.g., "A teacher assistant, taught by an SLP, will check Mary Ann's hearing aids daily" is written in the student's education plan as a general support, not as a goal and objective).

- **Problem 5:** Goals are discipline-referenced and jargon filled (e.g., "Darren will improve articulation of bilabial sounds in speech therapy.").

  COACH alternative: Goals are discipline-free (e.g., "In conversations with classmates and teachers, Darren will recognize when his speech attempts to communicate are not understood and pair his speech attempt with an additional/augmentative way of communicating; for example, speak and gesture/point.").

These examples clarify what will be learned and where it will be learned, but do not specify how instruction will occur. Because COACH is used in a number of countries, the requirements and recommendations for writing annual goals vary. Therefore, we encourage you to consider these suggestions from COACH within your local context and refer to other sources that delve into writing goals and objectives in more depth (e.g., Bateman, 2007; Bateman & Linden, 2006) and the plethora of online resources.

Short-Term Objectives

Step 5 provides a straightforward format to break down an annual goal into a sequence of smaller parts based on the present level of performance and intent of the goal established in Step 4. Although short-term objectives may be written in a variety of ways, one of the widely accepted formats is to include three distinct components: 1) conditions, 2) behavior, and 3) criteria (Janney & Snell, 2011; see Figure 17).

Conditions under which the behavior will occur should be included and are crucial in order for the student to engage in the behavior. These conditions frequently refer to specific cues (e.g., "Show me what you want," "Turn on the switch"); special equipment or materials (e.g., ruled writing paper, spoon with a built-up handle, visual symbol schedule, plate secured with a suction cup); and/or contexts (e.g., in class, on the playground during recess, at work). Conditions may be stated in a variety of combinations. It is not necessary to include every condition, only those that are crucial and unique in order for the student to pursue the objective. It is also important to remember that, ultimately, it is desirable for students to respond to natural cues in natural contexts as much as possible, even if instruction begins with adding extra cues. Therefore, assistive (nonnaturally occurring) conditions should be used conservatively, and plans should be made to fade such conditions as soon as possible.

A behavior displayed by the learner is the central feature of any objective. The behavior must be observable and measurable. Sometimes people inappropriately write annual goals and objectives about what they, as teachers or related services personnel, are going to do for the student rather than what the student will be able to do as result of instruction. Avoid terms such as *understand* or *know*. Instead, write a behavior you can observe that may be an indicator that the student knows or understands (e.g., points, says, writes, washes, counts, purchases).

The objective should include criteria. Selecting the type of criteria is based on how it matches the behavior. For example, if you want a student to increase the number of times he or she initiates appropriate greetings with other people, then you might take a frequency count to determine how many times the student initiates or a percentage to compare the number of

Short-Term Objectives

Conditions	Skill/behavior	Criteria

Figure 17. Excerpt from Short-Term Objectives.

initiations with the number of opportunities the student had during a specified time period. Types of criteria may include, but are not limited to, frequency, percent, rate, quality, duration, or response latency. It can be helpful to include a second component to the criteria to indicate how stable the behavior must be before you feel comfortable reporting that the objective has been met (e.g., 4 out of 5 consecutive school days over a 2-week period).

Short-term objectives should assist in the instructional cycle of assessment, planning, instruction, and data-based decision making. In developing a sequence of three or four short-term objectives, any or all three of the component parts can change. In other words, you could have consistent conditions and criteria while the behavior changes in each objective. Similarly, the conditions and behavior might remain consistent with the criteria changing. In some cases, particularly for students who require a lot of cues, supports, or other conditions, the behavior and criteria might remain the same while the conditions change in each of the objectives. Two of the three components may vary, as may all three. Individualized decisions about which components to change and how much will depend on your assessment data and what you know about the student's characteristics and history of response to instruction, as well as the nature of the learning outcome being targeted for instruction. Some learning outcomes are amenable to increasing the criteria leading toward proficiency, whereas others (e.g., crossing the street) need to be with 100% accuracy for safety reasons, and therefore, it makes more sense to modify the conditions (e.g., levels of supports, cues, prompts) and the behavior (e.g., crossing an intersection with a crossing guard, crossing an intersection with a traffic light, crossing an intersection with a stop sign).

Like any tool, short-term objectives can be used or misused. Some people fear that the way short-term objectives are often written may trivialize what a student needs to learn, be limited to things easier to measure, or interfere with the team's creativity in planning or implementing—this need not be the case. Objectives can be trivial, boring, and confining or relevant, interesting, and creative depending on how the team approaches the challenge. Under the best circumstances, objectives can be used as a map of the path to be taken to reach an identified destination (annual goal). Like any travel plans, you may start out on one path and later change that path to match new information you have gained. Because most schools are in session for approximately 40 weeks, it is suggested that 3 or 4 objectives be written for each goal, making intervals of approximately 10–12 weeks, which coincides with the school's marking periods. Like most things related to education, objectives are never perfect and are often in a state of change. Therefore, although setting objectives is a valuable activity, it is important not to get bogged down with excessive details because they probably will need readjustment at a later date. The initial set of short-term objectives is your team's "best guess" at the time, given current information.

Program-at-a-Glance

Many classroom teachers find the full IEP document too cumbersome for everyday planning and use. The Program-at-a-Glance keeps critical information about a student's curricular and support needs available throughout the school day (see Figure 18). Therefore, it should be kept in a handy spot for quick access, while being maintained in a manner to ensure student confidentiality. The Program-at-a-Glance typically is a concise list of the educational program components presented in an abbreviated format, including 1) Annual Goals (Step 4) based on family-selected priorities (Step 1.5), 2) Additional Learning Outcomes from COACH (Step 2.1), 3) additional learning outcome starting points from the general education curriculum and the primary type of participation (e.g., multilevel, curriculum overlapping) (Step 2.2), and 4) General Supports (Step 3).

Step 6

Program-at-a-Glance

COACH3

Student's name: _____ Date: _____

*List education program components: 1) highest priorities from Family Interview to be included in IEP;
2) Additional Learning Outcomes from COACH by curriculum area; 3) Additional Learning Outcomes
from General Education (Step 2.2) by curriculum area, also indicate primary type of participation and
example "starting point" learning outcomes; and 4) general supports by category and items.*

Figure 18. Excerpt from Program-at-a-Glance.

The Program-at-a-Glance offers a concise format to document and communicate a student's educational program components. It is a useful summary to share with classroom teachers, special area teachers (e.g., art, music, physical education, library), related services personnel (e.g., SLPs, physical therapists, occupational therapists), and paraprofessionals who work with the student.

Answering Common Questions About COACH

HOW DOES COACH FIT INTO IEP DEVELOPMENT?

COACH is designed to be one part of an overall approach to planning an appropriate education for a student with disabilities. Therefore, it is considered an individualized education program (IEP) planning tool and has proven to be a useful component of transition planning (e.g., preschool to kindergarten, grade to grade, school to postschool). COACH is meant to assist in educational planning by

- Identifying family-centered priorities
- Identifying additional learning outcomes (e.g., from general education curricula)
- Identifying general supports to be provided to or for the student
- Translating priorities into IEP goals and objectives
- Summarizing the educational program as a Program-at-a-Glance
- Scheduling participation in general education classes/activities
- Planning and adapting lesson plans to facilitate learning
- Evaluating the affect of educational efforts

COACH is

- Not designed to determine eligibility for special education
- Not designed to provide a comprehensive assessment profile
- Not designed to assign grade or developmental levels
- Not designed to be used to the exclusion of other planning tools
- Not designed to justify segregation of students with disabilities

Typically, COACH is used to assist in identifying IEP goals and objectives and providing some information to document a student's present level of functioning in reference to selected goals and objectives. This information also can be used by teams to determine educationally relevant support services (Giangreco, 2000) necessary to implement the educational program components identified using COACH. COACH fits into a sequence of major events of IEP development. Although presented sequentially, varying amounts of overlap are to be expected.

Sequence of Events for IEP Development Using COACH

1. Eligibility for special education is determined (before using COACH).

2. A student planning *team is formed.*

3. An *overall plan* to learn about the student's strengths, interests, and needs is developed. The team generates descriptive information about the student, not separate goals from each discipline.

4. *Educational program components* (i.e., priority learning outcomes, additional learning outcomes, general supports) are determined using *Part A of COACH.*

5. Priority learning outcomes are translated into annual goals and short-term objectives using *Part B of COACH.*

6. The student's *educational placement* is determined. This should be the least restrictive option in which the student can pursue his or her individually determined educational program (Steps 1, 2, and 3). First consideration should always be given to the educational placement options the student would have if he or she did not have a disability label (e.g., general education class in neighborhood school), given supplemental supports and services.

7. *Related services* are determined necessary to support the student's educational program in the identified educational placement (Giangreco, 1996b, 2000; Giangreco, Edelman, Luiselli, & MacFarland, 1996, 1998; Giangreco, Edelman, Nelson, Young, & Kiefer-O'Donnell, 1999). The educational program (e.g., IEP goals) and the placement must be known prior to making informed related services decisions (Giangreco, 2001).

8. Information generated using COACH and other sources (e.g., literacy assessment, speech-language evaluation) is transferred to the *official IEP document.* Quality IEP planning is a process rather than a single event.

9. At this point the team knows what is to be learned, the student's placement, and who will be involved in supporting the program and how. It is now time for more refined and ongoing planning by using the tools to *implement the COACH-generated plan* (see Section IV).

FOR WHOM SHOULD COACH BE USED?

COACH is designed to assist in planning educational programs for students with disabilities, ages 3–21, who have educational needs that extend beyond what is typically reflected in the general education curriculum and supports corresponding to their chronological age. In other words, some of the most important things these students need to learn have already been mastered by most other students their age and, therefore, are not reflected in typical general education curricula and supports. Students for whom COACH is an appropriate tool often are characterized as having moderate or severe disabilities. The international organization TASH (formerly The Association for Persons with Severe Handicaps) identified these individuals as people

who require ongoing support in one or more major life activities in order to participate in an integrated community and enjoy a quality of life similar to that available to all citizens. Support may be required for life activities such as mobility, communication, self-care, and learning as necessary for community living, employment, and self-sufficiency. (2000, p. 1)

Although terms such as *severe disabilities* are commonly used, without necessarily clear or agreed-on definitions, organizations such as the American Association on Intellectual and Developmental Disabilities (Schalock et al., 2010) have shifted away from describing people based on the severity of their intellectual disability (e.g., mild, moderate, severe, profound) and toward a multidimensional classification system (e.g., intellectual abilities, adaptive behavior, health, participation, context) that also considers classification based on an individual's pattern and intensity of support needs. This shift is meant to facilitate a better match between a person's current abilities and the demands of an environment or context, which is consistent with the purpose of COACH.

Although a disability diagnosis or classification is not particularly relevant to deciding whether using COACH is appropriate for a particular student, it may be helpful to know some of the common disability conditions of students for whom COACH has historically been utilized—Down syndrome, autism, cerebral palsy, deafblindness, fragile X syndrome, Rett syndrome, Williams syndrome, Cornelia de Lange syndrome, Angelman syndrome, Lesch-Nyhan syndrome, and Dandy-Walker syndrome. With modifications, components of COACH may be used with students who are younger, older, or who have milder disabilities; but in general, COACH is not designed for students with high-incidence disabilities (e.g., specific learning disabilities, speech-language impairments), those with emotional disturbance/behavior disorders, or those exclusively with sensory disabilities (e.g., hearing impairment, visual impairment) or orthopedic disabilities not occurring in combination with other disabilities (e.g., intellectual disabilities). Typically, COACH is not needed for these students because they are pursuing the general education curriculum at or near grade level. They do not need to pursue the types of learning outcomes listed in COACH that extend beyond the general education curriculum. COACH does not include many of the developmental skills frequently considered when working with infants and toddlers. Some people have successfully used COACH for younger children or those with milder disabilities by substituting other curriculum listings of learning outcomes while retaining the COACH process steps.

HOW LONG DOES IT TAKE TO COMPLETE COACH?

Because COACH is a flexible tool, completion time varies widely. The Family Interview (Step 1) can be completed in approximately 1 hour. Completion time varies based on factors such as 1) the familiarity, experience, and skillfulness of the facilitator; 2) the number of family members involved in the interview; it typically takes slightly longer with two parents than one; and 3) which curriculum areas are selected by the family for full review during the Family Interview (Step 1.2) because the number of learning outcomes varies across the curriculum areas. It almost always takes longer for facilitators who are new to using COACH. In any case, if the Family Interview goes beyond 90 minutes, then it is likely that there is some kind of facilitation problem. Table 2 shows an approximate breakdown of the time it takes to complete the various steps and substeps for Part A. The time it takes to complete Part B activities is more variable, in part, because the activities in Part B are ongoing.

WHO CAN FACILITATE COACH?

Any team member who is familiar with the process (e.g., special educator, general educator, school psychologist, guidance counselor, SLP, family support personnel) can facilitate COACH. The team should agree on who will assume responsibility for facilitating the various parts of COACH. COACH can be facilitated by a person who is familiar with the student and family (to enhance individualization of the tool) or by a neutral party who is naive to the dynamics of the situation and, therefore, can minimize the potential for bias during question asking. Either

Table 2. Approximate breakdown of the time it takes to complete the various steps and substeps for Part A of COACH

Step	Time range (minutes)
Step 1. Family Interview	60–85
Introducing COACH to participants	5–10
Step 1.1. Valued Life Outcomes	10–15
Step 1.2. Selecting Curriculum Areas	5–10
Step 1.3. Rating Learning Outcomes	15–20
Step 1.4. Prioritizing Learning Outcomes	12–15
Step 1.5. Cross-Prioritization	13–15
Step 2. Additional Learning Outcomes	45–60
Step 2.1. Additional Learning Outcomes from COACH	10–20
Step 2.2. Additional Learning Outcomes from General Education	35–40
Step 3. General Supports	10–15
Step 4. Annual Goals	Time varies
Step 5. Short-Term Objectives	Time varies
Step 6. Program-at-a-Glance	10–15

approach can be effective; it depends on team choice and dynamics. A person familiar with the family and student must guard against asking questions to elicit parent responses that reflect the interviewer's perspectives. A person unfamiliar with the family must be able to adapt questioning style, vocabulary, pacing, and so forth. COACH has been successfully facilitated under both circumstances, and we have found that familiarity and skillfulness with COACH is an essential common denominator to using the process effectively.

WHO PARTICIPATES IN COACH?

Different team members participate in different steps of COACH. Because each situation is unique, rather than providing definitive rules on who participates in the various steps of COACH, the team must understand the purpose and outcome of each step and make an individual determination about who needs to be involved in the various steps. The entire team should be aware of the plan so they have opportunities to be involved when appropriate. There is one notable exception to this individualization of participants—the Family Interview must include the family.

Occasionally we are asked if the professionals can complete the Family Interview themselves. Our answer is unequivocally "no." Professionals who are unable to get parent involvement in COACH might be able to use some concepts and ideas from COACH. Please be aware we are using the terms *family* and *parents* broadly to refer to the adults who live with and care for the child.

Although the full team should be aware of the Family Interview processes and outcomes, the interview itself is designed to be a more intimate activity involving the facilitator, the special educator (who often is the facilitator), the classroom teacher(s), the parent(s), and the student, when appropriate. In cases such as a middle school or high school where a student has more than one classroom teacher, a representative classroom teacher should be identified, and the special educator should be in communication with the others prior to the Family Interview.

The family should make an individual determination about the presence and participation of the student during the Family Interview. When students participate in COACH, particularly young adults (ages 17–21), it is important to clarify who holds the authority for selecting the priorities—the student or the parents. We suggest that students with disabilities be extended the same rights and responsibilities offered to their peers without disabilities. Typically, this means that students assume increasing decision-making control as they get older. By the time students are 17 or 18 years old, the same age when their peers would be graduating from high school, they should be given as much control of priority selection as is possible and culturally acceptable to their family—such decisions will necessarily be individual ones.

It is important for the general education teacher to be present during the Family Interview because it provides a rich opportunity to hear the perspectives of the family in ways difficult to capture on paper. If the team wants to invite more people to the Family Interview, then it should be discussed with the family in advance to ensure they are comfortable with the situation and not overwhelmed or intimidated by the number of people.

The same core group (i.e., facilitator, special educator, classroom teacher, parents, student) should be present for the completion of Step 2 (Additional Learning Outcomes) and Step 3 (General Supports). Again, in cases in which not all of the general education teachers or related services providers are present (and they need not be), someone, typically the special educator or classroom teacher representative, should be knowledgeable about the general education curriculum areas/classes and perspectives of related services providers not present at the meeting. This will require meeting with those personnel prior to the COACH meeting to gather information from the teachers about the curriculum content and potential participation and support for the target student in class (see directions for Step 2.2 and Step 3). Regardless of who the team designates to complete the various steps of COACH, the facilitator is responsible to gather and share the information and decisions generated with all team members for their feedback. Although this may be accomplished with face-to-face meetings (large or small groups), it can also be accomplished through telephone or correspondence (e.g., e-mail).

In Part B, Step 4 (Annual Goals) and Step 5 (Short-Term Objectives) can be completed by a designated group of team members at a different time and does not necessarily need to include the parents. The information generated is translated into a format that is suitable for inclusion in the IEP document and is helpful instructionally. Short-term objectives can be completed by designated subteams that reflect related services providers involved with particular goals. For example, when considering the priority learning outcome, "Makes choices when presented with two options using eye gaze," the team may have agreed that this goal required support from the occupational therapist and SLP. Therefore, these staff members would join with the core team members to formulate the short-term objectives pertaining to that annual goal. Different configurations of team members are used to develop short-term objectives for other annual goals. The Program-at-a-Glance (Step 6) can be prepared by an individual and, therefore, does not require the team to meet.

WHERE SHOULD COACH BE COMPLETED?

The location where the team chooses to complete COACH should be individually negotiated with the family to maximize the opportunity for their participation. The setting should be one where the family feels comfortable, is reasonably free of distractions, and allows for confidentiality. When facilitating Part A of COACH, two of the most common locations are family homes and schools. Other sites, such as a meeting room at a community center, also can be appropriate locations. School personnel should be open to other locations that match a family's preference.

WHEN SHOULD COACH BE COMPLETED?

The time of day COACH is scheduled will depend on finding a mutually agreeable time for all participants. We encourage school personnel to be as accommodating as possible to parents in an effort to demonstrate respect for their work schedules and child care needs. In terms of when

COACH should be completed during the school year, keep in mind that its intended use is to develop a student's IEP; therefore, COACH should be initiated sufficiently prior to the IEP meeting date to allow the results to contribute to IEP development. For example, the team might initiate COACH activities 2–3 weeks prior to the scheduled IEP meeting date. IEPs developed using COACH usually result in a relatively brief IEP meeting because team members have been involved in preparatory activities and are familiar with the components to be included on the IEP. In such cases, the IEP meeting is used to review and summarize the components of the educational program generated using COACH and verify placement.

COACH has been used successfully during the intake process for new students regardless of the time of year. For those students already in the school system, a number of schools have found it beneficial to complete COACH in the spring in preparation for the coming school year. COACH can be used at any time of the year to coincide with either IEP development or transition planning.

SHOULD COACH BE COMPLETED EVERY YEAR?

The frequency of using COACH varies, but here are some general guidelines for its use. The first time a team uses COACH to plan an IEP or transition for a student, all of Parts A and B need to be completed. The next time Part A is used for that same student (e.g., the following year), the team decides if it needs to be 1) done again in its entirety, 2) done again partially or in a modified format, or 3) verified but not done again at that time. These choices depend on the extent of change that has occurred or is expected in the student's circumstances or level of functioning that would likely result in changes in valued life outcomes, priority learning outcomes, additional learning outcomes, and general supports.

If significant change has occurred, then the team might decide to complete all of Part A again. In some cases, it is unnecessary to repeat every aspect of Part A each year because certain aspects, such as the valued life outcomes and general supports, may not have changed significantly. In such cases, the team may decide to simply verify last year's valued life outcomes and general supports, noting minor adjustments, and then complete Steps 1.2–1.5, 2.1, and 2.2 in their entirety to determine updated learning outcome priorities from COACH and additional learning outcomes respectively. Updated information can be used to update IEP goals and objectives (Steps 4 and 5) and then can be summarized on the Program-at-a-Glance (Step 6).

In any case, new team members should become oriented to COACH, and the team makes an individualized decision about the subsequent use of Part A after its initial use. This subsequent use should remain consistent with the principles forming the basis of COACH. We recommend that teams complete Part A for their student at least once every 3 years or to coincide with significant transitions such as from preschool to kindergarten or middle school to high school.

WHAT ARE KEY COACH "DON'TS"?

Although most of the feedback we have received about COACH has generally been positive, we have also received some constructive feedback incorporated into revisions of the tool and continue to identify examples of misuse. These misuses generally stem from lack of preparation and violation of the underlying principles forming the basis of COACH. The following are behaviors you should actively avoid when using COACH:

- Do not use COACH without first having thoroughly read the manual at least once.
- Do not complete the COACH Family Interview unless you plan to complete the rest of Part A.

- Do not send home a blank COACH Student Record form and ask the parents to complete it.
- Do not initiate COACH without first getting team consensus and ensuring that the related services providers (e.g., SLP, occupational therapist, physical therapist) understand the implications of using COACH.
- Do not invite parents to attend a meeting and then start using COACH without having first oriented them to the process in advance and getting their agreement to use the process.
- Do not invite people to join the COACH meeting without the agreement of the family.
- Do not create an additional scoring level below early/emerging skill, such as no skill—this is unhelpful and may be damaging to the process and interactions.
- Do not invite the family to participate in COACH unless you are willing to relinquish the exclusive decision making for the small set of highest priorities to the family.
- Do not automatically use COACH for all of your students for whom it is potentially appropriate—it is simply one tool you can consider with families on an individual basis.
- Do not use COACH to justify restricting inclusive opportunities for students with disabilities.

Directions for Completing COACH Steps

Throughout this section, each step and substep of COACH includes explicit directions stated as briefly as possible. Four types of information are provided:

♣ **Purpose**   ☞ **Directions**

 **Materials**   ✪ **Helpful Hints**

A Friendly Suggestion

The explicit directions provided throughout COACH are based on extensive use over many years. We encourage you to follow these directions closely, especially if you are a novice user of COACH, because we know they work. That said, we like to think of COACH as a thinking person's tool, not something to be completed in a rote, fill-in-the-blank fashion. We do not necessarily expect COACH to be used in a strictly standardized way, nor do we wish to constrain your own skills and creativity in making COACH work better. Therefore, we encourage you to individualize COACH in ways that match your unique circumstances. We caution you, however, that favorable results of any modifications to COACH will likely occur only if those changes are consistent with the principles on which COACH is based. Otherwise, it becomes something other than COACH. In our experience we find that once you have closely applied the directions in the manual three or four times, you will probably be ready and comfortable beginning to individualize your use of COACH.

Directions for completing COACH are illustrated using the example of Jake Gardener, a third-grade student with multiple disabilities (intellectual, physical, sensory). The CD-ROM accompanying the COACH manual includes two additional examples for students of different ages and characteristics: 1) a kindergarten student with developmental and sensory disabilities (Appendix G) and 2) a high school student with Down syndrome (Appendix H).

Jake Gardener

Jake is an engaging 8-year-old boy who lives with his father, stepmother, and older sister. He loves being with other people, especially other kids. He shows his enthusiasm for being with other people through his facial expressions, vocalizations, and laughter. He enjoys listening to music, being read to, roughhousing, going outside, and playing with his pet dog Blitz. It is unclear exactly how much Jake understands because he does not speak and currently responds to questions, somewhat inconsistently, using eye gaze and directional reaching/pointing with his hand. His team is trying to develop a more effective augmentative and alternative communication (AAC) system for Jake by building on his existing motor skills and exploring assistive technology options. Jake has severe physical disabilities resulting from cerebral palsy.

Jake's intellectual capabilities are unclear, and his current functioning level is substantially below other children his age. His parents and teachers think he understands more than he is presently able to communicate, so the team is careful not to put limits on assuming his intellectual capabilities. They expose him to the same experiences and information available to other children his age. Jake moves from place to place by having others push him in his wheelchair. Jake has limited use of his arms and hands; he needs assistance with activities of daily living. Jake wears glasses to improve his visual acuity, which is estimated at 20/40 after correction, and has been diagnosed with cortical visual impairment (CVI).

Jake attends a general education third-grade classroom in his neighborhood school. Jake's classroom teacher is supported by a special education teacher, a speech-language pathologist (SLP), an occupational therapist, a physical therapist, and an itinerant teacher for the visually impaired. A paraprofessional is assigned to Jake's classroom to provide targeted assistance to Jake and other students in the class (with and without disabilities). The team makes sure Jake receives the bulk of his instruction from the teacher and special educator and that the paraprofessional supports do not inadvertently isolate him within the classroom, create unnecessary dependencies, interfere with his peer interactions, or otherwise stigmatize him in the eyes of his classmates. The paraprofessional has clearly defined and appropriate roles, works from professionally prepared plans, receives ongoing training and supervision in key areas (e.g., implementing teacher-planned instruction, facilitating peer interactions, providing personal care supports), and is a integral member of the classroom team.

PART A   Determining a Student's Educational Program

Purpose

Part A of COACH is designed to assist the team in identifying and documenting the content of the student's educational program, including all three of the following components:

1. A small set of family-selected priority learning outcomes to provide curricular focus (from the Family Interview)

2. A set of additional learning outcomes, beyond the priority learning outcomes, from COACH and the general education curriculum, to provide curricular breadth (from additional learning outcomes)

3. A set of general supports that need to be provided to or for the student so he or she may gain access to educational environments and pursue identified learning outcomes

Materials

- COACH manual
- Photocopy of Appendix A
- Photocopy of Appendix B or printout from CD-ROM
- Pencils and erasers
- Clock/timer

 Directions

1. Identify a student for whom COACH is an appropriate educational planning tool.

2. Make sure all team members are sufficiently knowledgeable about COACH to make an informed decision about whether to use COACH (e.g., read Appendix A, read COACH manual, attend COACH training, discuss as a team).

3. Make a team decision about whether to use COACH to plan the student's educational program. This team decision must include an informed decision by the parent(s) and the student, as appropriate (e.g., transition age), to participate.

4. As a team, decide how COACH fits into the overall plan to develop the IEP. For example, what other assessment (e.g., language, literacy, motor) or planning tools also will be used, and how do they inform each other and the IEP planning and development process? What sequence makes the most sense?

5. Complete the steps listed on Preparation Checklist.

6. At one or more meetings, complete all three steps in Part A of COACH.
   - Step 1: Family Interview
   - Step 2: Additional Learning Outcomes
   - Step 3: General Supports

   Specific directions for these steps follow.

7. Part A can be completed during a single meeting. Plan 2 hours for the meeting, though you might finish sooner. If necessary, you can complete Part A during two meetings. If you decide to use the two-meeting option, then we recommend completing all of Step 1 at the first meeting and then completing Steps 2 and 3 at the second meeting.

⭐ **Helpful Hints**

1. Nothing can replace preparation. Taking the time to learn about COACH is a crucial first step. Practicing and getting feedback to refine your skills is invaluable.

2. COACH is a tool that has a specific purpose—to plan a student's educational program. It is not designed as a comprehensive assessment, so it can be used in combination with other planning tools and assessments. We encourage your team to consider COACH along with these other tools and choose the combination that matches your situation.

3. It is crucial to complete all three steps in Part A. Stopping after Step 1 results in an incomplete educational program. This is one of the most common mistakes we encounter and one that can be easily avoided by simply completing Steps 2 and 3.

4. Remember, Part A exclusively addresses what will be included in the student's educational program, not how.

5. Each family is unique. As your team considers the use of COACH, be sure to individualize to account for cultural practices of each family.

6. Novice users often exceed time estimates for completing the steps of COACH. Keep the time estimates and purpose of the step in mind to help you stay on course. Although it is important to be flexible in response to family comments and questions, be aware of straying too far from the purpose of the step or prematurely delving too deeply into a specific topic or issue. It is easy to go off on tangents. The better you understand and are able to communicate the steps of COACH and corresponding purposes, the better equipped you will be to stay on track.

7. Completing Part A is a beginning, not an ending. Completing Part A should lead to 1) translating COACH-generated information into a format that can be included in the IEP (e.g., family-selected priorities translated into annual goals and short-term objectives; see Part B), 2) sharing a Program-at-a-Glance with all team members (see Part B), 3) making related services decisions and coordinating those services, and 4) refining plans to implement the student's educational program.

8. Work in pencil because mistakes are made or a parent may change his or her mind.

9. Remember, although COACH is most frequently completed with the parent(s) as the main respondents on behalf of their child who currently may not have the communication skills to participate in such a language-heavy process, students themselves can be the primary respondents rather than the parents or in conjunction with their parents. If it is age appropriate and culturally appropriate for the student to participate, and he or she wishes to, then every effort should be made to include him or her. Even if he or she is not able to fully participate in all aspects of COACH, he or she may be able to partially participate, such as by helping to make priority selections once the process reaches Steps 1.4 or 1.5.

PREPARATION CHECKLIST

 ### Purpose

The Preparation Checklist is designed to enhance the likelihood that your team will have a fruitful experience using COACH. Most important, the Preparation Checklist provides initial guidance to ensure that team members, especially the parents, are making an informed decision to use COACH. Using the Preparation Checklist, parents have a voice in 1) whether to use COACH, 2) deciding where the meeting should be held, and 3) determining when the meeting should occur. The professionalism you show by being informed and prepared demonstrates your respect for the family and other team members. The following activities should be completed in the days or weeks prior to initiating the Family Interview and other parts of COACH.

 ### Materials

*   Blank copy of the Preparation Checklist
*   Pencils and erasers

Directions

1. Complete the six items on the Preparation Checklist (see Figure 19).

Helpful Hints

1. If the parents' primary language is other than English, plan ahead for translation or interpreter services. In most cases, when working in two languages, expect additional time to complete each step.

2. In situations in which the parents have difficulty reading, some background information from COACH (e.g., Appendix A) can be recorded and provided. Otherwise, you may decide to have a telephone or face-to-face conversation with the family to orient them to COACH and guide them through the process of deciding if they would like to use COACH.

3. Parents should not be pressured into using COACH, and we discourage schools or programs from automatically using COACH with all families of students who meet participation criteria. For example, it would be inappropriate to inform a parent, "We use COACH with all of our students who have intensive special education needs, so we want to schedule a time to do COACH with you." Parents do not have a choice if they are presented with only one option for offering their input into IEP preplanning. Therefore, in addition to offering COACH, you can offer the use of other tools you are aware of or less formalized approaches, such as a conversation. In presenting the options, you will want to explain the pros and cons of the options.

4. The whole team does not need to be present during Step 1. COACH is designed to be conducted in a small group (e.g., one or both parents, special educator, classroom teacher). Other team members may attend if it is requested by the family or is acceptable to them. In addition to the parent(s), special educator and classroom teacher involvement are essential.

5. The student's special educator typically facilitates COACH, but any person who is knowledgeable about COACH can facilitate it. The facilitator can be someone external to the team (e.g., consultant); this person does not need to be knowledgeable about the student or family as long as the parents, special educator, and classroom teacher are present. The parents should be comfortable with the person designated to facilitate COACH. If a facilitator cannot be agreed on, then it is better not to use COACH than to compromise the relationship with the family by asking them to engage in a voluntary activity in which they are not comfortable.

6. When deciding to use COACH, related services professionals on the team representing different disciplines (e.g., speech-language pathology, physical therapy, occupational therapy) agree to not retain separate goals for their respective disciplines. Rather, in keeping with the role of related services as being educationally necessary, all team members agree to apply the knowledge and skills of their disciplines to support the student's educational program (e.g., family-selected priorities, additional learning outcomes, identified aspects of the general education curriculum).

7. Because of the wide variation in the configuration of families, it is crucial to clarify the appropriate family participants from the outset. This can be a sensitive or challenging issue for some families in situations in which the student's parents are divorced or the student lives with a foster family. In cases of divorce, many noncustodial parents remain closely involved with their child and participate in educational planning. Even in cases in which one parent has primary physical custody of his or her child, the noncustodial parent may share legal custody and, therefore, may share decision making regarding issues such as health and education. In cases of a foster family, it is advisable to coordi-

Preparation Checklist

Before proceeding with COACH (Part A), ensure that all items below are completed. Check (✓) inside the ○ when completed.

☑ 1. All professional team members understand the COACH process and at least one member has the skills to facilitate all parts of COACH.

☑ 2. The family understands the COACH process and makes an informed decision to complete COACH with professional team members to develop their childís educational program. (See Appendix A and/or Sections I and II.)

☑ 3. All professional team members agree to accept and act on the educational priorities identified by the family during the Family Interview.

☑ 4. Mutually agreeable times and locations for the Steps 1, 2, and 3 are arranged so that at least the family, facilitator, special educator, and general educator can attend.

  Family member(s): _Sofie Gardener, Tom Gardener_

  Facilitator: _Karen Green_

  Special educator: _Karen Green_

  General educator(s): _Maryann Booth_

  Others: _____

  Step 1:
  Date: _May 5_ Start time: _2:00_ End time: _3:15_ Location: _Little Mountain Community Center (LMCC)_

  Step 2:
  Date: _May 12_ Start time: _2:00_ End time: _2:45_ Location: _LMCC_

  Step 3:
  Date: _May 12_ Start time: _2:00_ End time _2:45_ Location: _LMCC_

☑ 5. A Student Record booklet or a copy of the COACH forms is ready for use.

☑ 6. Plans are made to complete Step 4 (Annual Goals), Step 5 (Short-Term Objectives), and Step 6 (Program-at-a-Glance).

Figure 19. Jake's Preparation Checklist.

nate with the agency responsible for the foster placement to clarify who will appropriately participate in COACH (e.g., biological parent, foster parent, agency representative). Clarifying these issues from the outset with sensitivity and care will allow the work to proceed more smoothly and ensure that the appropriate family members have voice in the educational decision making.

8. If you are considering using the digital version of the blank forms, then you will want to check with the family in advance to make sure they are comfortable with the technology or whether they would be more comfortable using the paper version. If you decide to use the digital forms, then you may want to use a projector and screen (or wall space) to display the forms so everyone can readily see them and what is written.

STEP 1 ‖ FAMILY INTERVIEW

 Purpose

Step 1 is designed to assist the family in identifying a small set of high-priority learning outcomes to be included in the student's educational program in the coming year.

 Materials

- COACH manual
- Photocopy of Appendix A
- Photocopy of Appendix B or printout from CD-ROM
- Pencils and erasers
- Clock/timer
- Table and chairs

☞ **Directions**

1. Introduce the Family Interview and then complete Steps 1.1–1.5. Directions for substeps follow.

 Helpful Hints

1. Be yourself by adding your own personal style and warmth to the way you ask questions and verify your understanding of the family's comments.

2. Respect families' personal preferences and cultural traditions regarding issues such as formality of greetings and interactions, seating, eye contact, use of language, partaking of food, and visiting before or after attending to the COACH-related tasks.

3. Be aware of your own biases. Remember, the role of the facilitator is to ask questions, listen, and help the family zero in on their priorities (not yours). Subconsciously, it can be easy to ask questions in a way that guides a family toward what you think are priorities and not even realize you are doing it. It helps to be aware of your own biases so you can avoid them throughout the process. This is one reason why it sometimes can be helpful to have a person facilitate COACH who is knowledgeable about the process, but

does not know the student or family and, therefore, does not have preconceived ideas about what are the highest priorities. As a professional, you will have opportunities in later steps of COACH to share what you think is important. For COACH to have its maximum benefit, both as a planning tool and as way to promote communication and trust between school and home, it is essential that professionals ensure the process is used to help families identify their priorities.

4. As each substep is introduced, 1) briefly review its purpose, 2) provide an estimated time parameter for how long it will take to complete, and 3) request short answers to help maintain a steady pace of moving forward without rushing.

5. Write on the COACH forms in pencil to allow for changes.

6. Do not ask parents to fill out the COACH Student Record forms by themselves. The Family Interview is not to be used as a written questionnaire to be filled out by the family (or professionals) in isolation. Part of the value of COACH results from the interactions that occur between the family and school personnel.

7. Throughout the Family Interview, position the Student Record form so the family can see what is being written. This may mean turning the materials to face the family after you have marked or written something.

8. Feel free to write clarifying notes anywhere on the forms if they would be helpful to you later in translating the family-selected priorities into annual goals and corresponding objectives.

Introducing the Family Interview

♣ Purpose

Introducing the Family Interview is intended to welcome the family to the COACH planning session and review basic information with them about its purpose, content, activities, time frame, and desired outcomes. This information is a review or clarification because the family already should have been oriented to COACH and made an informed decision to participate as part of the Preparation Checklist activities.

Materials

From the COACH Student Record forms:

- Introducing the Family Interview script
- Steps of COACH
- Circles diagram

Directions

1. As participants gather for the Family Interview at the scheduled time and place, the facilitator welcomes the family and asks them how they would like to be seated so they can participate (see the forms) and feel comfortable. Arrangements may vary based on personal preferences, cultural traditions, or both.

2. Review all of the information included in the script, "Introducing the Family Interview" (see Figure 20).

Helpful Hints

1. Having the parents sit next to you (rather than across from you) is generally preferred. For example, if you are seated at rectangular table, then the facilitator might be seated at the short end with the parents seated close by (next to each other) on the long side of the table. If the facilitator is right handed, then it can be helpful to have the parents on the right side to facilitate seeing the paper version of the forms. In general, the facilitator should not be seated between two parents unless it is something the parents explicitly request. Seating arrangements can send subtle, yet powerful, messages.

2. Novice users are encouraged to tell the parents they are new at using COACH and will be reading some of the directions to them verbatim. As facilitators become more familiar with COACH, they can use the script as a guideline and explain the points in their own way.

3. The introduction to the Family Interview should take about 5 minutes.

Step 1.1 Valued Life Outcomes

 Purpose

Step 1.1 helps to set the context for later parts of the Family Interview, such as selecting curriculum areas and learning outcomes of interest. It does this by exploring the family's perspectives on the status of a set of valued life outcomes as they pertain to the student now and in the future. By responding to a series of questions, the family provides information that assists the team in understanding student strengths, interests, and challenges. Step 1.1 culminates in a rating of the valued life outcomes so the team has a sense of which ones are most important to the family this year. Figure 22 shows Jake's valued life outcomes.

 Materials

From the COACH Student Record forms:

- Forms for Step 1.1

 Directions

1. Explain the purpose and procedures by reading the Step 1.1 script to the person(s) being interviewed (on the first page of the Step 1.1 form; see Figure 21).

2. Remind the parent(s) that this step should take 10–15 minutes to complete.

3. Starting with the first valued life outcome (safety and health), ask the parent(s), "Are you interested in answering questions on this topic?" and record the response by checking *yes* or *no*.

   - If the parent(s) respond *no*, then move on to the next category.
   - If the parent(s) respond *yes*, then ask the listed question(s), listen carefully, and record a summary of the response.

4. Ask follow-up questions if needed to clarify the response.

5. Repeat Directions 2 and 3 for each of the valued life outcome categories.

Introducing the Family Interview

To be read to person(s) being interviewed.

Welcome and the Importance of Family Involvement
Thank you for agreeing to meet with us to use COACH to help plan for your child's IEP. We are glad you are here to help us understand your family's perspectives about his or her educational needs and priorities.

Purpose of the Family Interview
The purpose of the COACH Family Interview is for all of us to gain a better understanding of what you think is important for [student's name] so the educational team can develop and implement an appropriate IEP.

Curriculum Content Included in the Family Interview
COACH includes nine categories of curriculum with corresponding learning outcomes that typically are not included in the general education curriculum. These learning outcomes are not designed to replace the general education curriculum—they are meant to augment or extend it. That is why it is so important to complete later steps of COACH where we will ensure that [student's name] has appropriate access to the general education curriculum available to his or her classmates without disabilities.

Interview Activities and Time Frame
It will take about 60–90 minutes to complete the interview. I will ask you a series of questions, listen carefully to your responses, and record them. The questions start broadly in order to consider many possibilities. As we proceed, the questions are designed to help you focus in on what you think are the most important learning outcomes for [student's name] to work on this year. Because the interview includes so many questions, we will be asking you to share brief answers. If there is anything you do not want to answer, then feel free to say so.

Outcomes of the Family Interview
By the end of the COACH Family Interview, you will have a selected a small set (e.g., 5–7) of learning outcomes that you think are the most important for [student's name] to work on in the coming year and should be listed on the IEP as annual goals.

Next Steps
After the interview is completed, we will share your selections with the other team members who were not present today. The priorities you identified to be included in the IEP will be worded as annual goals with short-term objectives or benchmarks for your review. Next, we need to complete Steps 2.1 and 2.2 of COACH to identify the additional learning outcomes and Step 3.0 to identify the general supports that will be part of [student's name] overall educational plan. Do you have any questions before we get started?

Figure 20.   Introducing the Family Interview.

Step 1.1

Valued Life Outcomes

To be read to the person(s) being interviewed:

The valued life outcomes listed were identified by asking parents who have children with disabilities what makes their child's life a "good life." These valued life outcomes should be interpreted individually to match each family's situation and culture.

Valued Life Outcomes

- Safety and health (physical and emotional)
- A home—now and in the future
- Meaningful relationships
- Control over personal choices (suited to the student's age and culture)
- Meaningful activities in various and valued places

You will be asked if you would like to answer questions for each valued life outcome. If you do, then you will be asked a small number of questions before moving on to the next valued life outcome topic. If for any reason you do not wish to answer a question, then you can simply decline and you do not need to explain why. In such cases, we will move on to the next topic.

There are a total of 11 questions in this section, and some may require follow-up questions for clarification. We hope to complete this part in about 10–15 minutes, so I will be asking you to provide brief responses. After all of the questions are asked, I will ask you to rate each of the five valued life outcomes in terms of its level of importance for your child in the coming year. By listening to and recording your responses, we hope to better understand your perspectives and help set the context for planning your child's IEP with you.

Figure 21. Valued life outcomes script.

6. On the last page of the Step 1.1 form, read the script to the family describing the rating task.

7. Ask the parent(s) to rate the first valued life outcome category on the scale provided, and record the response by checking the corresponding rating.

8. Repeat the rating of the remaining valued life outcomes categories.

 ## Helpful Hints

1. If family members indicate they do not wish to answer questions about a particular valued life outcome, then the interviewer simply acknowledges that choice in a nonjudgmental manner and moves on to the next question. The interviewer should not inquire about the reasons the person declines to answer and should not pressure the family member to explain him- or herself.

2. When asking questions, you are encouraged to word them in ways that make sense in the situation.

3. If the family begins telling numerous or relatively long stories, then it may substantially alter and extend the time it takes to complete the Family Interview. This is problematic because you want the parent(s) to be reasonably fresh when they reach the final decisions in Step 1.5 (Cross-Prioritization); if early steps take too long, then parents may be physically or emotionally tired when they get to the final decision points. The facilitator reminds them that you are seeking relatively brief responses and redirects the COACH session to get it back to the suggested time track. Step 1.1 is one spot in COACH many users tend to go far off the recommended time frame because they either inadvertently invite long, in-depth responses or are not conscious of the time. So be aware and keep track with a clock or timer.

Step 1.2   Selecting Curriculum Areas to Explore During the Family Interview

 ## Purpose

Step 1.2 is intended to 1) familiarize the participants with the nine curriculum areas included in COACH and their corresponding lists of learning outcomes and 2) have the family identify up to a maximum of four of the most important curriculum areas to be examined more closely during the Family Interview (marked *Now*). Those areas not selected for closer examination during the Family Interview will be marked to address later in Step 2.1 (Additional Learning Outcomes from COACH) or to skip this year. Figure 23 shows a completed form for Jake.

 ## Materials

From the COACH Student Record forms:

*   Forms for Step 1.2

 ## Directions

1. Explain the purpose of Step 1.2 and remind participants that this substep should take about 5–10 minutes to complete.

Safety and Health
(physical and emotional)

"Are you interested in answering questions on this topic?"
Mark (✓): ✓ Yes or ○ No

1. Do you have any current health or safety concerns about [student's name] that you would like to see change over the next year?

    Needs to drink more liquids; prone to dehydration; insufficient liquids causes constipation. No other health or safety concerns.

A Home—Now and in the Future

"Are you interested in answering questions on this topic?"
Mark (✓): ✓ Yes or ○ No

2. Where and with whom does [student's name] currently live? (e.g., at home with parents and siblings, in foster home, in group home)

    Jake lives at home with his Dad (Tom), step mom (Sofie), and older sister (Rose)

    If everything goes as you hope, then do you anticipate that [student's name] will continue to live in this same type of setting throughout the school years?

    Mark (✓): ✓ Yes or ○ No

    If no, what would be a desirable type of setting?

3. Would you like to talk about where a desirable type of setting would be for [student's name] to live as a young adult? Feel free to say no or that it's too soon if you feel that decision is too far in the future to discuss at this time.

    Mark (✓): ○ Yes or ○ No or ✓ It's too soon

    If yes, what type of setting? _____

4. Is there any type of future living setting for [student's name] that you would like to avoid?

    Never in an institution or large facility (e.g., nursing home)

Figure 22. Excerpt from Jake's Valued Life Outcomes.   *(continued)*

Figure 22. *(continued)*

Meaningful Relationships

"Are you interested in answering questions on this topic?"
Mark (✓): ☑ Yes or ○ No

5. Who are the people (e.g., family, neighbors, friends) that [student's name] spends the most time with during a typical week?
    Immediate family; cousins Robert and Gail; classmates (but only at school)

6. How, if at all, would you like to see [student's name] relationships change or expand in the near future (e.g., more time with same-age peers)?
    Expand relationships with kids his age in school, after-school organized groups, and in informal settings (friends coming to play)

Control Over Personal Choices
(suited to the student's age and culture)

"Are you interested in answering questions on this topic?"
Mark (✓): ☑ Yes or ○ No

7. Does [student's name] have opportunities to have similar control over personal choices that are available to others of the same age? Mark (✓): ○ Yes or ☑ No
    Examples: *Makes a few choices about toys, but choices have been made mostly by others for him.*

8. How, if at all, would you like to see [student's name] control over personal choices change or expand in the near future?
    Expand the kinds of choices he has (e.g., food, clothes, places, people, activities)

Figure 22. *(continued)*

Meaningful Activities in Various and Valued Places

"Are you interested in answering questions on this topic?"
Mark (✓): ☑ Yes   or   ○ No

9. What are some of [student's name] favorite or most frequent activities? Where do these activities happen? (e.g., school, recreation center, work)
   Loves playing with his dog; enjoys music; likes being in a pool (if it's warm); likes going to public places with the family where there is a lot of activity (e.g., stores, farmer's market, local festivals)

10. How, if at all, would you like to see these activities, or the places where they happen, change or expand in the near future?
    Needs more options to be actively involved—tends to be a passive participant. May need more assistive technology to open up participation. Also needs activities he can do when alone.

11. Ask only if the student is age 14 or older:
    Have you and [student's name] thought about how he or she might spend his or her time as a young adult once high school is over (e.g., working, volunteering, continuing education)? What are your hopes about these possibilities?
    NA

Figure 22. *(continued)*

Rating Valued Life Outcomes of Concern This Year

To be read to the person(s) being interviewed:

Thank you for taking this time to share your perspectives about valued life outcomes for your child. While all of the valued life outcomes may be important, it would be helpful for the school staff to understand what you think is most important for the coming year. So please rate their importance for your child for this coming year on a scale of 1 to 5, in which 1 means *not a concern this year* and 5 means *extremely important this year.* Each one will be marked (✓). Just because something is not a topic of concern this year does not mean it is unimportant or might not be important in the future. For example, although a child's health and safety are always important to parents, if a child has a recent history of being safe and healthy, then this may not be an important concern this year. Similarly, if a young child has a stable home situation, then having a home now and in the future may not be an important concern this year—but may be later if the person is making a transition to an adult living option. As you rate the five valued life outcomes, please focus your ratings on the present and coming year.

1 = Not a concern this year   5 = Extremely important this year

Safety and health (physical and emotional)
1 ○   2 ○   3 ✓   4 ○   5 ○

A home—now and in the future
1 ✓   2 ○   3 ○   4 ○   5 ○

Meaningful relationships
1 ○   2 ○   3 ○   4 ○   5 ✓

Control over personal choices
1 ○   2 ○   3 ○   4 ✓   5 ○

Meaningful activities in various and valued places
1 ○   2 ○   3 ○   4 ○   5 ✓

Step 1.2

Selecting Curriculum Areas to Explore During the Family Interview

Consider all nine COACH curriculum areas and select up to four areas to address *now* in the Family Interview. For those remaining areas, indicate whether to address *later* or *skip* for this year. Only one box will be marked (✓) for each area.

Curriculum areas	Now Address in Family Interview	Later Address in Step 2.1	Skip for this year
Communication	✓		
Socialization	✓		
Personal management			✓
Recreation		✓	
Access academics	✓		
Applied academics	✓		
School		✓	
Community Consider for transition-age students (14–21 years)			✓
Vocational Consider for transition-age students (14–21 years at community worksites)			✓

Figure 23. Jake's completed form for Step 1.2.

2. Display and review the Step 1.2 reference information, which lists all the curriculum areas and learning outcomes.

3. Remind the parent(s) that this content includes learning outcomes typically not included in the general education curriculum and is not meant to replace the general education curriculum content, which will be explored in Step 2.2 (Additional Learning Outcomes from General Education).

4. For each curriculum area, ask the parent to make a choice from among these options:

   - *Now* can be checked for up to four curriculum areas that represent the highest priority areas for the student this year that the parent(s) would like to examine in more detail during the Family Interview.

   - *Later* (address in Step 2.1) can be checked for curriculum areas that include at least some learning outcomes that the parent(s) would like to see included in the student's educational program, but are not among the four highest priorities curriculum areas. This is designed to ensure important content is not ignored.

   - *Skip* can be checked if the parent(s) do not think this is a vital curriculum area to explore this year. The decision to skip an area may be because 1) the student is doing well and does not need work in that curriculum area; 2) the curriculum area includes learning outcomes that the parents consider far beyond what should be pursued within the coming year; 3) although it is an important area, it is not important this year but may be in the future years (e.g., vocational); or 4) the content will be primarily addressed through General Supports (Step 3) that are done to or for the student (e.g., personal care supports).

5. Mark each curriculum area as 1) now, 2) later, or 3) skip, corresponding with the parent's choices.

6. Remember, you will only complete Steps 1.3 and 1.4 for up to four curriculum areas that were selected as *now*.

⭐ Helpful Hints

1. This step includes both a divergent component (considering all nine curriculum areas in COACH) and a convergent component (narrowing to select up to a maximum of four curriculum areas to be included in the Family Interview). Having a good understanding of the various parts, steps, and purpose of COACH is essential in helping parents understand how convergence is leading them toward selecting their top priorities. At the same time, the overall design of COACH ensures important curriculum content is not lost by shifting some examination of it to Step 2. It can be helpful to revisit Figure 4 if the parents need further clarification.

2. There may be times when it is appropriate to review only a single item or a small set of items from a particular curriculum area. For example, if the student has severe physical disabilities that require personal supports (e.g., eating, drinking, dressing, using the bathroom) to be attended by others, the parents may decide that the one item, *Gives permission and/or directs others to provide personal care supports*, may be a potential priority to include without the need to review all of the other items in that area, many of which may end up being addressed in Step 3 (General Supports). So, if the facilitator notices the parent(s) hesitating over an area because it includes only one or two learning outcomes of interest, the option to look at a subset of items can be offered.

3. An effective facilitator will demonstrate his or her knowledge of COACH and make connections to earlier parent input. For example, when considering the socialization cur-

riculum area, the facilitator might say, "As you consider whether you want to explore this area in the Family Interview, you will be interested to know that it includes several learning outcomes designed to encourage positive social interactions. I know this is important to you because during the valued life outcomes step you mentioned how much Jake likes being around other people, you identified a need to expand his relationships with other children his age, and rated meaningful relationships as extremely important this year."

Step 1.3   Rating Learning Outcomes in Selected Curriculum Areas

Purpose

Step 1.3 has two primary purposes. The first is a fact-finding function designed to gather information about the family's perspective on the student's current level of performance in reference to each of the learning outcomes within selected curriculum areas using a three-level rating system (i.e., early/emerging skill, partial skill, skillful). The second purpose is for the family to decide whether they think the learning outcomes needs work this year. Step 1.3 narrows the set of possible priorities because some learning will not need work this year and, thus, will be eliminated from consideration as possible priorities. Figure 25 shows Jake's rated learning outcomes for communication.

Materials

From the COACH Student Record forms:

• Forms for Step 1.3

Directions

1. Explain the purpose of Step 1.3 and remind participants that this substep should take about 15–20 minutes to complete.

2. Only complete Step 1.3 for the four high-priority curriculum areas selected in Step 1.2 (leave the others blank).

3. Orient the parent(s) to this step by explaining that you will be asking them to do two things related to each listed learning outcome. First, the facilitator will present a learning outcome from the selected curriculum area and will ask the parent(s) to rate their child's present level of performance (from their perspective) using one of three rating levels.

   • E: early/emerging skill

   • P: partial skill

   • S: skillful

Tell the parents that the ratings will not be added up or used to offer any kind of overall score or assign any level or label to their child. It is simply a way to get a sense of how they are thinking about their child's skill level. Therefore, although parent(s) are encouraged to select one of the three options, it is fine to combine two ratings (e.g., *E-P*; *P-S*) if the parents think it is a more accurate characterization of their child's skill level. Second, the facilitator will ask the parent(s) whether the learning outcome they just rated needs work *this year.* It is important to inform the parent(s) that regardless of the learn-

Learning outcomes	STEP 1.3		STEP 1.4
	Mark score	Needs work this year?	Rank up to four priorities
1. Displays consistent communication mode(s) (e.g., gestures, points, vocalizes, uses facial expressions, uses AAC)	E P S ☑ ○ ○	N Y ○ ☑	
2. Expresses continuation or "more" (e.g., makes sounds or movement to indicate continuation)	E P S ○ ☑ ○	N Y ☑ ○	
3. Makes selection when given options (e.g., story, food, clothes, activities, peers, personal needs)	E P S ○ ☑ ○	N Y ○ ☑	
4. Makes requests of others (e.g., objects, food, interactions, activities, personal care)	E P S ☑ ○ ○	N Y ○ ☑	
5. Signals desire/need for attention (e.g., gesture, vocalization, assistive technology)	E P S ☑ ○ ○	N Y ☑ ○	

Figure 24. Sequence of use within Step 1.3.

ing outcome's rating, it may or may not need work this year. In other words, the three rating options and the yes/no option can occur in any combination. For example, a parent may rate a particular learning outcome as *early skill* and decide it does need work this year and rate another learning outcome as *early skill* and decide it does not need work this year. Similarly, a parent could rate a particular learning outcome as *skillful* and decide it does need work this year and rate another learning outcome as *skillful* and decide it does not need work this year.

So, as depicted by the arrows in Figure 24, the sequence is to present a learning outcome, determine and mark the score, then determine whether it needs work this year before moving to the next item on the list. This process will be repeated for each of the learning outcomes listed within the selected curriculum area before completing Step 1.4 (prioritizing learning outcomes in selected curriculum areas) within that same curriculum area.

4. Remind the parent(s) that this step should take about 15–20 minutes to complete.

5. The following actions need to be completed in the first of the four selected curriculum areas:

   • Present a listed learning outcome.

   • Have the parents rate their child's present level of performance by asking them to choose between the three rating options. The facilitator could say something such as. "The next item is *Makes selection when given options* (e.g., stories, food, activities, personal needs). How would you rate your child's level on this learning outcome, *early/emerging skill*, *partial skill*, or *skillful*?"

   • Listen and record the parent(s) response in the column labeled *mark score* by checking *E*, *P*, or *S*.

   • For the same learning outcome that was just rated, the facilitator asks the parent(s), "Do you think your child needs work on this learning outcome this year?"

   • Listen and record the parent(s) response by checking *Y* (yes) or *N* (no) in the column labeled *needs work this year*.

Communication

*Complete only if **Now** was selected in Step 1.2.*

How does the student communicate (e.g., vocalization, AAC device, sign language, body language, speech)?   Expressively: *Facial expressions, eye gaze, vocalizations, pointing*
Receptively: *Speech*

Learning outcomes	STEP 1.3 Mark score	STEP 1.3 Needs work this year?	STEP 1.4 Rank up to four priorities
1. Displays consistent communication mode(s) (e.g., gestures, points, vocalizes, uses facial expressions, uses AAC)	E ☑ P ○ S ○	N ○ Y ☑	
2. Expresses continuation or "more" (e.g., makes sounds or movement to indicate continuation)	E ○ P ☑ S ○	N ☑ Y ○	
3. Makes selection when given options (e.g., story, food, clothes, activities, peers, personal needs)	E ○ P ☑ S ○	N ○ Y ☑	
4. Makes requests of others (e.g., objects, food, interactions, activities, personal care)	E ☑ P ○ S ○	N ○ Y ☑	
5. Signals desire/need for attention (e.g., gesture, vocalization, assistive technology)	E ☑ P ○ S ○	N ☑ Y ○	
6. Expresses rejection/refusal (e.g., indicates he or she wants something to stop or not begin)	E ○ P ○ S ☑	N ☑ Y ○	
7. Sustains communication with others (e.g., takes turn, listens to others communicate, stays on topic)	E ○ P ☑ S ○	N ☑ Y ○	
8. Recognizes if misunderstood and uses another way (e.g., uses "repair strategy," perseveres)	E ☑ P ○ S ○	N ○ Y ☑	
9. Expresses greetings and farewell	E ○ P ☑ S ○	N ☑ Y ○	
10. Follows instructions (e.g., one step, multistep)	E ○ P ☑ S ○	N ○ Y ☑	
11. Answers questions (e.g., yes/no, who, what, where, why, when, how)	E ○ P ☑ S ○	N ○ Y ☑	
12. Comments/describes (e.g., vocabulary for events, objects, interactions, feelings)	E ☑ P ○ S ○	N ○ Y ☑	
13. Asks questions of others	E ☑ P ○ S ○	N ○ Y ☑	

Scoring key (use scores for Step 1.3 alone or in combination):
E = Early/emerging skill (1%–25%); P = Partial skill (25%–80%); S = Skillful (80%–100%).

Figure 25. Jake's rated learning outcomes for communication.

- Repeat this process for each of the learning outcomes listed with the selected curriculum area.

Note: Unique items not included in COACH can be added in the blank spaces provided.

6. Complete Step 1.4 after finishing Step 1.3 for all the learning outcomes listed in this curriculum area, but before leaving this page, complete Step 1.4. In other words, within a selected curriculum area, both Steps 1.3 and 1.4 are completed before moving to the next selected curriculum area.

7. Write any clarifying or reminder notes that you find helpful in the spaces provided or anywhere on the page.

8. Repeat Steps 5, 6, and 7 for each of the four curriculum areas selected in Step 1.2.

 ## Helpful Hints

1. Facilitators will benefit from familiarity with the lists of learning outcomes and their potential relationship to valued life outcomes.

2. Individualize the wording of items to match the situation.

3. Use your knowledge of the student to avoid asking unnecessary questions. Rather than simply not asking about certain learning outcomes and assuming that asking the question is unnecessary, check with the parent(s) first. If you find that more than a couple of questions are considered unnecessary, then it is probable that a facilitation error occurred back in Step 1.2 when the curriculum area was initially selected.

4. The process moves along more quickly and smoothly in Step 1.3 if parents are asked to choose between the three discrete rating options as per the directions. The time it takes to complete the process is unnecessarily extended when parent(s) are asked about a learning outcome in an open-ended manner (e.g., How does your child do with making selections when given options?); this type of question asking tends to invite longer, more detailed responses. Although the information gained from such extended responses certainly can be valuable, going into detail at this point in the process can be premature and adversely affect the overall outcome of the Family Interview. If parents start to go substantially beyond what the facilitator is asking for, then politely redirect the process and remind them that once their priorities are determined, more time and detail will be focused on those learning outcomes. Sometimes, it is best just to listen. Be flexible yet aware of your overall time use and the purpose of the process.

5. Do not spend extra time having parents make distinctions between two rating levels when the parents feel their child is in between two levels or when two parents disagree. So, if one parent feels the level is early/emerging skill and the other parent feels the level is partial skill, then the facilitator is encouraged to record the rating score as *E-P*.

6. We strongly discourage using the *no skill* option. Part of the philosophy of COACH is to build on strengths and acknowledge capabilities. No matter how severe a student's disability may be, he or she always has some skill on which to build. It is much more affirming (and accurate) for parents to indicate their child has early or emerging skill, than no skill at all. This is a small but powerful bit of language that can make a big difference in the tone and outcome of the Family Interview as well as interactions that follow. Remember, all students have some level of skill on which to build.

Step 1.4 Prioritizing Learning Outcomes in Selected Curriculum Areas

 Purpose

Step 1.4 is designed to narrow the field of possibilities that lead to selecting the highest priority learning outcomes by the family. This is accomplished within each of the four selected curriculum areas by having the family consider the subset of learning outcomes that they identified as "needs work this year" (those marked yes in Step 1.3) and rank the four highest priorities. Figure 26 shows Jake's four highest ranked priorities.

 Materials

From the COACH Student Record forms:

*   Forms for Step 1.4

 Directions

1. Explain the purpose of Step 1.4 and remind participants that this substep should take about 15 minutes or less to complete.

2. Orient the parent(s) to this step by explaining that you will be asking them to consider only those learning outcomes they identified as *needs work this year* (those marked *yes* in Step 1.3) and to rank order the four highest priorities among them. Remind the parent(s) that selecting the priorities is the family's decision.

3. Point out which learning outcomes were marked *yes*, and ask the parent(s) to rank the four most important to address this year. It can be helpful to read off the available learning outcomes aloud, leaving spaces for the parent(s) to ponder and reply.

4. Listen to the parent(s) and record their responses in the column labeled *rank up to four priorities*.

5. Repeat Step 1.4 within each selected curriculum area. Remember, Steps 1.3 and 1.4 are completed for the same curriculum area sequentially before moving on to the next curriculum area. Do not complete all of Step 1.3 in all four selected curriculum areas and then move back to complete Step 1.4 in all four curriculum areas.

6. After completing Steps 1.3 and 1.4 for all four selected curriculum areas, it is advisable to offer the parents a short break before starting Step 1.5 (Cross-Prioritization). This not only allows the parent(s) the opportunity for a break before the final decision making, but also gives the facilitator the opportunity to transfer the priorities to the Step 1.5 form.

 Helpful Hints

1. Ranking priorities can be facilitated by reading the learning outcomes aloud and making connections to earlier comments made by parents, such as during Step 1.1.

2. It is okay to have fewer than four priorities within a selected curriculum area. In some cases, fewer than four items are identified as needing work this year.

3. Do not waste time ranking more than four priorities because only a maximum of four from each selected curriculum area move forward to be considered in Step 1.5 (Cross-Prioritization).

Communication

*Complete only if **Now** was selected in Step 1.2.*

How does the student communicate (e.g., vocalization, AAC device, sign language, body language, speech)?   Expressively: *Facial expressions, eye gaze, vocalizations, pointing*

Receptively: *Speech*

Learning outcomes	STEP 1.3 Mark score	STEP 1.3 Needs work this year?	STEP 1.4 Rank up to four priorities
1. Displays consistent communication mode(s) (e.g., gestures, points, vocalizes, uses facial expressions, uses AAC)	E ✓ P ○ S ○	N ○ Y ✓	1
2. Expresses continuation or "more" (e.g., makes sounds or movement to indicate continuation)	E ○ P ✓ S ○	N ✓ Y ○	
3. Makes selection when given options (e.g., story, food, clothes, activities, peers, personal needs)	E ○ P ✓ S ○	N ○ Y ✓	2
4. Makes requests of others (e.g., objects, food, interactions, activities, personal care)	E ✓ P ○ S ○	N ○ Y ✓	3
5. Signals desire/need for attention (e.g., gesture, vocalization, assistive technology)	E ✓ P ○ S ○	N ✓ Y ○	
6. Expresses rejection/refusal (e.g., indicates he or she wants something to stop or not begin)	E ○ P ○ S ✓	N ✓ Y ○	
7. Sustains communication with others (e.g., takes turn, listens to others communicate, stays on topic)	E ○ P ✓ S ○	N ✓ Y ○	
8. Recognizes if misunderstood and uses another way (e.g., uses "repair strategy," perseveres)	E ✓ P ○ S ○	N ○ Y ✓	
9. Expresses greetings and farewell	E ○ P ✓ S ○	N ✓ Y ○	
10. Follows instructions (e.g., one step, multistep)	E ○ P ✓ S ○	N ○ Y ✓	
11. Answers questions (e.g., yes/no, who, what, where, why, when, how)	E ○ P ✓ S ○	N ○ Y ✓	
12. Comments/describes (e.g., vocabulary for events, objects, interactions, feelings)	E ✓ P ○ S ○	N ○ Y ✓	
13. Asks questions of others	E ✓ P ○ S ○	N ○ Y ✓	4

Scoring key (use scores for Step 1.3 alone or in combination):
E = Early/emerging skill (1%–25%); P = Partial skill (25%–80%); S = Skillful (80%–100%).

Figure 26.   Jake's four highest ranked priorities.

STEP 1

4. If the parents are struggling to distinguish between any of the top four rankings, it is not worth spending too much time on it. For example, if the parents cannot decide which learning outcome is first and which is second, then you can let them know that this distinction is not as important as knowing that they are both among the top four priorities. Therefore, label them both as first and have the parents select two more priorities.

5. Sometimes, when parents are having difficulty selecting the top four priorities, it may be easier to eliminate learning outcomes by identifying which of the remaining possibilities are not among the top four.

6. Occasionally, parents request input from school personnel when the parents may have less opportunity to observe than the teachers (e.g., school, vocational). In such cases, dialogue can be helpful and appropriate as long as it is understood that the family retains decision making regarding selecting and ranking the priorities.

7. Having the student involved in Steps 1.4 and 1.5 is an option when it is age appropriate for the student to participate in COACH.

8. Always remember it is the family, not the professionals, who are selecting the priorities for the student during the Family Interview. Professionals will have an opportunity to share what potential program content they feel is important in the other steps of COACH (e.g., Step 2).

9. Some teams find it helpful to have a nonfacilitating team member (e.g., the classroom teacher, SLP) transfer the ranked priorities to the Step 1.5 form while the facilitator continues to work through Steps 1.3 and 1.4 with the family. Not only does this save time, but it also allows the facilitator a short break as well.

Step 1.5   Cross-Prioritization

 Purpose

Step 1.5 is designed to 1) determine a maximum of the top six overall priorities from the family perspective, 2) clarify which valued life outcomes are being sought by selecting each overall priority, and 3) determine which of the overall priorities should be included on the IEP as goals and objectives, as opposed to being documented as additional learning outcomes or being primarily a home responsibility. Step 1.5 acknowledges that not all overall priorities necessarily need to be documented as IEP goals and objectives. Something can be important and, after further consideration, be appropriate to document as an additional learning outcome. Some other learning outcomes, such as personal management or community skills, may be high priorities to the family, but they may decide that they would rather work on these at home or during nonschool hours. More time at school can then be devoted to outcomes less amenable to working on at home (e.g., academics, peer interactions). Figure 27 shows Jake's cross-prioritization.

 Materials

From the COACH Student Record forms:

• Forms for Step 1.5

 Directions

1. Have the participants take a short break. This gives the family some time to recharge and the facilitator time to transfer the priorities from Step 1.4 to the first page of the Step 1.5 form.

Step 1.5

Cross-Prioritization

Transfer priority learning outcomes in their ranked order from each COACH curriculum area reviewed with the family in Step 1.4.

	Communication	Socialization	Personal management	Recreation	Access academics
1	Displays consistent communication mode	Sustains social interactions			Directs/sustains attention
2	Makes selections given options	Offers assistance	Skip for now	A.L.O.	Explores surroundings
3	Makes requests	Advocates for self (asks for help)			Differentiates/discriminates
4	Asks questions	Ends social interactions			Understands nontext symbols

	Applied academics	School	Community	Vocational	Other
1	Uses computer				
2	Understands text has meaning	A.L.O.	Skip for now	Skip for now	NA
3	Uses schedule				
4	Uses writing/drawing tools				

Step 1.5

Cross-Prioritization

COACH 3

Rank	Overall priority learning outcomes (Word priorities to explicitly clarify what the student will be expected to learn)	Safety/health	Home	Relationships	Control/choices	Activities	IEP goal	Additional learning outcomes	Home
		Indicate which valued life outcomes the priority is meant to support					Check (✓) only one box for each priority		
1	Displays consistent communication mode			✓	✓	✓	✓		
2	Makes selections when given options			✓	✓	✓	✓		
3	Differentiates/discriminates between things				✓	✓	✓	✓	
4	Asks questions of others (including help)	✓		✓	✓	✓	✓		
5	Offers assistance to others			✓	✓	✓		✓	
6	Uses computer			✓	✓	✓	✓		

Next step: The interviewer explains Steps 2.1, 2.2, and 3 and the relationship of the Family Interview to the next steps.

Figure 27. Jake's cross-prioritization.

2. When the group reconvenes, explain the purpose of Step 1.5 and remind participants this substep should take about 15 minutes or less to complete.

3. Orient the parent(s) to this step by explaining that all of their selected priorities have been transferred onto a single page (first page of Step 1.5 form), thus they can see them all together in ranked order. The parent's job will be to 1) consider the priorities across the selected curriculum areas and rank the top six priority learning outcomes overall, 2) help ensure that the team understands the meaning behind their selections (e.g., their connection to the valued life outcomes), and 3) reach consensus with the school representatives about which overall priorities should be included in the IEP as goals and objectives as opposed to being documented as additional learning outcomes or primarily a home responsibility.

4. Remind the participants that any high priorities not selected as overall priorities will not be lost, but will be captured and documented in Step 2.1 (Additional Learning Outcomes from COACH).

5. Ask the parents to review the list of available priorities (first page of Step 1.5) and select one as the top overall priority. Make sure the parent(s) know their selections may come from any of the ranked curriculum areas and may come from any ranking. For example, something that was the third-ranked learning outcome in a selected curriculum area in Step 1.4 may end up being selected before something that was rated higher in the earlier step. It can be helpful to read aloud the available learning outcomes, leaving spaces for the parent(s) to ponder and reply.

6. Listen to the parent(s) and record their response in the column labeled *Overall Priority Learning Outcomes*.

7. Repeat this process until six overall top priorities have been identified by the family and documented.

8. Once the overall priorities have been identified, have the family verify their agreement with the list by saying something such as, "As you look at this list of overall priorities, do you feel comfortable that these represent the most important priorities you would like to see your child work on in the coming year?" Make any adjustments or clarifications as needed.

9. Verify which valued life outcomes are sought by the family's selection of each overall priority learning outcome. This is an active listening substep in which the responsibility is on the facilitator to synthesize and restate what they have heard during the Family Interview from the parent(s). The facilitator might say something such as,

    > I'd like to briefly review each of the overall priorities you selected to make sure I have an accurate understanding of how they relate to improving Jake's valued life outcomes. You selected *Offers assistance to others*. My understanding is that you are concerned that because Jake needs so much support from others that his peers might not see him as contributing to others. You are hopeful that when peers see and experience him offering assistance, not just always receiving it, it will have a positive influence on his relationships. Am I understanding you correctly?

    The family then has the opportunity to verify, clarify, or correct the meaning behind their selections.

10. Listen to the parent(s) and record the identified valued life outcomes pertaining to each learning outcome by checking the corresponding boxes under the heading labeled *Indicate which valued life outcomes the priority is meant to support*.

11. For each overall priority, check one of the three boxes in the column labeled *Check only one box for each priority* to indicate whether the family would like to have the priority written as an IEP goal, documented as an additional learning outcome in Step 2.1, or remain primarily a home responsibility. This should be a negotiated decision between the parent(s) and the school personnel in attendance. The facilitator should begin this final aspect of Step 1.5 by clarifying the distinction between these three options and asking the parents for their choices. If the school representatives agree, then this is verified. If the school personnel notice something they would like the parents to reconsider, then they can explain their perspective and attempt to reach consensus with the parent. For example, if among the six overall priorities, the parents only care about having two on the IEP, then a special educator might advocate for including four or five.

12. Provide the parent(s) with important information related to next steps. Explain that those overall priorities checked to be translated into IEP goals will be included as the team moves forward to develop the IEP. Also, remind the parents that these priorities reflect a small subset of the highest priority learning outcomes that typically are not addressed in the general education curriculum. Last, remind the parent(s) that these priorities for the IEP reflect only the focal point for their child's program—the breadth of the program, namely a broader range of learning outcomes, will be added in Step 2.

13. Conclude the Family Interview by thanking the participants and explain the next steps.

 Helpful Hints

1. Sometimes during cross-prioritization, parents may switch the ranked order of selected learning outcomes. Such reordering is not only acceptable, but it is also desirable because it demonstrates that parents can refine and adjust their priorities given multiple opportunities to consider the importance of learning outcomes. Be sure to let parents know it is okay to move things around in this fashion.

2. Cross-prioritization can be facilitated by stating the listed priorities aloud and leaving pauses for responding. For example, a facilitator might say, "What would be your top overall priority for this year? Would it be [then read off a few top priorities across curriculum areas]?" Conversely, some parents prefer silence while they scan the possibilities and formulate their thoughts. Facilitators should be sensitive to the participants' styles of interaction and adjust the interview process accordingly.

3. You can help the family visually keep track of which items have been selected by putting checkmarks or another indicator next to learning outcomes once they have been selected.

4. If the family is having difficulty selecting the top priority, then it can be helpful to say, "If you are having difficulty picking out the top priority, then can you identify the top two or three? At this stage the order is less important than the learning outcomes being identified among the top six overall priorities." Conversely, if participants get stuck, then sometimes it can be helpful to converge on the top priorities by eliminating learning outcomes. The facilitator might say, "As you look at the list of possibilities, are there any learning outcomes you know are not among your highest six priorities and can be eliminated?" Ultimately, if the family is having difficulty selecting the top six priorities in a ranked order, then the facilitator can simply ask the family to identify the top six priorities without concern for ranked order.

5. Once the Family Interview gets to this stage, selecting overall priorities can occur in any combination. For example, overall priorities could end up coming from all four curriculum areas or only two or three.

6. Always remember it is the family, not the professionals, who are selecting the priorities for the student during the Family Interview.

STEP 2 || ADDITIONAL LEARNING OUTCOMES

 ### Purpose

Step 2 is designed to identify additional learning outcomes beyond the priorities selected during the Family Interview. Selecting individually determined additional learning outcomes is designed to ensure the student has access to a broad range of learning opportunities and the contents of the educational program are not artificially narrow. This could happen if only a small set of priorities were identified and is the key reason why it is important to continue past Step 1 of COACH. In addition, whereas Step 1 was designed to have the family retain exclusive decision making over the selection of priority learning outcomes, Step 2 is intended to provide opportunities for all participants to share their perspectives in an effort to reach consensus about which additional learning outcomes should be targeted for instruction.

 ### Materials

From the COACH Student Record forms:

*   Forms for Step 2.1: Additional Learning Outcomes from COACH
*   Forms for Step 2.2: Additional Learning Outcomes from General Education

 ### Directions

1. Make a team decision about which substep to complete first: Step 2.1 or 2.2 (either way is acceptable as long as you complete both substeps).

2. After completing both steps, consider the combined list of learning outcomes, applying your selected criteria, to ensure the list is a reasonable size, doable, does not detract from the priority learning outcomes, and guides the team's educational instruction and support.

⭐ Helpful Hints

1. Selecting additional learning outcomes in Step 2 partially addresses the content of a student's educational program (with the highest priorities already identified in Step 1). Like Step 1, Step 2 deals exclusively with what educational content (learning outcomes) will be targets of instruction, but does not offer guidance on where or how the student will receive instruction. Sometimes people confuse the what, where, and how and draw inferences that may not be accurate. For example, if a student has no identified additional learning outcomes in science, then it does not mean the student will not be included in science class or activities. The student may still be included in science class and activities through curriculum overlapping, whereby the science activities are the mechanism

to focus on targeted learning outcomes from other curriculum areas (e.g., communication, socialization, access academics, applied academics).

2. Step 2 is not meant to document every conceivable learning outcome that a student might be exposed to. Rather, it is designed to identify and document critical learning outcomes that will be targeted for instruction. Therefore, it is vital to select a quantity of learning outcomes the team agrees can be reasonably pursued during a school year.

3. Team members have expressed concern that if additional learning outcomes are not documented as IEP annual goals and short-term objectives, then they will not be given adequate attention and accountability will suffer. This can be addressed by attaching the additional learning outcomes to the IEP as an addendum. Remember, IDEA spells out minimum requirements for an IEP but does allow your team to include information that extends beyond those minimum requirements (e.g., attaching additional learning outcomes).

4. Be sure to know, or have available, the general education grade-level curricular content for the projected class placement. This will be necessary when the team completes Step 2.2.

STEP 2.1   Additional Learning Outcomes from COACH

 Purpose

Step 2.1 is designed to ensure that learning outcome areas in COACH not considered within the Family Interview and those not selected as priorities for inclusion on the IEP as annual goals are reviewed for consideration as additional learning outcomes from COACH. Figure 28 displays Jake's additional learning outcomes from COACH.

 Materials

- Forms for Step 2.1

 Directions

1. Explain the purpose of Step 2.1 and remind participants that this substep should take about 10–15 minutes or less to complete.

2. Refer to the list of overall priority learning outcomes completed in Step 1.5. For those priorities selected as additional learning outcomes (see the second column from the left), check the learning outcomes in Step 2.1 corresponding to those priorities; this is simply a transfer of information from Step 1.5 to Step 2.1. By checking the learning outcome in Step 2.1, you are ensuring that these non–IEP goal priorities are not ignored.

3. Refer to the ranked priority learning outcomes listed by curriculum area shown on the first page of Step 1.5. Consider if any of those ranked learning outcomes that did not make it to the second page of the Cross-Prioritization should be checked as additional learning outcomes. Check the spaces in Step 2.1 corresponding to those priorities. The team may decide that some of these learning outcomes do not need to be designated as additional learning outcomes if they do not rise to the level of critical learning outcomes that will be targeted for instruction.

4. Consider if any other learning outcomes that were marked *Y* (yes) for *needs work this year*, but were not among the priorities listed in Step 1.5, should be included as addi-

Step 2.1

Additional Learning Outcomes from COACH

Select and mark (✓) only those additional learning outcomes to be targeted for instruction (limit to reasonable number). See manual for directions.

Date: _May 12th_   Participants: _Sophie & Tom Gardener, Karen Green, Maryann Booth_

Communication

___ 1. Displays consistent communication mode
___ 2. Expresses continuation or "more"
___ 3. Makes selection when given options
✓ 4. Makes request of others
___ 5. Signals desire/need for attention
___ 6. Expresses rejection/ refusal
___ 7. Sustains communication with others
___ 8. Recognizes when misunderstood and uses another way
___ 9. Expresses greetings and farewells
___ 10. Follows instructions
___ 11. Answers questions
___ 12. Comments/describes
___ 13. Asks questions of others

Socialization

___ 14. Responds to the presence and interactions of others
___ 15. Initiates social interactions
✓ 16. Sustains social interactions
✓ 17. Ends social interactions

___ 18. Distinguishes and interacts differently with friends/family, acquaintances, and strangers
___ 19. Maintains safe and healthy behaviors when alone and with others
___ 20. Accepts assistance from others
✓ 21. Offers assistance to others
___ 22. Makes transitions between routine activities
___ 23. Adjusts to unexpected changes in routine
___ 24. Shares with others
✓ 25. Advocates for self

Personal Management

___ 26. Gives permission and/ or directs others to provide personal care support
___ 27. Drinks and eats
___ 28. Feeds self
___ 29. Cares for bowel and bladder needs
___ 30. Selects appropriate clothing to wear
___ 31. Dresses/undresses
___ 32. Cares for personal hygiene

___ 33. Is mobile between locations
___ 34. Manages personal belongings
___ 35. Gives self-identification information
___ 36. Uses telephone
___ 37. Responds to emergency alarm
___ 38. Recognizes and avoids potentially dangerous situations
___ 39. Maintains safe and healthy behaviors

Recreation

___ 40. Engages in spectator events with others
___ 41. Engages in recreation activities on his or her own
___ 42. Engages in recreation activities with others

Figure 28. Jake's additional learning outcomes from COACH.

Figure 28. *(continued)*

Step 2.1

Additional Learning Outcomes from COACH

Access Academics

___ 43. Reacts to objects, activities, and/or interactions

✓ 44. Directs and sustains attention to activity

✓ 45. Explores surroundings and objects

✓ 46. Differentiates/ discriminates between things

___ 47. Imitates skills used in daily life

___ 48. Uses objects as intended

✓ 49. Understands meaning of nontext symbols

Applied Academics

___ 50. Uses computer

✓ 51. Understands text has meaning

___ 52. Reads (decodes) words/phrases

___ 53. Understands what is read

✓ 54. Uses writing/drawing tools

___ 55. Writes letters or words

___ 56. Counts with correspondence

___ 57. Computes numbers

___ 58. Uses money

✓ 59. Uses schedule or calendar

School

___ 60. Travels to and from school

___ 61. Participates in small groups

___ 62. Participates in large groups

___ 63. Completes tasks/ assignments independently

___ 64. Manages school-related belongings

___ 65. Follows school procedures/routines

___ 66. Does classroom or school jobs

___ 67. Uses school facilities

___ 68. Participates in extracurricular activities

Community

___ 69. Travels safely in the community

___ 70. Uses restaurants

___ 71. Uses recreation facilities

___ 72. Makes purchases of merchandise or services

___ 73. Uses vending machines

___ 74. Uses banking facilities

___ 75. Uses public transportation

Vocational

___ 76. Applies for jobs(s)

___ 77. Travels to and from worksite

___ 78. Uses check-in procedure

___ 79. Interacts appropriately with others

___ 80. Follows worksite rules for appearance, safety, and conduct

___ 81. Follows schedule of work activities

___ 82. Completes assigned work

___ 83. Uses worksite facilities

Other

___ _____

___ _____

___ _____

___ _____

___ _____

___ _____

___ _____

___ _____

___ _____

___ _____

___ _____

tional learning outcomes because they are critical learning outcomes that will be targeted for instruction. Again, remember you want to limit the total number of additional learning outcomes from COACH to a relatively small number because the team will be identifying more learning outcomes from the general education curriculum in Step 2.2, and the entire listing needs to be implemented reasonably.

5. Consider learning outcomes from the subset of curriculum areas not reviewed in detail in Step 1. These curriculum areas can be found in two places. 1) You can look at the completed Step 1.2 to see which curriculum areas are marked *later*. In Figure 27, two areas are marked (i.e., recreation, school). 2) Looking on the first page of Step 1.5, you will see the same two curriculum areas coded as *ALO* (for additional learning outcomes). Review the ALO designated curriculum areas to determine if any of the listed learning outcomes should be targeted for instruction this year. Check the spaces in Step 2.1 corresponding to those learning outcomes.

6. Regardless of the order in which your team decided to complete Step 2.1 or Step 2.2, once both substeps have been completed, the team should review the combined list of targeted additional learning outcomes to ensure it is a reasonable number. This may require reducing the number or deferring certain learning outcomes for attention later in the school year.

7. These additional learning outcomes should be revisited throughout the school year to add new items as initial learning outcomes are achieved.

★ Helpful Hints

1. Alternate using divergent and convergent thinking as your team makes decisions about additional learning outcomes. This will encourage the team to consider a broad set of learning outcomes and converge by selecting a smaller (manageable) set to work on this year.

2. If certain team members are unable to attend the meeting (e.g., related services providers) to select additional learning outcomes, then their input can be obtained prior to the meeting and represented by a team member in attendance.

3. There may be some overlap between the learning outcomes listed in COACH and the general education curriculum. Most likely this occurs when the team is considering preschool, kindergarten, and primary grade general education curriculum and applied academics. Be aware of these potential overlaps to avoid duplicating items in Steps 2.1 and 2.2.

Step 2.2   Additional Learning Outcomes from General Education

Purpose

Step 2.2 provides a systematic way to ensure that students with disabilities have access to appropriate general education curricular content available to students without disabilities. Although Step 1 provides focus for a student's educational program, and Step 2.1 further explores learning outcomes that extend or augment the general education curriculum, Step 2.2 broadens the student's curriculum even more. Step 2.2 assists the team in considering a range of general education learning outcomes for the student in areas such as language arts, math, science, social studies, art, music, physical education, technology, foreign language, and others. Most important, Step 2.2 is designed to assist team members in developing shared expectations for the primary type of participation (e.g., same, multilevel, curriculum overlapping) students with disabilities have in general education classes. Step 2.2 provides opportunities for all team members to share their perspectives in an effort to reach consensus on the primary type of participation and an initial starting point for instruction. Figure 30 shows Jake's additional learning outcomes from general education.

 ## Materials

- Forms for Step 2.2

Directions

1. Be familiar with the four types of participation options: 1) same (grade-level expectations), 2) multilevel (same content), 3) multilevel (different content), and 4) curriculum overlapping. See definitions on the subsequent pages of these directions and embedded within the Student Record forms.

2. Explain the purpose of Step 2.2 and remind participants that this substep should take no more than 35–40 minutes to complete. It can be completed in a shorter amount of time if all team members have a thorough understanding of 1) the four types of participation options, 2) the general education curriculum, 3) and the characteristics of the student.

3. Review the list of general education curriculum areas and put a checkmark in the box to the left of all the classes 1) that are typically part of the general education curriculum at the grade-level placement for which your team is planning and 2) in which the team anticipates the student will participate. Typically, the default expectation—in other words, the starting point—is that the student will be included in all the same classes available to his or her peers without disabilities. At the elementary and middle school levels these tend to be same for most students. More variation exists at the high school level where students tend to have more options and elective courses. In those cases the team provides the student the same level of choice about those options as is available to other students in the same grade.

4. In space provided for each checked curriculum area, list examples of the curricular content at that grade level (e.g., major units of study). For example, some major units of study for third-grade science might include life cycle, plants, animals, weather/climate, astronomy, magnets, energy, and scientific method. This step is meant to ensure that parents and school personnel have a shared understanding of the curricular content at the grade level where the student is placed, even though the student may be functioning below the academic level of his or her classmates. The space provided is purposefully small because this substep is meant to give a flavor of the curricular content, not to document the entire grade-level curriculum. Understanding the grade-level curriculum is necessary to complete the next substep within Step 2.2.

5. By considering the grade-level curricular content expectations and what the team members know about the characteristics and needs of the student, they select one of four primary types of participation the student would be expected to have within that curriculum area—same, multilevel (same content), multilevel (different content), or curriculum overlapping (see Figure 30 for definitions of these terms). See the two-page key defining these terms on the pages preceding the Step 2.2 forms. Record the team's consensus by marking one of the four primary types of participation. Selecting the primary type of participation does not imply that other types of participation might not be appropriate within the same class. Frequently, there are opportunities to address multiple learning outcomes across multiple types of participation within a single class or even activity. The purpose here is not to identify all types of participation, but only the primary type of participation.

The student may require access or instructional supports (e.g., assistive technology, AAC device, extended time, modified materials) across each of the four types of participation.

Same curriculum with supports (same content, same level)
- Within a curriculum area class or activity (e.g., reading, math, science), the expectation for the student with a disability is that he or she will pursue and can reasonably achieve the same grade-level expectations as his or her classmates without disabilities.
- Same curriculum means same content, level, amount, and rate.
- It is expected that the student will gain access to the same curriculum in the general education classroom with supports as needed.

Multilevel curriculum (same content, different level)
- Within a curriculum area class or activity (e.g., reading, math, science), the expectation for the student with a disability is that he or she will pursue an individually determined subset of the learning outcomes within the same curriculum area and have the same content as his or her classmates without disabilities, but at a different level.
- Multilevel curriculum means the same curriculum area and content, but at a different level, amount, and/or rate. For example, in math, most students are working on computing numbers (e.g., three digits). The student with a disability is also working on computing numbers, but at a different level (e.g., single digits), typically a lesser amount, and potentially at a slower rate.
- Multilevel curriculum is delivered within shared educational activities in a large or small group with a natural proportion of students with and without disabilities.

Multilevel curriculum (different content, different level)
- Within a curriculum area class or activity (e.g., reading, math, science), the expectation for the student with a disability is that he or she will pursue an individually determined subset of the learning outcomes within the same curriculum area, but have different content than his or her classmates without disabilities and at a different level.
- Multilevel curriculum means the same curriculum area, but different content, at a different level, amount, and/or rate. For example, in math, most students are working on computing numbers (e.g., three digits). The student with a disability is also working on math curriculum, but is learning a different content (e.g., counting, geometric shapes), typically a lesser amount, and potentially at a slower rate.
- Multilevel curriculum is delivered within shared educational activities in a large or small group with a natural proportion of students with and without disabilities.

Curriculum overlapping (different curriculum area, different level)
- Within a curriculum area class or activity (e.g., social studies, health), the expectation for the student with a disability is that he or she will pursue an individually determined subset of the learning outcomes from curriculum areas different from his or her classmates without disabilities and at a different level.
- Curriculum overlapping means different curriculum areas and different content at a different level, amount, and/or rate. For example, in social studies, most students are working on geography. The student with a disability is exposed to and involved in geography activities (e.g., a geography game with classmates), but the primary learning outcomes he or she is focusing on are from other curriculum areas (e.g., communication, socialization, access academics), such as developing a consistent pointing response, making a selection when given options, or exploring objects.
- The student with a disability may require access or instructional supports (e.g., assistive technology, AAC device, extended time, modified materials) when exploring curriculum overlapping.
- Curriculum overlapping is delivered within shared educational activities in a large or small group with a natural proportion of students with and without disabilities.
- Curriculum overlapping does not preclude also encouraging learning outcomes in the curriculum area targeted for the majority of the class.

Figure 29. Definitions of the four primary types of participation a student would be expected to have within a curriculum area. (See pp. 150–151.)

6. In the space labeled *Provide example* (far right column on Step 2.2 form), develop a short, noncomprehensive list of appropriate learning outcomes designed to give teachers a starting point for instruction and an opportunity to learn more about the student. If either of the two multilevel types of participation were selected, then these examples should be learning outcomes within the curriculum area (as per the definition of multi-

Step 2.2

Additional Learning Outcomes from General Education

COACH3

✓	General education curriculum areas (provide brief description)	Indicate primary participation option	Provide example — Starting points if multilevel or curriculum overlapping
✓	Language arts: Oral and silent reading Writing stories and poems Spelling, dictionary skills, synonyms, antonyms	○ Same (grade-level expectation) ○ Multilevel (same content) ✓ Multilevel (different content) ○ Curriculum overlapping	Orients to books Identifies photographs, objects and symbols Follows one-step instructions
✓	Math: Word problems Add, subtract, multiply, divide, fractions, geometry, metric measurement, Roman numerals	○ Same (grade-level expectation) ○ Multilevel (same content) ○ Multilevel (different content) ✓ Curriculum overlapping	Use math activities to work on Priority Learning Outcomes in other curriculum areas
✓	Science: Life cycle, plants, animals, weather/climate, astronomy, magnets, energy	○ Same (grade-level expectation) ✓ Multilevel (same content) ○ Multilevel (different content) ○ Curriculum overlapping	Distinguishes between plants and animals Matches weather with clothes
✓	Social studies: human needs, folk customs, Native Americans, community helpers, citizenship, social responsibility	○ Same (grade-level expectation) ✓ Multilevel (same content) ○ Multilevel (different content) ○ Curriculum overlapping	Identifies classmates, school personnel, provides help to others in class or at job

Figure 30. Jake's additional learning outcomes from general education. APE, adapted physical education. (Note: No Child Left Behind [NCLB] Act of 2001 [PL 107-110] required assessment in language arts, math, and science. States may require assessment in additional curriculum areas.)

(continued)

Figure 30. *(continued)*

Step 2.2 *(continued)*

Additional Learning
Outcomes from General Education

COACH3

	General education curriculum areas (provide brief description)	Indicate primary participation option	Provide example Starting points if multilevel or curriculum overlapping
✓	Physical education: *Games & sports, fitness, outdoor pursuits (orienteering)*	○ Same (grade-level expectation) ✓ Multilevel (same content) ○ Multilevel (different content) ○ Curriculum overlapping	*Adapted, partial participation in some activities with guidance from APE and physical therapist*
✓	Health education: *Dental health, parts of the body, nutrition, safety hazards, healthy leisure, eye and ear care*	○ Same (grade-level expectation) ✓ Multilevel (same content) ○ Multilevel (different content) ○ Curriculum overlapping	*Identify body parts, healthy leisure activities with peers*
✓	Art (visual/performing): *Use of various media; differentiate landscape portraits and still life; art vocabulary*	○ Same (grade-level expectation) ✓ Multilevel (same content) ○ Multilevel (different content) ○ Curriculum overlapping	*Uses a variety of media—explore self-expression*
✓	Music (vocal/instrumental): *Sing or play music of different cultures, create and echo music patterns, arrange music to accompany stories, music notation*	○ Same (grade-level expectation) ✓ Multilevel (same content) ○ Multilevel (different content) ○ Curriculum overlapping	*Uses adapted devices (e.g., with switches) to produce rhythms, notes, songs, and so forth*

level). For example, if the student's primary type of participation is multilevel (different content) in language arts and the class is focusing on new spelling words, then the target student is learning to identify photos, objects, or symbols. If the primary type of participation in math is curriculum overlapping, then the student's focus might be to work on his or her priority learning outcomes identified in the Family Interview (e.g., displays consistent response mode, makes selections given options, differentiates/discriminates between things, uses computer with adapted switch) within the context of math activities.

7. Regardless of the order in which your team decided to complete Step 2.1 or Step 2.2, once both substeps have been completed, the team should review the combined list of targeted additional learning outcomes to ensure it is a reasonable number. This may require reducing the number or deferring certain learning outcomes for attention later in the school year.

8. These additional learning outcomes should be revisited throughout the school year to add new items as initial learning outcomes are achieved.

 Helpful Hints

1. In cases in which there are several general education teachers (e.g., high school), the team may have at least one general education representative at the COACH meeting. The special educator should contact each teacher in advance to get input and perspectives pertaining to the curricular area: 1) description of primary units of study, 2) primary type of participation, and 3) potential examples of starting point learning outcomes. Any teacher who is feeling unsure or unclear about what makes the most sense should attend this aspect of the COACH planning process.

2. Include any curriculum areas that are state or district requirements (e.g., physical education, health education).

3. Although you are attempting to select additional learning outcomes at an appropriate level of difficulty for the student, be sure you are providing opportunities for your student to surprise you by exceeding your expectations. These learning outcomes are provided to guide a student's learning, never to limit a student's opportunities.

4. Be careful to select a quantity of additional learning outcomes your team feels they can reasonably address given the number of hours in the school day. Try to balance your optimism with realism.

STEP 3 | | **GENERAL SUPPORTS**

 Purpose

Step 3 is designed to determine and document general supports that are necessary for the student to gain access to or participate in his or her IEP across six key areas of support: 1) personal needs, 2) physical needs, 3) teaching others about the student, 4) sensory needs, 5) providing access and opportunities, and 6) other general supports. Unlike learning outcomes identified in Steps 1 and 2, which focus on changes in the student's behavior (e.g., skill acquisition), Step 3 does not require changes in student behavior, but rather actions that need to be taken by other team members for the student. Figure 31 shows Jake's general supports.

Step 3

General Supports

COACH 3

Select and mark (✓) all necessary general supports. See manual for directions.

Participants: _Sofie & Tom Gardener, Karen Green, Maryann Booth_

Personal Needs

✓ 1. Needs to be fed food and drinks

✓ 2. Needs to be dressed

✓ 3. Needs assistance with bowel and bladder management

✓ 4. Needs assistance with personal hygiene

___ 5. Needs to be given medication

___ 6. Needs suctioning and/or postural drainage

___ _____

___ _____

___ _____

___ _____

___ _____

___ _____

___ _____

Physical Needs

✓ 7. Needs to be physically repositioned at regular intervals

✓ 8. Needs to have environmental barriers modified to allow access

✓ 9. Needs to have physical equipment managed (e.g., wheelchair, braces, orthotics)

✓ 10. Needs specialized transportation accommodations

✓ 11. Needs to be moved and positioned in specialized ways

✓ 12. Needs to be physically moved from place to place

___ _____

___ _____

___ _____

___ _____

___ _____

Teaching Others About the Student

✓ 13. Teach staff and classmates about the student's AAC system and other communicative behaviors

✓ 14. Teach staff and students how to communicate with the student

___ 15. Teach staff seizure management procedures

___ 16. Teach staff emergency procedures (e.g., medical, evacuation)

___ 17. Teach staff preventive behavior management procedures

___ 18. Teach staff behavioral crisis intervention procedures

___ 19. Teach peers and adults to ask the student to repeat or communicate in another way if not understood

___ _____

___ _____

___ _____

Figure 31. Jake's general supports.

Step 3

General Supports

COACH 3

Sensory Needs

___ 20. Needs to have hearing aids monitored (e.g., batteries, settings)

___ 21. Needs to have people use FM unit/auditory trainer

___ 22. Needs people to manually communicate (e.g., American Sign Language, gestures)

✓ 23. Needs to have glasses managed (e.g., adjusted, cleaned)

___ 24. Needs tactile materials

✓ 25. Needs enlarged materials

___ 26. Needs materials in braille

___ 27. Needs to be positioned to accommodate sensory needs (e.g., specified distance from source)

✓ 28. Needs environmental modifications to accommodate for sensory needs (e.g., lighting, location background, volume, color)

___ _____

___ _____

___ _____

___ _____

Providing Access and Opportunities

✓ 29. Provide access to general education classes and activities

✓ 30. Needs to have instructional accommodations to general education activities and materials prepared in advance to facilitate multilevel instruction and/or curriculum overlapping

___ 31. Provide access to community-based experiences with people without disabilities

___ 32. Provide exposure to a variety of career/work experiences

___ 33. Provide access to cocurricular activities with people without disabilities

___ 34. Provide access to materials in the student's native language

___ 35. Provide access to materials and activities associated with the student's cultural background as well as other cultures

___ 36. Provide access to nonaversive approaches to dealing with challenging behaviors

___ _____

Other General Supports (not listed elsewhere)

___ 37. Needs time limits extended or waived

___ 38. Needs class notes recorded or scribed

___ 39. Needs alternative testing modification

___ _____

___ _____

___ _____

___ _____

___ _____

___ _____

___ _____

___ _____

___ _____

Materials

- Forms for Step 3

Directions

1. Explain the purpose of Step 3 and remind participants that this substep should take no more than 10–15 minutes to complete.

2. Review the listed items in the first general support category (personal needs).

3. Reach consensus on which supports need to be provided for the student.

4. Document the group's decision by putting a checkmark by those items that need support.

5. Add any unique items (not already listed) in the spaces provided.

6. Proceed to the next general support category (physical needs) and all subsequent categories and repeat directions 3–5.

Helpful Hints

1. Although the core group of participants, namely the parent(s), general education teacher(s), and special educator can usually complete this step, input from related services personnel (e.g., SLP, physical therapist, occupational therapist) can be helpful and, for some students, essential. When related services personnel are not present at the meeting, their input can be solicited by the special educator or other team member in advance.

2. Be aware that some students will not require any general supports in certain categories. For example, the section on sensory needs is likely to be blank for a student without sensory disabilities, or the section on physical needs may be blank for a student without orthopedic disabilities. There may be times when particular items in those categories are relevant for other reasons. For example, a student with certain behavioral characteristics may require specialized transportation accommodations (e.g., seating arrangement, bus monitor) if the behavior poses a safety risk during transport.

3. These general supports are meant to be cross-situational—they are not meant to be specific instructional supports and accommodations.

4. IEP terminology varies by locale. All IEPs have a space for what we are calling general supports in COACH. Although the language used may be different, the meaning is the same. Some terminology we have seen includes adaptations, accommodations, and management needs.

 PART B | Translating the Family-Identified Priorities into Goals and Objectives

 Purpose

Part B of COACH is designed to assist teams in translating the family-identified priorities into

1. Annual Goals (Step 4)

2. Short-Term Objectives (Step 5)

3. A Program-at-a-Glance (Step 6) consisting of the annual goals, additional learning outcomes, and general supports is summarized in a short, easily accessible format.

 ## Materials

- COACH manual
- Blank photocopies of Steps 4 and 5 (see Appendix C or the CD-ROM)
- Blank photocopy of Step 6 (see Appendix C or the CD-ROM)
- Pencils and erasers

Directions

1. Identify team members and establish a time line to complete Step 4 (Annual Goals) and Step 5 (Short-Term Objectives) as an initial draft of the IEP goals and objectives based on family-selected priorities identified in Step 1.5.

2. See specific directions for completing Steps 4 and 5.

3. Identify team member to summarize information from Steps 1–4 into a Program-at-a-Glance.

4. See specific directions for completing Step 6 (Program-at-a-Glance).

 ## Helpful Hints

1. Plan ahead so there is enough time between completing COACH and the date of the IEP meeting.

2. Throughout Steps 4–6, involve team members (including the parents and student) in ways that 1) tap their respective areas of knowledge and skill, 2) contribute to team members developing a unified and shared understanding of the student's educational program, and 3) contribute to documenting a plan that is both workable and leads to improvements in valued life outcomes.

STEP 4 | ANNUAL GOALS

Purpose

To translate priority learning outcomes selected during the Family Interview into annual goal statements for the IEP. See Figure 32 for an example of one of Jake's annual goals.

Directions

1. Record the priority to be included on the IEP from Step 1.5 (Cross-Prioritization) in the space labeled "Priority learning outcome from Step 1.5."

2. Describe the student's current level of functioning related to the priority learning outcome. As indicated in the description of this step, your team may need to collect addi-

Steps 4 and 5

Goal __1__   **Annual Goals**   COACH3

1. Priority learning outcome from Step 1.5: *Displays consistent communication response mode.*

2. Present level of performance based on current assessment of the priority learning outcome:
   Uses eye gaze and directional reaching/pointing in an effort to respond, though inconsistently and only about 30% of the time. Needs stable positioning with head fully supported and lap tray on wheelchair for his best responding, within 5 seconds of request. Currently responds somewhat more consistently to unfamiliar teachers and peers (50%) more so than familiar people.

3. What are the natural, age-appropriate contexts (places and activities) in which the student will be expected to use the skill/behavior this year? *During classroom and school activities in response to questions from teachers and classmates.*

4. What aspect of the priority learning outcomes should be reflected in the annual goal? Check all those to be addressed this year.

   __ Decreasing extra cues/supports

   __ Respond to natural supports

   _X_ Generalization across settings, people, materials/cues

   _X_ Acquiring core skills

   __ Expand repertoire

   __ Extend or reduce duration

   __ Other

   __ Quality of performance

   __ Tempo, rate, or fluency

   __ Retention over time

   __ Other

   __ Other

5. What is the specific observable, measurable skill/behavior the team wants the student to learn this year? *Uses eye gaze and directional reaching/pointing to consistently respond within 5 seconds of a request*

6. Final annual goal (include contexts and skill/behavior): *During classroom and school activities in response to questions from teachers and classmates, Jake will use eye gaze and/or directional reaching/pointing to consistently respond within 5 seconds of a request*

Figure 32. Example of one of Jake's annual goals.

tional assessment information if currently available assessment information does not adequately address the learning priority.

3. Describe the primary natural, age-appropriate contexts (places and activities) in which the student will be expected to use the skill/behavior this year. Sometimes learning outcomes cross many contexts. In other cases, it can be crucial when attaining the learning outcome depends on access to the context. For example, this most frequently occurs when the behavior must be exhibited 1) in a particular location (e.g., at a worksite, on the playground), 2) during a particular activity (e.g., eating lunch, participating in whole-class instruction), or 3) with particular people (e.g., peers without disabilities).

4. Consider (and indicate by checking) what aspects of the priority learning outcome should become the focus of the annual goal. The Step 1.5 form offers some common aspects of potential focus (e.g., acquiring core skills, decreasing extra cues/supports, gen-

eralization, rate, tempo, fluency, retention over time). If the focus for a student is different than those listed, then check *other* and write the focus in the space provided. The identified focus will not only influence the wording of the annual goals, but will also have implications for the short-term objectives.

5. Identify a measurable/observable behavior that will be sought as an annual goal. Remember, the learning outcomes within the COACH Family Interview are not all necessarily stated in terms that would be suitable for a quality annual goal. To increase clarity, add a response mode to the behavior if it is not already clear. For example, how will Josh *make choices when given options*? Observable response modes might include speaking, pointing, eye gaze, or others. Include other clarifying information that will assist in clearly stating the goal. For example, *responds to questions* could be clarified by "Josh will respond to yes/no questions using head and eye movements (i.e., yes for *up*; no for *down*)."

6. Combine the information and ideas that have been collected to state the annual goal in a way that includes a context and a behavior that the team agrees is attainable within a year.

7. The completed annual goals can then be shared with team members face to face, by telephone, by fax, or by e-mail to verify its contents and make any final adjustments before the goals are transferred to the IEP document.

 Helpful Hints

1. Clarify among the team members who will assume or share responsibility for developing the annual goals based on the selected priorities.

2. The student's annual goals are meant to provide a general road map for your instruction. Do a thorough job developing the goals, but at the same time, do not spend too much time on details that are likely to change. These initial goals represent your collective "best guess"; they are not written in stone and should not constrain your instruction.

3. It is always helpful to get feedback and ideas from team members by routing the annual goals to the team members.

4. As suggested earlier in COACH, we favor IEPs that list a small set of top priority learning outcomes that are discipline-free. Problems have arisen when professional staff generate priorities using the Family Interview in COACH and then either 1) do not translate those priorities to IEP goals or 2) do so and then include additional annual goals representing their individual priorities based on the orientation of their various disciplines. Avoid these problems by using the Additional Learning Outcomes (Steps 2.1 and 2.2) and the General Supports (Step 3) to help clarify additional learning outcomes and the roles of related services personnel.

| STEP 5 | | **SHORT-TERM OBJECTIVES** |

 Purpose

The purpose of Step 5 is to develop a series of short-term objectives for each annual goal that provide smaller, teachable steps leading toward the attainment of the annual goal. Figure 33 shows an example of one of Jake's short-term objectives.

Directions

1. Refer to the annual goal statement and related information (e.g., present level of performance) with the intent of breaking it down into smaller instructional targets. Consider the following ideas as you develop the short-term objectives.

2. Using the short-term objectives grid (left and middle columns), list any crucial conditions that must be present for the student to learn the behavior, and list a behavior that includes the information identified when clarifying the intent of the goals (e.g., observable mode of response).

3. To write the measurable criteria, ask yourself, "How far might we expect the student to progress from his or her current level of functioning given 10–15 weeks of instruction?" The criteria also should include a measure of stability (e.g., 4 out of 5 days for 2 consecutive weeks).

4. Combining the three components (i.e., conditions, behavior, criteria) forms an initial short-term objective.

5. Write additional short-term objectives by changing one or more of the three components (i.e., conditions, behavior, criteria). In some cases, the conditions and behavior remain constant and the criteria increases. In other cases, the conditions (e.g., fading of prompts) change, the behavior remains constant, and the criteria may or may not change. In still other cases, the behavior changes (e.g., learning new sets of words) and the conditions and criteria remain constant. Any combination of the short-term objectives can change to create an individualized program for the student.

 Helpful Hints

1. List only crucial conditions that are cross-situational. There will be opportunities to describe more situation-specific conditions when you are engaged in specific lesson planning (see Section IV and Appendix D for formats for planning and adapting instruction).

2. Undoubtedly, you will find it helpful to seek input from various team members about what makes the most sense as short-term objectives are developed.

3. Short-term objectives are focused on what the student will learn and do not include all the information about how they will achieve those objectives (e.g., prompts, cues, correction procedures, reinforcement, feedback).

4. After you have completed your initial draft, share it with team members prior to the IEP meeting for their feedback.

5. Use all of the information generated from COACH to help the team determine what related services are educationally relevant and necessary for the student to gain access to and participate in the identified educational program.

| STEP 6 || PROGRAM-AT-A-GLANCE |

 Purpose

Step 6 summarizes the student's educational program components in approximately two pages so it can be used as a handy way to communicate student needs to a variety of school staff (e.g.,

Short-Term Objectives

Conditions	Skill/behavior	Criteria
When asked a direct question by a teacher in morning circle and during reading and math groups and properly positioned in his wheelchair with adequate head and trunk support	Jake will use eye gaze and/or directional reaching/pointing to consistently respond	Within 8 seconds of a request, 50% of the time, for 5 consecutive school days
As above	As above	Within 6 seconds of a request, 80% of the time, for 5 consecutive school days
When asked a direct question by a teacher or a peer in busier environments (e.g., lunch, recess, choice time) and properly positioned in his wheelchair with adequate head and trunk support	As above	As above
When asked a direct question by a teacher or a peer in any classroom or school activity and properly positioned in his wheelchair with adequate head and trunk support	As above	Within 5 seconds of a request, 100% of the time, for 5 consecutive school days

Figure 33. Sample of Jake's short-term objectives.

classroom teachers, related services personnel, instructional assistants, special area teachers). The Program-at-a-Glance can serve as a ready reference and reminder to school personnel about the focus and breadth of a student's educational program, facilitating implementation of the agreed-on educational program. It may also assist in planning for educationally necessary related services. See Figure 34 for Jake's Program-at-a-Glance.

Materials

- Forms for Step 6

Directions

1. This substep need not be completed during a group meeting. A designated team member can complete it once the needed information is available. It should take no more than 10–15 minutes to complete Step 6 because it is exclusively a transfer of information from other steps of COACH.

Step 6

Program-at-a-Glance

COACH 3

Student's name: _Jake Gardener_   Date: _5/27/10_

List education program components: 1) highest priorities from Family Interview to be included in IEP; 2) Additional Learning Outcomes from COACH by curriculum area; 3) Additional Learning Outcomes from General Education (Step 2.2) by curriculum area, also indicate primary type of participation and example "starting point" learning outcomes; and 4) general supports by category and items.

Family-Selected Priorities (Annual Goals)

1. During classroom and school activities in response to questions from teachers and classmates, Jake will use eye gaze and/or directional reaching/pointing to consistently respond within 5 seconds of a request.

2. During class and school activities (e.g., recess, lunch), when presented with four options, Jake will use eye gaze and/or directional reaching/pointing to make choices.

3. During class and school activities, Jake will use assistive technology (e.g., switch attached to voice output device) to ask questions of others (e.g., for help with a task, to take a break, to change activities).

4. During classroom and computer lab class activities, Jake will use an adapted switch to operate a cursor (move it to desired locations on the screen) to activate various computer program features (e.g., activities, games, voice output, letters, symbols).

Additional Learning Outcomes from COACH

5. Communication/Socialization: (a) makes requests of others, (b) sustains and ends social interactions, (c) offers assistance to others, (d) advocates for self

6. Access Academics: (a) directs and sustains attention to activity, (b) explores surroundings and objects, (c) differentiates/discriminates between things, (d) understands meannig of non-text symbols

7. Applied academics: (a) understands text has meaning, (b) uses writing/drawing tools, (c) uses schedule or calendar

Additional Learning Outcomes from the General Education Curriculum

8. Language Arts   Primary Type of Participation: Multilevel (different content)
   Starting Point: (a) orients to books; (b) identifies photographs, objects, and symbols; (c) follows one-step instructions

(continued)

Figure 34. Jake's Program-at-a-Glance.

Step 6   *(continued)*

Program-at-a-Glance

9. Math   *Primary Type of Participation:* Curriculum overlapping
    Starting Point: uses math activities to work on family-selected priority learning outcomes listed on
    the previous page (1–4)

10. Science   *Primary Type of Participation:* Multilevel (same content)
    Starting Point: (a) distinguishes between plants/animals, (b) matches weather with clothes

11. Social Studies   *Primary Type of Participation:* Multilevel (same content)
    Starting Point: (a) identifies classmates and school personnel, (b) offers help to others doing class jobs

12. Physical Education and Health   *Primary Type of Participation:* Multilevel (same content)
    Starting Point: (a) adapted partial participation in same activites as classmates with guidance from
    adapted physical education teacher and physical therapist, (b) identify body parts, (c) participate in
    healthy leisure activities with peers

13. Art and Music   *Primary Type of Participation:* Multilevel (same content)
    Starting Point: (a) use a variety of art media for self-expression, (b) use adapted devices (e.g.,
    switches) to produce rhymes, notes, songs, and so forth

General Supports

14. Personal Needs: (a) needs to be fed food and drink, (b) needs to be dressed, (c) needs assistance
    with bowel and bladder management, (d) needs assistance with personal hygiene

15. Physical Needs: (a) needs to be physically repositioned at regular intervals, (b) needs to have
    environmental barriers modified to allow access, (c) needs to have physical equipment managed (e.g.,
    wheelchair, braces, orthotics), (d) needs specialized transportation accommodations, (e) needs to be
    moved and positioned in specialized ways, (f) needs to be physically moved from place to place

16. Teaching Others About the Student: (a) teach staff and classmates about the student's system and
    other communicative behaviors, (b) teach staff and students how to communicate with the student

17. Sensory Needs: (a) needs to have glasses managed (e.g., adjusted, cleaned), (b) needs enlarged
    materials, (c) needs environmental modifications to accommodate for sensory needs (e.g., lighting,
    location background, volume, color)

18. Providing Access and Opportunites: provide access to general education classes and activities, needs
    to have instructional accommodations to general education activities and materials prepared in
    advance to facilitate multilevel instruction and/or curriculum overlapping

2. Write the student's name and date in the spaces provided at the top of the page.

3. Transfer the student's educational program components from the various parts of COACH to the Program-at-a-Glance and include

   • Annual goals from family-selected priorities and all the family-selected learning outcomes to be included in the IEP (originally from Step 1.5) that were restated as annual goals (Step 4)

   • Additional Learning Outcomes from COACH by curriculum area and all the learning outcomes checked on the completed pages of Step 2.1

   • Additional Learning Outcomes from General Education by curriculum areas and examples of starting points listed on the completed pages of Step 2.2

   • General supports by categories (e.g., personal needs, physical needs, sensory needs) and all checked items from Step 3

4. Categorize and number the Program-at-a-Glance entries to provide easy reference for team members.

 Helpful Hints

1. Organize the components of the Program-at-a-Glance in whatever sequence makes the most sense to your team, keeping in mind the purpose is a quick reference guide to a student's educational program components for team members. As shown in Figure 34, some users find it helpful to note the primary type of participation (e.g., multilevel same content, multilevel different content, curriculum overlapping), whereas others find ways to combine the learning outcomes from COACH and the general education curriculum. You can find examples of such variations to the Program-at-Glance in Appendixes G and H on the accompanying CD-ROM.

2. Some teams find it advantageous to organize Program-at-a-Glance entries so related items are reordered or grouped together. For example, in the additional learning outcomes sections of the Program-at-a-Glance, curriculum areas conceptually related can be grouped together (e.g., communication and socialization; physical education/health; art/music). This streamlines the document and facilitates team communication.

3. Although the Program-at-a-Glance can be completed by hand, we encourage you to use the blank digital form on the accompanying CD-ROM, which allows for easy updating.

4. Although it is important to have the Program-at-a-Glance readily available to staff working with the student, it is also important to maintain student confidentiality. Be keenly aware of how and where the Program-at-a-Glance is used and stored.

Section IV

Implementing COACH-Generated Plans

You have successfully identified learning outcomes and supports for your student when your team has completed COACH (Steps 1–6). When you adequately follow through on your COACH work (e.g., incorporating elements in the IEP document, making plans to embed learning opportunities into daily routines, designing explicit instructional plans), your team can realize the full benefits of the front-end expenditure of time and energy devoted to completing COACH. If follow through is inadequate, not only will the time your team devoted have been at least partially wasted, it can also damage relationships with families that hopefully have been enhanced by using COACH. Few things will diminish trust and confidence more than involving a family in planning and then not following through on the agreed-on plans.

COACH provides your team with foundational elements of an individualized education program (IEP) you can rely on to initiate instruction and build on throughout the school year. At its heart, COACH focuses on the "what" of educational planning, rather than the "how." Although it is beyond the scope of COACH to provide a comprehensive "how to," we want to send you forward in a constructive direction.

To help you in this endeavor, we have provided a series of forms in Appendix D and on the CD-ROM that include 1) a scheduling matrix format designed to help you identify opportunities for embedding targeted learning outcomes in the daily/weekly schedule, 2) three formats for planning and adapting instruction designed to help you think through the details of individual lesson/activity planning, and 3) forms you can employ in conjunction with your other data collection efforts to assist in evaluating the affect of learning outcomes and supports on valued life outcomes.

Successfully implementing a COACH-generated educational program (or one generated using other approaches) in an inclusive context always depends heavily on what team members do individually and collaboratively. Appendix F and the CD-ROM include the document titled "Roles of Team Members Supporting Students with Disabilities in Inclusive Classrooms." Based on research and literature about inclusive schools, this document provides proposed roles for teachers, special educators, paraprofessionals, administrators, related services providers (e.g., speech-language pathologists, occupational therapists, physical therapists, school psychologists, orientation and mobility specialists), as well as students and families.

A main reason why we have decided to not expand COACH more into the "how to" realm is because there are so many excellent "how to" resources already available. Some of our favorites include the following: Browder and Spooner (2006); Downing (2005, 2008, 2010); Janney and Snell (2011); Jorgensen et al. (2010); Peterson and Hittie (2010); and Snell and Brown (2011).

The additional resources included in the appendixes of COACH and the other sources will help you implement your COACH-generated educational plans. Together, these greatly increase the probability of success for your students. Ultimately, whether your team realizes the potential COACH offers will depend on what you choose to do next. We encourage you to continue to rely on the collaboration of your teammates, work constructively with the family, and explore ways to involve your students in decisions that effect their lives.

CONCLUSION

In closing, we remind you that COACH, like any tool, must be used with care and skill to achieve optimal results. Such care and skill on your part means you are constantly thinking about what you are doing rather than filling out forms in a rote manner. You must individualize what you do to match the situation, continually seek to improve your own skills, deepen your own understanding, and judge your collective success by the affect your team's actions have on the lives of your students and their families. We know through our experiences that many of you will find new and creative ways to use the ideas in COACH to improve on the work we offer to you—we applaud those efforts and hope you will share them with us. We hope that the ideas and skills you bring to using COACH will improve it beyond our current conceptualization of the process to match the needs in your community and the children you serve.

References

Baer, D. (1981). A hung jury and a Scottish verdict: "Not proven." *Analysis and Intervention in Developmental Disabilities, 1*(1), 91–98.

Bateman, B. (2007). *From gobbledygook to clearly written annual IEP goals.* Verona, WI: IEP Resources/Attainment.

Bateman, B.D., & Linden, M.A. (2006). *Better IEPs: How to write legally correct and educationally useful programs* (4th ed.). Champaign, IL: Research Press.

Baumgart, D., Brown, L., Pumpian, I., Nisbet, J., Ford, A., Sweet, M., Messina, R., & Schroeder, J. (1982). Principle of partial participation and individualized adaptations in educational programs for severely handicapped students. *Journal of The Association for the Severely Handicapped, 7*(2), 17–27.

Biklen, D.P., & Knoll, J. (1987). The disabled minority. In S. Taylor, D. Biklen, & J. Knoll (Eds.), *Community integration for people with severe disabilities* (pp. 3–21). New York: Teachers College Press.

Blue-Banning, M., Summers, J.A., Frankland, H.C., Nelson, L.L., & Beegle, G. (2004). Dimensions of family and professional partnerships: Constructive guidelines for collaboration. *Exceptional Children, 70,* 167–184.

Browder, D.M., & Spooner, F. (Eds.). (2006). *Teaching language arts, math, and science to students with significant cognitive disabilities.* Baltimore: Paul H. Brookes Publishing Co.

Brown, F., Evans, I., Weed, K., & Owen, V. (1987). Delineating functional competencies: A component model. *Journal of The Association for Persons with Severe Handicaps, 12,* 117–124.

Brown, F., Lehr, D., & Snell, M.E. (2011). Conducting and using student assessment. In M.E. Snell & F. Brown (Eds.), *Instruction of students with severe disabilities* (7th ed., pp. 73–121). Upper Saddle River, NJ: Pearson Education/Prentice Hall.

Brown, F., & Snell, M.E. (2011). Measuring student behavior and learning. In M.E. Snell & F. Brown (Eds.), *Instruction of students with severe disabilities* (7th ed., pp. 186–223). Upper Saddle River, NJ: Pearson Education/Prentice Hall.

Brown, L., Branston, M.B., Hamre-Nietupski, S., Pumpian, I., Certo, N., & Gruenewald, L. (1979). A strategy for developing chronologically age-appropriate and functional curricular content for severely handicapped adolescents and young adults. *Journal of Special Education, 13,* 81–90.

Brown, L., Nietupski, J., & Hamre-Nietupski, S. (1976). The criterion of ultimate functioning and public school services for severely handicapped students. In M.A. Thomas (Ed.), *Hey, don't forget about me! Education's investment in the severely, profoundly, and multiply handicapped* (pp. 2–15). Reston, VA: Council for Exceptional Children.

Campbell, C., Campbell, S., Collicott, J., Perner, D., & Stone, J. (1988). Individualized instruction. *Education New Brunswick—Journal Education, 3,* 17–20.

Certo, N.J., Luecking, R.G., Murphy, S., Brown, L., Courey, S., & Belanger, D. (2008). Seamless transition and long-term support for individuals with severe intellectual disabilities. *Research and Practice for Persons with Severe Disabilities, 33,* 85–95.

Council for Chief State School Officers and National Governors' Association. (March 2010a). *Common core state standards for English language arts, and literacy in history, social studies, and science.* Retrieved April 5, 2010, from http://www.corestandards.org/Files/K12ELAStandards.pdf

Council for Chief State School Officers and National Governors' Association. (March 2010b). *Common core state standards in mathematics.* Retrieved April 5, 2010, from http://www.corestandards.org/Files/K12MathStandards.pdf

Dalton, B., & Gordon, D. (2007). Universal design for learning. In M.F. Giangreco & M.B. Doyle (Eds.), *Quick-Guides to inclusion: Ideas for educating students with disabilities* (2nd ed., pp. 123–136). Baltimore: Paul H. Brookes Publishing Co.

Davern, L., Sapon-Shevin, M., D'Aquanni, M., Fisher, M., Larson, M., Black, J., & Minondo, S. (1997). Drawing the distinction between coherent and fragmented efforts at building inclusive schools. *Equity and Excellence in Education, 30*(3), 31–39.

Davis, A. (1999). *The enormous potato.* Toronto: Kids Can Press.

Dennis, R., & Giangreco, M.F. (1996). Creating conversation: Reflections on cultural sensitivity in Family Interviewing. *Exceptional Children, 63,* 103–116.

Dennis, R.E., Williams, W., Giangreco, M.F., & Cloninger, C.J. (1993). Quality of life as a context for planning and evaluation of services for people with disabilities. *Exceptional Children, 59,* 499–512.

Donnellan, A. (1984). The criterion of the least dangerous assumption. *Behavior Disorders, 9,* 141–150.

Downing, J.E. (2005). *Teaching literacy to students with significant disabilities.* Thousand Oaks, CA: Corwin.

Downing, J.E. (2008). *Including students with severe and multiple disabilities in typical classrooms: Practical strategies for teachers* (3rd ed.). Baltimore: Paul H. Brookes Publishing Co.

Downing, J.E. (2010). *Academic instruction for students with moderate and severe intellectual disabilities in inclusive classrooms.* Thousand Oaks, CA: Corwin.

Doyle, M.B. (2008). *The paraprofessional's guide to the inclusive classroom: Working as a team* (3rd ed.). Baltimore: Paul H. Brookes Publishing Co.

Doyle, M.B. & Giangreco, M.F. (2009). Making presentation software accessible for high school students with moderate and severe intellectual disabilities. *TEACHING Exceptional Children, 41*(3), 24–31.

Dymond, S.K., Renzaglia, A., Gilson, C.L., & Slagor, M.T. (2007). Defining access to the general curriculum for high school students with significant cognitive disabilities. *Research and Practice for Persons with Severe Disabilities, 32,* 1–15.

Education for All Handicapped Children Act of 1975, PL 94-142, 20 U.S.C. §§ 1400 *et seq.*

Feldman, R., Fialka, J. (Producers), & Rossen, P. (Director/Producer). (2006). *Through the same door: Inclusion includes college* [Motion picture]. (Available from Dance of Partnerships Publications; http://www.danceofpartnership.com/index.htm)

Ferguson, D.L., & Baumgart, D. (1991). Partial participation revisited. *Journal of The Association for Persons with Severe Handicaps, 16,* 218–227.

Firestien, R. (1989). *Why didn't I think of that? A personal and professional guide to better ideas and decision making.* East Aurora, NY: D.O.K. Publishing.

Flowers, C., Ahlgrim-Delzell, L., Browder, D.M., & Spooner, F. (2005). Teachers' perceptions of alternate assessments. *Research and Practice for Persons with Severe Disabilities, 30,* 81–92.

Ford, A., Davern, L., & Schnorr, R. (2001). Learners with significant disabilities: Curricular relevance in an era of standards-based reform. *Remedial and Special Education, 22,* 214–222.

Gartner, A., & Lipsky, D.K. (2007). *Inclusion: A service, not a place. A whole school approach.* Port Chester, NY: National Professional Resources.

Giangreco, M.F. (1985). *Cayuga-Onondaga assessment for children with handicaps: Version 1.0 (COACH).* Stillwater, OK: National Clearinghouse of Rehabilitation Training Materials.

Giangreco, M.F. (1996a). Choosing options and accommodations for children (COACH): Curriculum planning for students with disabilities in general education classrooms. In W. Stainback & S. Stainback (Eds.), *Inclusion: A guide for educators* (pp. 237–254). Baltimore: Paul H. Brookes Publishing Co.

Giangreco, M.F. (1996b). *Vermont Interdependent Services Team Approach: A guide to coordinating educational support services.* Baltimore: Paul H. Brookes Publishing Co.

Giangreco, M.F. (1998). *Ants in his pants: Absurdities and realities of special education.* Thousand Oaks, CA: Corwin.

Giangreco, M.F. (2000). Related services research for students with low incidence disabilities: Implications for speech-language pathologists in inclusive classrooms. *Language, Speech, and Hearing Services in the Schools, 31,* 230–239.

Giangreco, M.F. (2001). *Guidelines for making decisions about I.E.P. services.* Montpelier: Vermont Department of Education. Retrieved February 13, 2010, from http://www.uvm.edu/~cdci/iepservices/pdfs/decision.pdf

Giangreco, M.F. (2007). Extending inclusive opportunities. *Educational Leadership, 64*(5), 34–37.

Giangreco, M.F. (2009). Opportunities for children and youth with intellectual developmental disabilities: Beyond genetics. *Life Span and Disability: An Interdisciplinary Journal (Cicio Evolutivo e Disabilita), 12*(2), 129–139.

Giangreco, M.F. (2011). Educating students with severe disabilities: Foundational concepts and practices. In M.E. Snell & F. Brown (Eds.), *Instruction of students with severe disabilities* (7th ed., pp. 1–30). Upper Saddle River, NJ: Pearson Education/Prentice Hall.

Giangreco, M.F., Carter, E.W., Doyle, M.B., & Suter, J.C. (2010). Supporting students with disabilities in inclusive classrooms: Personnel and peers. In R. Rose (Ed.), *Confronting obstacles to inclusion: International responses to developing inclusive schools* (pp. 247–263). London: Routledge.

Giangreco, M.F., Cloninger, C.J., Dennis, R.E., & Edelman, S.W. (1993). National expert validation of COACH: Congruence with exemplary practice and suggestions for improvement. *Journal of The Association for Persons with Severe Handicaps, 18,* 109–120.

Giangreco, M.F., Cloninger, C.J., Dennis, R.E., & Edelman, S.W. (2002). Problem-solving methods to facilitate inclusive education. In J.S. Thousand, R.A. Villa, & A.I. Nevin (Eds.), *Creativity and collaborative learning: The practical guide to empowering students, teachers, and families* (2nd ed., pp. 111–134). Baltimore: Paul H. Brookes Publishing Co.

Giangreco, M.F., Cloninger, C., Mueller, P., Yuan, S., & Ashworth, S. (1991). Perspectives of parents whose children have dual sensory impairments. *Journal of The Association for Persons with Severe Handicaps, 16,* 14–24.

Giangreco, M.F., Dennis, R., Cloninger, C., Edelman, S., & Schattman, R. (1993). "I've counted Jon": Transformational experiences of teachers educating students with disabilities. *Exceptional Children, 59,* 359–372.

Giangreco, M.F., Dennis, R., Edelman, S., & Cloninger, C. (1994). Dressing your IEPs for the general education climate: Analysis of IEP goals and objectives for students with multiple disabilities. *Remedial and Special Education, 15,* 288–296.

Giangreco, M.F., Edelman, S., & Dennis, R. (1991). Common professional practices that interfere with the integrated delivery of related services. *Remedial and Special Education, 12,* 16–24.

Giangreco, M.F., Edelman, S., Dennis, R., & Cloninger, C.J. (1995). Use and impact of COACH with students who are deaf-blind. *Journal of The Association for Persons with Severe Handicaps, 20,* 121–135.

Giangreco, M.F., Edelman, S., Luiselli, T.E., & MacFarland, S.Z. (1996). Support service decision-making for students with multiple service needs: Evaluation data. *Journal of The Association for Persons with Severe Handicaps, 21,* 135–144.

Giangreco, M.F., Edelman, S., Luiselli, T.E., & Mac-Farland, S.Z. (1997). Helping or hovering? Effects of instructional assistant proximity on students with disabilities. *Exceptional Children, 64,* 7–18.

Giangreco, M.F., Edelman, S.W., Luiselli, T.E., & Mac-Farland, S.Z. (1998). Reaching consensus about educationally necessary support services: A qualitative evaluation of VISTA. *Special Services in the Schools, 13*(1/2), 1–32.

Giangreco, M.F., Edelman, S., Nelson, C., Young, M.R., & Kiefer-O'Donnell, R. (1999). Improving support service decision-making: Consumer feedback regarding updates to VISTA. *International Journal of Disability, Development, and Education, 46,* 463–473.

Giangreco, M.F., Prelock, P.A., Reid, R.R., Dennis, R.E., & Edelman, S.W. (2000). Role of related services personnel in inclusive schools. In R.A. Villa & J.S. Thousand (Eds.), *Restructuring for caring and effective education: Piecing the puzzle together* (2nd ed., pp. 360–388). Baltimore: Paul H. Brookes Publishing Co.

Giangreco, M.F., & Putnam, J. (1991). Supporting the education of students with severe disabilities in regular education environments. In L.H. Meyer, C. Peck, & L. Brown (Eds.), *Critical issues in the lives of people with severe disabilities* (pp. 245–270). Baltimore: Paul H. Brookes Publishing Co.

Giangreco, M.F., & Snell, M.E. (1996). Severe and multiple disabilities. In R. Turnbull & A. Turnbull (Eds.), *Improving the implementation of the individuals with disabilities education act: Making schools work for all of America's children* (pp. 97–132). Washington, DC: National Council on Disability.

Grisham-Brown, J., & Kearns, J.F. (2001). Creating standards-based individualized educational programs. In H.L. Kleinert & J.F. Kearns (Eds.), *Alternate assessment: Measuring outcomes and supports for students with disabilities* (pp. 17–28). Baltimore: Paul H. Brookes Publishing Co.

Hanson, M.J., & Lynch, E.W. (2003). *Understanding families: Approaches to diversity, disability, and risk.* Baltimore: Paul H. Brookes Publishing Co.

Harry, B. (2008). Collaboration with culturally and linguistically diverse families: Ideal versus reality. *Exceptional Children, 74,* 372–388.

Harry, B., & Klingner, J. (2005). *Why are so many minority students in special education? Understanding race and disability in schools.* New York: Teachers College Press.

Individuals with Disabilities Education Act Amendments (IDEA) of 1997, PL 105-17, 20 U.S.C. §§ 1400 *et seq.*

Individuals with Disabilities Education Improvement Act (IDEA) of 2004, PL 108-446, 20 U.S.C. §§ 1400 *et seq.*

Jackson, L., Ryndak, D.L., & Billingsly, F. (2000). Useful practices in inclusive education: A preliminary view of what experts in moderate to severe disabilities are saying. *Journal of The Association for Persons with Severe Handicaps, 25,* 129–141.

Jackson, L., Ryndak, D., & Wehmeyer, M. (2008/2009). The dynamic relationship between context, curriculum, and student learning: A case for inclusive educa-tion as a research-based practice. *Research and Practice in Severe Disabilities, 33/34,* 175–195.

Janney, R. & Snell, M.E., (2004). *Teachers' guides to inclusive practices: Modifying schoolwork* (2nd ed.). Baltimore: Paul H. Brookes Publishing Co.

Janney, R., & Snell, M.E. (2011). Designing and implementing instruction for inclusive classes. In M.E. Snell & F. Brown (Eds.), *Instruction of students with severe disabilities* (7th ed., pp. 224–256). Upper Saddle River, NJ: Pearson Education/Prentice Hall.

Johnson, D.R., McGrew, K., Bloomberg, L., Bruininks, R.H., & Lin, H.C. (1996). *Postschool outcomes and community adjustment for young adults with severe disabilities.* Minneapolis: University of Minnesota, Institute on Community Integration. (ERIC Document Reproduction Service No. ED392209)

Jorgensen, C.M., McSheehan, M., & Sonnenmeier, R.M. (2010). *The Beyond Access model: Promoting membership, participation, and learning for students with disabilities in the general education classroom.* Baltimore: Paul H. Brookes Publishing Co.

Kauffman, J.M., & Krouse, J. (1981). The cult of educability: Searching for the substance of things hoped for; the evidence of things not seen. *Analysis and Intervention in Developmental Disabilities, 1*(1), 53–60.

Kearns, J.F., & Quenemoen, R. (2010). Alternate assessments, families, and the individualized education program. In H.L. Kleinert & J.F. Kearns (Eds.), *Alternate assessment for students with significant cognitive disabilities: An educator's guide* (pp. 291–302). Baltimore: Paul H. Brookes Publishing Co.

Kearns, J.F., Towles-Reeves, E., Kleinert, H.L., Kleinert, J.O., & Thomas, M. (in press). Characteristics of and implications for students participating in alternate assessments based on alternate academic achievement standards. *Journal of Special Education.*

Kleinert, H.L., Collins, C., Wickham, D., Riggs, L., & Hager, K. (2010). Embedding life skills, self-determination, and other evidence-based practices. In H.L. Kleinert & J.F. Kearns (Eds.), *Alternate assessment for students with significant cognitive disabilities: An educator's guide* (pp. 267–290). Baltimore: Paul H. Brookes Publishing Co.

Kleinert, H., Kearns, J., & Kennedy, S. (1997). Accountability for all students: Kentucky's alternate portfolio system for students with moderate and severe cognitive disabilities. *Journal of The Association for Persons with Severe Handicaps, 22,* 88–101.

Kleinert, H.L., Quenemoen, R., & Thurlow, M. (2010). An introduction to alternate assessments: Historical foundations, essential parameters, and guiding principles. In H.L. Kleinert & J.F. Kearns (Eds.), *Alternate assessment for students with significant cognitive disabilities: An educator's guide* (pp. 3–18). Baltimore: Paul H. Brookes Publishing Co.

Kronberg, R.M. (2007). Reaching and teaching diverse learners through differentiated instruction. In M.F. Giangreco & M.B. Doyle (Eds.), *Quick-Guides to inclusion: Ideas for educating students with disabilities* (2nd ed., pp. 137–150). Baltimore: Paul H. Brookes Publishing Co.

Lynch, E.W., & Hanson, M.J. (Eds.). (2004). *Developing cross-cultural competence: A guide for working with children and their families* (3rd ed.). Baltimore: Paul H. Brookes Publishing Co.

McDonnell, J. (1998). Instruction for students with severe disabilities in general education settings. *Education and Training in Mental Retardation and Developmental Disabilities, 33,* 199–215.

McDonnell, J., & McGuire, J. (2007). Community-based instruction. In M.F. Giangreco & M.B. Doyle (Eds.), *Quick-Guides to inclusion: Ideas for educating students with disabilities* (2nd ed., pp. 307–314). Baltimore: Paul H. Brookes Publishing Co.

McKenzie, B. (2008). *Reflections of Erin: The importance of belonging, relationships and learning with each other.* Seaman, OH: Art of Possibility Press.

McWilliam, R.A. (1996). *Rethinking pull-out services in early intervention: A professional resource.* Baltimore: Paul H. Brookes Publishing Co.

Nisbet, J. (Ed.). (1992). *Natural supports in school, at work, and in the community for people with severe disabilities.* Baltimore: Paul H. Brookes Publishing Co.

No Child Left Behind Act of 2001, PL 107-110, 115 Stat. 1425, 20 U.S.C. §§ 6301 *et seq.*

Orelove, F.P., Sobsey, D., & Silberman, R.K. (2004). *Educating children with multiple disabilities: A collaborative approach* (4th ed.). Baltimore: Paul H. Brookes Publishing Co.

Osborn, A.F. (1993). *Applied imagination: Principles and procedures of creative problem-solving* (3rd ed.). Buffalo, NY: Creative Education Foundation Press. (Original work published 1953)

Parnes, S.J. (1988). *Visionizing: State-of-the-art processes for encouraging innovative excellence.* East Aurora, NY: D.O.K. Publishing.

Parnes, S.J. (1992). *Source book for creative problem-solving: A fifty year digest of proven innovation processes.* Buffalo, NY: Creative Education Foundation Press.

Parnes, S.J. (1997). *Optimize the magic of your mind.* Buffalo, NY: Creative Education Foundation Press.

Peterson, J.M., & Hittie, M.M. (2010). *Inclusive teaching: The journey towards effective schools for all learners* (2nd ed.). Columbus, OH: Charles E. Merrill.

Rainforth, B., Giangreco, M.F., & Dennis, R. (1989). Motor skills. In A. Ford, R. Schnorr, L. Meyer, L. Davern, J. Black, & P. Dempsey (Eds.), *The Syracuse community-referenced curriculum guide for students with moderate and severe disabilities* (pp. 211–230). Baltimore: Paul H. Brookes Publishing Co.

Roach, A. (2006). Influences on parent perceptions of an alternate assessment for students with severe cognitive disabilities. *Research and Practice for Persons with Severe Disabilities, 31,* 267–274.

Rose, D.H., Meyer, A., & Hitchcock, C. (2005). *The universally designed classroom: Accessible curriculum and digital technologies.* Cambridge, MA: Harvard Press.

Ryndak, D., Moore, M., Orlando, A., & Delano, M. (2008/2009). Access to the general curriculum: The mandate and the role of context in research-based practice for students with extensive support needs. *Research and Practice in Severe Disabilities, 33/34,* 199–213.

Schalock, R.L., Borthwick-Duffy, S.A., Bradley, V.J., Buntinx, W.H.E., Coulter, D.L., & Craig, E.M. (2010). *Intellectual disability: Definition, classification, and systems of supports* (11th ed.). Washington, DC: American Association on Intellectual and Developmental Disabilities.

Snell, M.E. (2003). Education of individuals with severe and multiple disabilities. In J.W. Guthrie (Ed.), *Encyclopedia of education* (2nd ed., pp. 2210–2213). New York: Macmillan.

Snell, M.E., & Brown, F. (2011). *Instruction of students with severe disabilities* (7th ed.). Upper Saddle River, NJ: Pearson Education/Prentice Hall.

Soodak, L.C., & Erwin, E.J. (2000). Valued member or tolerated participant: Parents' experiences in inclusive early childhood settings. *Journal of The Association for Persons with Severe Handicaps, 25,* 29–41.

Speight, S., Myers, L., Cox, C., & Highlen, P. (1991). A redefinition of multicultural counseling. *Journal of Counseling and Development, 70,* 29–36.

Spooner, F., & Browder, D.M. (2006). Why teach the general curriculum? In D.M. Browder & F. Spooner (Eds.), *Teaching language arts, math, and science to students with significant cognitive disabilities* (pp. 1–13). Baltimore: Paul H. Brookes Publishing Co.

TASH. (2000, March). *TASH resolution on the people for whom TASH advocates.* Retrieved February 13, 2010, from http://www.tash.org/resolutions/res02advocate.htm

Taylor, S.J. (1988). Caught in the continuum: A critical analysis of the principle of the least restrictive environment. *Journal of The Association for Persons with Severe Handicaps, 13,* 41–53.

Taylor, S.J. (2006). Supporting adults to live in the community: Beyond the continuum. In S.M. Pueschel (Ed.), *Adults with Down syndrome* (pp. 173–182). Baltimore: Paul H. Brookes Publishing Co.

Timothy W. v. Rochester School District, 559 EHLR 480 (D.N.H. 1988), 875 F.2d 954 (1st Cir. 1989), cert. denied, 493 U.S. 983 (1989).

Tomlinson, C.A. (2001). *How to differentiate instruction in mixed-ability classrooms* (2nd ed.). Alexandria, VA: Association for Supervision and Curriculum Development.

Tomlinson, C.A. (2003). *Fulfilling the promise of the differentiated classroom: Strategies and tools for responsive teaching.* Alexandria, VA: Association for Supervision and Curriculum Development.

Towles-Reeves, E., Kleinert, H., & Muhomba, M. (2009). Alternate assessment: Have we learned anything new? *Exceptional Children, 75,* 233–252.

U.S. Department of Education. (2004). *Standards and assessment peer review guidance.* Washington, DC: Author.

U.S. Department of Education. (2005). *Alternate achievement standards for students with the most significant cognitive disabilities: Non-regulatory guidance.* Washington DC: Author.

U.S. Department of Justice. (2002). *Brief for the United States as amicus curiae supporting appellee and urging affirmance in the case of Girty v. School District of Valley Grove on appeal from the United States District Court for the western district of Pennsylva-*

nia to the U.S. Court of Appeals for the Third Circuit. Retrieved April 10, 2007, from http://www.usdoj.gov/crt/briefs/girty.pdf

Vianello, R., & Lanfranchi, S. (2009). Genetic syndromes causing mental retardation: Deficit surplus in school performance and social adaptability compared to cognitive capacity. *Life Span and Disability (Cicio Evolutivo e Disabilita), 12*(1), 41–52.

Wehmeyer, M.L. (2006). Beyond access: Ensuring progress in the general education curriculum for students with severe disabilities. *Research and Practice for Persons with Severe Disabilities, 31,* 322–326.

Wehmeyer, M.L., & Agran, M. (2006). Promoting access to the general curriculum for students with signi-ficant cognitive disabilities. In D.M. Browder & F. Spooner (Eds.), *Teaching language arts, math, and science to students with significant cognitive disabilities* (pp. 15–37). Baltimore: Paul H. Brookes Publishing Co.

Wolfensberger, W. (1975). *The origin and nature of our institutional models.* Syracuse, NY: Human Policy Press.

Zuna, N., Turnbull, A.P., & Turnbull, H.R. (2011). Fostering family–professional partnerships. In M.E. Snell & F. Brown (Eds.), *Instruction of students with severe disabilities* (7th ed., pp. 31–69). Upper Saddle River, NJ: Pearson Education/Prentice Hall.

Questions and Answers for Team Members About COACH

Dear Team Member,

The following information is being shared with you so all team members, especially the family, can make an informed decision about using COACH. COACH is for use in situations in which team members (e.g., school personnel, parents, student) agree that it is appropriate. Here are commonly asked questions and brief answers to provide some initial information about COACH and assist you in deciding whether COACH is the right tool to use in your situation.

Q1: What does COACH stand for?

A1: *Choosing Outcomes and Accommodations for CHildren*

Q2: What is COACH?

A2: COACH is a six-step planning tool used by educational teams to assist in developing the individualized educational program (IEP) for students with intensive special educational needs.

Steps of COACH (after completing the Preparation Checklist)

Part A: Determining a Student's Educational Program

Step 1: Family Interview

The purpose of Step 1 is to enable the family to select learning priorities for the student for the upcoming school year. This is accomplished through a series of questions asked by a facilitator who is usually a current team member, such as the special education teacher. The questions during the Family Interview are about learning outcomes that extend beyond those typically included in the general education curriculum in the following curriculum areas: 1) communication, 2) socialization, 3) personal management, 4) recreation, 5) access academics, 6) applied academics, 7) school, 8) community, and 9) vocational.

Step 2: Additional Learning Outcomes

The purpose of Step 2 is to determine learning outcomes beyond the family-selected priorities, both from COACH and the general education curriculum. Additional learning outcomes from COACH ensure important items from the Family Interview not selected as priorities are not forgotten. Additional learning outcomes from the general education curriculum ensure 1) access to the general education curriculum within regular class activities, 2) team members have a shared understanding about the primary participation option (i.e., same, multilevel curriculum/instruction, curriculum overlapping) the student will pursue within regular class activities, and 3) a starting place for the general education teacher (e.g., sample learning outcomes).

Step 3: General Supports

The purpose of Step 3 is to determine what supports need to be provided to or for the student in order to successfully pursue his or her IEP. The general supports areas in COACH include 1) personal needs (e.g., needs to be dressed, needs assistance with personal hygiene); 2) physical needs (e.g., needs to be physically repositioned at regular intervals, needs to have environmental barriers modified to allow access); 3) teaching others about the student: (e.g., teach staff and classmates about the student's augmentative and alternative communication (AAC) system and other communicative behaviors); 4) sensory needs (e.g., needs tactile materials, needs to have hearing aids monitored), 5) providing access and opportunities (e.g., provide access to general education classes and activities, provide access to cocurricular activities); and 6) other general supports (e.g., needs alternative testing modifications such as extended time).

Part B: Translating the Family-Identified Priorities into Goals and Objectives

Step 4: Annual Goals

The purpose of Step 4 is to ensure the family's priorities are reflected as IEP goals.

Step 5: Short-Term Objectives

The purpose of Step 5 is to develop short-term objectives to pursue annual goals.

Step 6: Program-at-a-Glance

The purpose of Step 6 is to provide a concise summary of the educational program.

Q3: What are the principles on which COACH is based?

A3:   COACH is based on a set of six guiding principles.

Principle 1: All students are capable of learning and deserve a meaningful curriculum

Principle 2: Quality instruction requires ongoing access to inclusive environments

Principle 3: Pursuing valued life outcomes informs the selection of curricular content

- Safety and health (physical and emotional)
- A home—now and in the future
- Meaningful relationships

- Control over personal choices (suited to the student's age and culture)
- Meaningful activities in various and valued places

Principle 4: Family involvement is a cornerstone of educational planning

Principle 5: Collaborative teamwork is essential to quality education

Principle 6: Coordination of services ensures necessary supports are appropriately provided

Q4: COACH is designed for which students?

A4: COACH is meant to be used for students ages 3–21 with disabilities who have intensive special educational needs. Because COACH helps teams plan a student's educational program (e.g., curriculum content), it is designed for students who require modifications to the curriculum, such as learning basic life skills, in addition to gaining access to the general education program at a substantially different level than peers without disabilities. So, it is appropriate for some (but not all) students with disabilities such as autism, Down syndrome, intellectual disabilities, deafblindness, cerebral palsy, or other multiple or severe disabilities. It is not designed for students who typically are pursuing the full general education curriculum at or near grade level, even if they need some specialized supports. COACH is appropriate for students who take the alternate assessment and may also be appropriate for other students with disabilities who are not eligible for alternate assessment, but who have substantially different curriculum needs than his or her peers.

Q5: How does COACH relate to the IEP process?

A5: COACH is used as an IEP planning tool. It is a structured way to get family input and team involvement in the IEP process. COACH views IEP development as a process rather than an event.

Q6: Who should participate in COACH?

A6: COACH is designed to be used with a student's family, special educator, and general educator(s) together. Parents are essential to the process. Although having two parents participate is desirable, the process is often completed with one parent because of practical realities. It is essential to recognize that COACH is not COACH unless the family is involved face to face with the school personnel.

It is also essential for the student's special education teacher(s) to participate in the COACH process. Special educators are the most common facilitators of the process, although another person may facilitate COACH as long as he or she is familiar with its use and the family agrees to the selected facilitator.

General education classroom teachers are also essential participants in the COACH process. At the elementary level, in which a student typically has one primary classroom teacher, COACH is designed to include that person. At the middle and high school level, in which a student typically has multiple general education teachers, it is not essential (or typically practical) for all of them to attend. In these cases, it is appropriate to have at least one general education teacher who is knowledgeable about the student to attend the meeting(s). That person or the special educator will be in contact with the other general education teachers in advance of the meeting to complete Step 2.2 (Additional Learning Outcomes from General Education). This ensures that the perspectives of teachers not in attendance are represented by one of their colleagues.

Although other participants can be invited to join in the COACH process, we encourage you to keep the group as small as possible and to reach consensus with the family about who will be present. Not all team members need to attend, though in accordance with the COACH Preparation Checklist, they should have agreed as a team to use COACH, be knowledgeable about it, and agree to support the family-identified priorities.

Q7: Should the student participate in the COACH meeting?

A7: The student with a disability may attend and participate in the COACH meeting at the discretion of the family. This decision is often based on the age of the student and his or her language abilities. A limitation of COACH is that it is very language based. Because many of the students for whom COACH is an appropriate tool have significant challenges with language, it may require adaptations for them to participate. If a student is transition age (16 or older), then attendance and involvement are strongly encouraged. The most common scenario is that one or two parents or other primary caregiver representing the family attend the meetings.

Q8: Where does COACH happen?

A8: COACH can happen anywhere that is mutually agreed to by the family and facilitator. Although conducting COACH at school is one of the most common options, it can also happen around the kitchen table in the family's home, at a community center, or any other agreed-on location. The location should be a place where the family feels comfortable and is amenable to completing the process (e.g., free of distraction, available space, allows for confidentiality).

Q9: What happens during the COACH process?

A9: During the Family Interview (Step 1) the facilitator will ask the family a series of questions designed to help the team get a better understanding of the family perspective on a wide range of topics related to planning a quality education for their child. The family members (parents and/or student) are the exclusive responders and choice makers during the Family Interview. The primary role of the professionals at the meeting is to listen to the family's responses to the facilitator's questions to gain a better understanding of the family's perspectives. During Steps 2.1 (Additional Learning Outcomes from COACH), 2.2 (Additional Learning Outcomes from General Education), and 3 (General Supports), all those in attendance at the meeting work together to provide input to the questions posed by the facilitator in an effort to reach consensus decisions.

Q10: How long does it take to complete COACH?

A10: Typically it takes 1.5–2 hours to complete COACH Part A (Steps 1, 2, and 3). The time varies based on 1) whether one or two parents participate, 2) whether the student participates and the level of adaptation necessary for him or her to participate, and 3) the familiarity and skillfulness of the facilitator in using COACH. The time to complete Part B (Steps 4, 5, and 6) varies and is typically completed by school personnel based on the information gathered from the family.

Q11: Should parents prepare by filling out the COACH forms in advance?

A11: No. COACH is not just a form to be filled out by parents or professionals in isolation. It is a process designed to be completed together. Parents already know everything about their child in order to participate in the COACH process. In fact, when parents try to complete the forms in advance (in an effort to be prepared), it can actually interfere with the dynamics of the process. If parents want more information about COACH than these questions and answers supply, then the COACH manual can be shared with them. Regardless, parents are strongly discouraged from trying to prepare their responses to the questions in COACH ahead of time.

Q12: If our team does the Family Interview, then have we completed COACH?

A12: No. One of the most common mistakes made when using COACH is to stop after completing the Family Interview. When entering into the COACH process, teams deciding to use COACH must commit to completing all three steps in Part A. Part B of COACH can be helpful to the team, although they may have other ways of completing these tasks. So, if you plan to use COACH, that means completing at least Steps 1, 2, and 3.

Q13: What happens after the team has completed Steps 1–3?

A13: After completing Steps 1–3, the facilitator shares the collected information with any team members who did not attend the COACH meeting(s). The school personnel use the information provided by the family to begin drafting the IEP. The content and number of IEP goals drafted by the team should reflect the decisions made during the COACH meeting, especially the priorities identified by the family for inclusion in the IEP. In other words, the family should clearly and easily see their perspectives reflected in the drafted IEP goals before they are finalized.

Q14: Where do related services providers fit into COACH?

A14: Related services, such as transportation, and support services, such as speech-language pathology, occupational therapy, physical therapy, and others, are provided when they are both educationally relevant and necessary in order for a student with a disability to gain access to and/or participate in his or her educational program (i.e., IEP goals, general education curriculum, general supports). Therefore, the need for related services can only be appropriately determined after the educational program has been developed and after the educational placement decision has been made. These provide the characteristics of the context for learning, which then enables appropriate determination of necessary related services. Although COACH does not explicitly address these related services decisions, information in the manual offers advice on these decisions and directs team members to related resources that may be of assistance.

Q15: What if I have other questions that are not answered here?

A15: If you have additional questions, then refer to the COACH manual or talk with other team members knowledgeable about COACH.

Blank COACH Student Record Forms for Part A: Steps 1–3

Student Record

by
Michael F. Giangreco, Ph.D.
Chigee J. Cloninger, Ph.D.
Virginia S. Iverson, M.Ed.

_____

Student's name

_____

Date of birth

Planning is for the 20_____ – 20_____ school year

_____

Educational placement(s) (e.g., school, grade)

Preparation Checklist

Before proceeding with COACH (Part A), ensure that all items below are completed. Check (✓) inside the ○ when completed.

○ 1. All professional team members understand the COACH process and at least one member has the skills to facilitate all parts of COACH.

○ 2. The family understands the COACH process and makes an informed decision to complete COACH with professional team members to develop their child's educational program. (See Appendix A and/or Sections I and II.)

○ 3. All professional team members agree to accept and act on the educational priorities identified by the family during the Family Interview.

○ 4. Mutually agreeable times and locations for the Steps 1, 2, and 3 are arranged so that at least the family, facilitator, special educator, and general educator can attend.

   Family member(s): _____

   _____

   Facilitator: _____

   Special educator: _____

   General educator(s): _____

   _____

   Others: _____

   Step 1:

   Date: _____ Start time: _____ End time: _____ Location: _____

   Step 2:

   Date: _____ Start time: _____ End time: _____ Location: _____

   Step 3:

   Date: _____ Start time: _____ End time _____ Location: _____

○ 5. A Student Record booklet or a copy of the COACH forms is ready for use.

○ 6. Plans are made to complete Step 4 (Annual Goals), Step 5 (Short-Term Objectives), and Step 6 (Program-at-a-Glance).

Introducing the Family Interview

To be read to person(s) being interviewed.

Welcome and the Importance of Family Involvement
Thank you for agreeing to meet with us to use COACH to help plan for your child's IEP. We are glad you are here to help us understand your family's perspectives about his or her educational needs and priorities.

Purpose of the Family Interview
The purpose of the COACH Family Interview is for all of us to gain a better understanding of what you think is important for [student's name] so the educational team can develop and implement an appropriate IEP.

Curriculum Content Included in the Family Interview
COACH includes nine categories of curriculum with corresponding learning outcomes that typically are not included in the general education curriculum. These learning outcomes are not designed to replace the general education curriculum—they are meant to augment or extend it. That is why it is so important to complete later steps of COACH where we will ensure that [student's name] has appropriate access to the general education curriculum available to his or her classmates without disabilities.

Interview Activities and Time Frame
It will take about 60–90 minutes to complete the interview. I will ask you a series of questions, listen carefully to your responses, and record them. The questions start broadly in order to consider many possibilities. As we proceed, the questions are designed to help you focus in on what you think are the most important learning outcomes for [student's name] to work on this year. Because the interview includes so many questions, we will be asking you to share brief answers. If there is anything you do not want to answer, then feel free to say so.

Outcomes of the Family Interview
By the end of the COACH Family Interview, you will have a selected a small set (e.g., 5–7) of learning outcomes that you think are the most important for [student's name] to work on in the coming year and should be listed on the IEP as annual goals.

Next Steps
After the interview is completed, we will share your selections with the other team members who were not present today. The priorities you identified to be included in the IEP will be worded as annual goals with short-term objectives or benchmarks for your review. Next, we need to complete Steps 2.1 and 2.2 of COACH to identify the additional learning outcomes and Step 3.0 to identify the general supports that will be part of [student's name] overall educational plan. Do you have any questions before we get started?

Part A: Determining a student's educational program

Preparation Checklist

Step 1: Family Interview

Purpose: To determine family-selected learning priorities for the student through a series of questions asked by an interviewer

Step 2: Additional Learning Outcomes

Purpose: To determine learning outcomes beyond family priorities

> 2.1: Select additional learning outcomes from COACH to ensure important items from the Family Interview that were not selected as priorities are not forgotten.

> 2.2: Identify additional learning outcomes from the general education curriculum to 1) ensure access to the general education curriculum, 2) ensure team members have a shared understanding about what general education content the student will pursue, 3) determine a starting place for the general education teacher (e.g., sample learning outcomes).

Step 3: General Supports

Purpose: To determine what supports need to be provided to or for the student

Part B: Translating the family-identified priorities into goals and objectives

Step 4: Annual Goals

Purpose: To ensure that the family's priorities are reflected as IEP goals

Step 5: Short-Term Objectives

Purpose: To develop short-term objectives to achieve annual goals

Step 6: Program-at-a-Glance

Purpose: To provide a concise summary of the educational program

---

Use COACH-generated information to assist in completing the IEP (e.g., inform present levels of performance, make related services decisions, document accommodations, finalize placement decision).

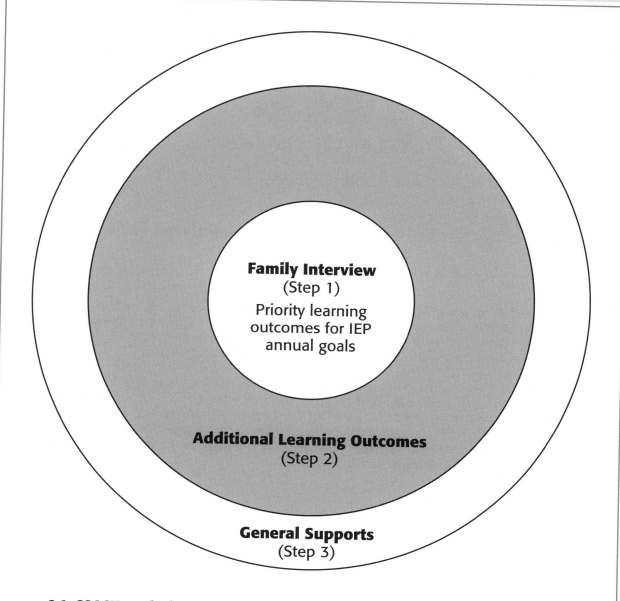

Family Interview
(Step 1)

Priority learning
outcomes for IEP
annual goals

Additional Learning Outcomes
(Step 2)

General Supports
(Step 3)

2.1. COACH curriculum areas

Communication	Applied academics
Socialization	School
Personal management	Community
Recreation	Vocational
Access academics	Other

2.2. General education curriculum areas

Reading/language arts	Foreign language
Math	Science
Arts	Music
Physical education	Health education
Social studies	Others

Valued Life Outcomes

To be read to the person(s) being interviewed:

The valued life outcomes listed were identified by asking parents who have children with disabilities what makes their child's life a "good life." These valued life outcomes should be interpreted individually to match each family's situation and culture.

Valued Life Outcomes

- Safety and health (physical and emotional)
- A home—now and in the future
- Meaningful relationships
- Control over personal choices (suited to the student's age and culture)
- Meaningful activities in various and valued places

You will be asked if you would like to answer questions for each valued life outcome. If you do, then you will be asked a small number of questions before moving on to the next valued life outcome topic. If for any reason you do not wish to answer a question, then you can simply decline and you do not need to explain why. In such cases, we will move on to the next topic.

There are a total of 11 questions in this section, and some may require follow-up questions for clarification. We hope to complete this part in about 10–15 minutes, so I will be asking you to provide brief responses. After all of the questions are asked, I will ask you to rate each of the five valued life outcomes in terms of its level of importance for your child in the coming year. By listening to and recording your responses, we hope to better understand your perspectives and help set the context for planning your child's IEP with you.

Safety and Health
(physical and emotional)

"Are you interested in answering questions on this topic?"
Mark (✓): ○ Yes or ○ No

1. Do you have any current health or safety concerns about [student's name] that you would like to see change over the next year?

_____

_____

_____

A Home—Now and in the Future

"Are you interested in answering questions on this topic?"
Mark (✓): ○ Yes or ○ No

2. Where and with whom does [student's name] currently live? (e.g., at home with parents and siblings, in foster home, in group home)

_____

_____

_____

If everything goes as you hope, then do you anticipate that [student's name] will continue to live in this same type of setting throughout the school years?

Mark (✓): ○ Yes or ○ No

If no, what would be a desirable type of setting?

_____

3. Would you like to talk about where a desirable type of setting would be for [student's name] to live as a young adult? Feel free to say no or that it's too soon if you feel that decision is too far in the future to discuss at this time.

Mark (✓): ○ Yes or ○ No or ○ It's too soon

If yes, what type of setting? _____

4. Is there any type of future living setting for [student's name] that you would like to avoid?

_____

_____

(continued)

(continued)

Meaningful Relationships

"Are you interested in answering questions on this topic?"
Mark (✓): ○ Yes or ○ No

5. Who are the people (e.g., family, neighbors, friends) that [student's name] spends the most time with during a typical week?

_____

_____

_____

_____

6. How, if at all, would you like to see [student's name] relationships change or expand in the near future (e.g., more time with same-age peers)?

_____

_____

_____

_____

Control Over Personal Choices
(suited to the student's age and culture)

"Are you interested in answering questions on this topic?"
Mark (✓): ○ Yes or ○ No

7. Does [student's name] have opportunities to have similar control over personal choices that are available to others of the same age? Mark (✓): ○ Yes or ○ No
Examples: _____

_____

_____

8. How, if at all, would you like to see [student's name] control over personal choices change or expand in the near future?

_____

_____

_____

_____

(continued)

(continued)

Meaningful Activities in Various and Valued Places

"Are you interested in answering questions on this topic?"
Mark (✓):   ○ Yes   or   ○ No

9. What are some of [student's name] favorite or most frequent activities? Where do these activities happen? (e.g., school, recreation center, work)

    _____
    _____
    _____
    _____
    _____
    _____
    _____
    _____
    _____

10. How, if at all, would you like to see these activities, or the places where they happen, change or expand in the near future?

    _____
    _____
    _____
    _____
    _____
    _____
    _____
    _____

11. Ask only if the student is age 14 or older:
    Have you and [student's name] thought about how he or she might spend his or her time as a young adult once high school is over (e.g., working, volunteering, continuing education)? What are your hopes about these possibilities?

    _____
    _____
    _____
    _____
    _____
    _____
    _____
    _____

Rating Valued Life Outcomes of Concern This Year

To be read to the person(s) being interviewed:

Thank you for taking this time to share your perspectives about valued life outcomes for your child. While all of the valued life outcomes may be important, it would be helpful for the school staff to understand what you think is most important for the coming year. So please rate their importance for your child for this coming year on a scale of 1 to 5, in which 1 means *not a concern this year* and 5 means *extremely important this year.* Each one will be marked (✓). Just because something is not a topic of concern this year does not mean it is unimportant or might not be important in the future. For example, although a child's health and safety are always important to parents, if a child has a recent history of being safe and healthy, then this may not be an important concern this year. Similarly, if a young child has a stable home situation, then having a home now and in the future may not be an important concern this year—but may be later if the person is making a transition to an adult living option. As you rate the five valued life outcomes, please focus your ratings on the present and coming year.

---

1 = Not a concern this year   5 = Extremely important this year

Safety and health (physical and emotional)
1 ○   2 ○   3 ○   4 ○   5 ○

A home—now and in the future
1 ○   2 ○   3 ○   4 ○   5 ○

Meaningful relationships
1 ○   2 ○   3 ○   4 ○   5 ○

Control over personal choices
1 ○   2 ○   3 ○   4 ○   5 ○

Meaningful activities in various and valued places
1 ○   2 ○   3 ○   4 ○   5 ○

Notes

Selecting Curriculum Areas to Explore During the Family Interview

Consider all nine COACH curriculum areas and select up to four areas to address *now* in the Family Interview. For those remaining areas, indicate whether to address *later* or *skip* for this year. Only one box will be marked (✓) for each area.

Curriculum areas	**Now** Address in Family Interview	**Later** Address in Step 2.1	**Skip** for this year
Communication			
Socialization			
Personal management			
Recreation			
Access academics			
Applied academics			
School			
Community Consider for transition-age students (14–21 years)			
Vocational Consider for transition-age students (14–21 years at community worksites)			

Reference Information

Communication

Displays consistent communication mode • Expresses continuation or "more" • Makes selection when given options • Makes requests of others • Signals desire/need for attention • Expresses rejection/refusal • Sustains communication with others • Recognizes when misunderstood and uses another way • Expresses greetings and farewells • Follows instructions • Answers questions • Comments/describes • Asks questions of others

Socialization

Responds to the presence and interactions of others • Initiates social interactions • Sustains social interactions • Ends social interactions • Distinguishes and interacts differently with friends/family, acquaintances, and strangers • Maintains prosocial behaviors when alone and with others • Accepts assistance from others • Offers assistance to others • Makes transitions between routine activities • Adjusts to unexpected changes in routine • Shares with others • Advocates for self

Personal Management

Gives permission and/or directs others to provide personal care support • Drinks and eats • Feeds self • Cares for bowel and bladder needs • Selects appropriate clothing • Dresses/undresses • Cares for personal hygiene • Is mobile between locations • Manages personal belongings • Gives self-identification information • Uses telephone • Responds to emergency alarm • Recognizes and avoids potentially dangerous situations • Maintains safe and healthy behaviors

Recreation

Engages in spectator events with others • Engages in recreation activities on his or her own • Engages in recreation activities with others

Access Academics

Reacts to objects, activities, and/or interactions • Directs and sustains attention to activity • Explores surroundings and objects • Differentiates/discriminates between things • Imitates skills used in daily life • Uses objects as intended • Understands meaning of nontext symbols

Applied Academics

Uses computer • Understands text has meaning • Reads (decodes) words/phrases • Understands what is read • Uses writing/drawing tools • Writes letters or words • Counts with correspondence • Computes numbers • Uses money • Uses schedule or calendar

School

Travels to and from school • Participates in small groups • Participates in large groups • Does classroom or school jobs • Completes tasks/assignments independently • Manages school-related belongings • Follows school procedures/routines • Uses school facilities • Participates in extracurricular activities

Community

Travels safely in the community • Uses restaurants • Uses recreational facilities • Makes purchases of merchandise or services • Uses vending machines • Uses banking facilities • Uses public transportation

Vocational

Applies for jobs(s) • Travels to and from worksite • Uses check-in procedure • Interacts appropriately with others • Follows worksite rules for appearance, safety, and conduct • Follows schedule of work activities • Completes assigned work • Uses worksite facilities

Communication

*Complete only if **Now** was selected in Step 1.2.*

How does the student communicate (e.g., vocalization, AAC device, sign language, body language, speech)? Expressively: _____

Receptively: _____

	STEP 1.3		STEP 1.4
Learning outcomes	Mark score	Needs work this year?	Rank up to four priorities
1. Displays consistent communication mode(s) (e.g., gestures, points, vocalizes, uses facial expressions, uses AAC)	E P S ○ ○ ○	N Y ○ ○	
2. Expresses continuation or "more" (e.g., makes sounds or movement to indicate continuation)	E P S ○ ○ ○	N Y ○ ○	
3. Makes selection when given options (e.g., story, food, clothes, activities, peers, personal needs)	E P S ○ ○ ○	N Y ○ ○	
4. Makes requests of others (e.g., objects, food, interactions, activities, personal care)	E P S ○ ○ ○	N Y ○ ○	
5. Signals desire/need for attention (e.g., gesture, vocalization, assistive technology)	E P S ○ ○ ○	N Y ○ ○	
6. Expresses rejection/refusal (e.g., indicates he or she wants something to stop or not begin)	E P S ○ ○ ○	N Y ○ ○	
7. Sustains communication with others (e.g., takes turn, listens to others communicate, stays on topic)	E P S ○ ○ ○	N Y ○ ○	
8. Recognizes if misunderstood and uses another way (e.g., uses "repair strategy," perseveres)	E P S ○ ○ ○	N Y ○ ○	
9. Expresses greetings and farewell	E P S ○ ○ ○	N Y ○ ○	
10. Follows instructions (e.g., one step, multistep)	E P S ○ ○ ○	N Y ○ ○	
11. Answers questions (e.g., yes/no, who, what, where, why, when, how)	E P S ○ ○ ○	N Y ○ ○	
12. Comments/describes (e.g., vocabulary for events, objects, interactions, feelings)	E P S ○ ○ ○	N Y ○ ○	
13. Asks questions of others	E P S ○ ○ ○	N Y ○ ○	

Scoring key (use scores for Step 1.3 alone or in combination):
E = Early/emerging skill (1%–25%); P = Partial skill (25%–80%); S = Skillful (80%–100%).

Socialization

*Complete only if **Now** was selected in Step 1.2.*

Learning outcomes	STEP 1.3 Mark score	STEP 1.3 Needs work this year?	STEP 1.4 Rank up to four priorities
14. Responds to the presence and interactions of others (e.g., family, peers, adults)	E P S ○ ○ ○	N Y ○ ○	
15. Initiates social interactions (e.g., approaches others, joins group)	E P S ○ ○ ○	N Y ○ ○	
16. Sustains social interactions (e.g., explores objects with others, takes turns, provides mutual attention)	E P S ○ ○ ○	N Y ○ ○	
17. Ends social interactions	E P S ○ ○ ○	N Y ○ ○	
18. Distinguishes and interacts differently with friends/family, acquaintances, and strangers	E P S ○ ○ ○	N Y ○ ○	
19. Maintains prosocial behaviors when alone and with others	E P S ○ ○ ○	N Y ○ ○	
20. Accepts assistance from others	E P S ○ ○ ○	N Y ○ ○	
21. Offers assistance to others	E P S ○ ○ ○	N Y ○ ○	
22. Makes transitions between routine activities	E P S ○ ○ ○	N Y ○ ○	
23. Adjusts to unexpected changes in routine	E P S ○ ○ ○	N Y ○ ○	
24. Shares with others	E P S ○ ○ ○	N Y ○ ○	
25. Advocates for self (e.g., directs personal care, selects projects/classes, asks for help if needed, makes decisions available to peers)	E P S ○ ○ ○	N Y ○ ○	

Comments:

Scoring key (use scores for Step 1.3 alone or in combination):
E = Early/emerging skill (1%–25%); P = Partial skill (25%–80%); S = Skillful (80%–100%).

Choosing Outcomes and Accommodations for Children, Third Edition.

Personal Management

Complete only if *Now* was selected in Step 1.2.

| | STEP 1.3 | | STEP 1.4 |
Learning outcomes	Mark score	Needs work this year?	Rank up to four priorities
26. Gives permission and/or directs others to provide personal care support (e.g., move wheelchair, feed, dress)	E P S ○ ○ ○	N Y ○ ○	
27. Drinks and eats (e.g., retains food/drink in mouth, chews, swallows)	E P S ○ ○ ○	N Y ○ ○	
28. Feeds self (e.g., eats with hands/fingers, uses utensils)	E P S ○ ○ ○	N Y ○ ○	
29. Cares for bowel and bladder needs	E P S ○ ○ ○	N Y ○ ○	
30. Selects appropriate clothing to wear (e.g., selects items appropriate to activity, weather, style)	E P S ○ ○ ○	N Y ○ ○	
31. Dresses/undresses	E P S ○ ○ ○	N Y ○ ○	
32. Cares for personal hygiene (e.g., washes hands, wipes nose, brushes hair/teeth, showers)	E P S ○ ○ ○	N Y ○ ○	
33. Is mobile between locations (e.g., walks, crawls, moves wheelchair, climbs stairs, uses elevator/escalators)	E P S ○ ○ ○	N Y ○ ○	
34. Manages personal belongings (e.g., toys, clothes, special equipment)	E P S ○ ○ ○	N Y ○ ○	
35. Gives self-identification information (e.g., names, address, telephone number)	E P S ○ ○ ○	N Y ○ ○	
36. Uses telephone (e.g., cellular telephone, pay telephone, land line)	E P S ○ ○ ○	N Y ○ ○	
37. Responds to emergency alarm (e.g., leaves building when smoke alarm sounds)	E P S ○ ○ ○	N Y ○ ○	
38. Recognizes and avoids potential danger	E P S ○ ○ ○	N Y ○ ○	
39. Maintains safe and healthy behaviors (e.g., copes with environmental stresses, shows impulse control, has self-regulation)	E P S ○ ○ ○	N Y ○ ○	

Comments:

Scoring key (use scores for Step 1.3 alone or in combination):
E = Early/emerging skill (1%–25%); P = Partial skill (25%–80%); S = Skillful (80%–100%).

Recreation

*Complete only if **Now** was selected in Step 1.2.*

Learning outcomes	STEP 1.3 Mark score	STEP 1.3 Needs work this year?	STEP 1.4 Rank up to four priorities
40. Engages in spectator events with others (e.g., movies, plays, concerts, performances, sports)	E P S ○ ○ ○	N Y ○ ○	
41. Engages in recreation activities on his or her own (e.g., toy play, games, sports, exercise, hobbies, music/media devices, books/ magazines)	E P S ○ ○ ○	N Y ○ ○	
42. Engages in recreation activities with others (e.g., read to by someone, games, clubs, sports, exercise, hobbies)	E P S ○ ○ ○	N Y ○ ○	
	E P S ○ ○ ○	N Y ○ ○	
	E P S ○ ○ ○	N Y ○ ○	
	E P S ○ ○ ○	N Y ○ ○	

Comments:

Scoring key (use scores for Step 1.3 alone or in combination):
E = Early/emerging skill (1%–25%); P = Partial skill (25%–80%); S = Skillful (80%–100%).

Access Academics

*Complete only if **Now** was selected in Step 1.2.*

All students are entitled access to academic curricula available to students without disabilities. Complete Step 2.2 to ensure the team identifies how the student will gain access to the general education curriculum (e.g., literacy, math, science, social studies, physical education, arts/music) as part of his or her educational program.

Learning outcomes	STEP 1.3 Mark score	STEP 1.3 Needs work this year?	STEP 1.4 Rank up to four priorities
43. Reacts to objects, activities, and/or interactions (e.g., recognizes someone is reading or playing with him or her)	E P S ○ ○ ○	N Y ○ ○	
44. Directs and sustains attention to activity (e.g., book pages, toys, interactions, class activities)	E P S ○ ○ ○	N Y ○ ○	
45. Explores surroundings and objects (e.g., scans, searches, explores toys/books)	E P S ○ ○ ○	N Y ○ ○	
46. Differentiates/discriminates between things (e.g., objects, activities, patterns, pictures, interactions, book cover, edibles versus nonedibles)	E P S ○ ○ ○	N Y ○ ○	
47. Imitates skills used in daily life	E P S ○ ○ ○	N Y ○ ○	
48. Uses objects as intended (e.g., plays with toy, eats with spoon, turns pages of a book)	E P S ○ ○ ○	N Y ○ ○	
49. Understands meaning of nontext symbols (e.g., line drawings, photographs, tactile material, gesture)	E P S ○ ○ ○	N Y ○ ○	
	E P S ○ ○ ○	N Y ○ ○	
	E P S ○ ○ ○	N Y ○ ○	

Comments:

Scoring key (use scores for Step 1.3 alone or in combination):
E = Early/emerging skill (1%–25%); P = Partial skill (25%–80%); S = Skillful (80%–100%).

Choosing Outcomes and Accommodations for Children, Third Edition.

Applied Academics

*Complete only if **Now** was selected in Step 1.2.*

All students are entitled access to academic curricula available to students without disabilities. Complete Step 2.2 to ensure the team identifies how the student will gain access to the general education curriculum (e.g., literacy, math, science, social studies, physical education, arts/music) as part of his or her educational program.

Learning outcomes	STEP 1.3 Mark score	Needs work this year?	STEP 1.4 Rank up to four priorities
50. Uses computer (e.g., controls cursor, navigates software)	E P S ○ ○ ○	N Y ○ ○	
51. Understands text has meaning (e.g., letters, words, numerals)	E P S ○ ○ ○	N Y ○ ○	
52. Reads (decodes) words/phrases (e.g., signs, labels, directions, stories)	E P S ○ ○ ○	N Y ○ ○	
53. Understands what is read (e.g., words, phrases, sentences, numerals)	E P S ○ ○ ○	N Y ○ ○	
54. Uses writing/drawing tools (e.g., pen/pencil, paintbrush, keyboard, assistive technology)	E P S ○ ○ ○	N Y ○ ○	
55. Writes letters or words (e.g., pencil, keyboard, stamp, arranging 3D letters)	E P S ○ ○ ○	N Y ○ ○	
56. Counts with correspondence	E P S ○ ○ ○	N Y ○ ○	
57. Computes numbers (e.g., adds, subtracts)	E P S ○ ○ ○	N Y ○ ○	
58. Uses money (e.g., making purchase, saves, discriminates values)	E P S ○ ○ ○	N Y ○ ○	
59. Uses schedule or calendar (e.g., now/next, time/activity schedule, daily/weekly schedule)	E P S ○ ○ ○	N Y ○ ○	

Comments:

Scoring key (use scores for Step 1.3 alone or in combination):
E = Early/emerging skill (1%–25%); P = Partial skill (25%–80%); S = Skillful (80%–100%).

School

*Complete only if **Now** was selected in Step 1.2.*

For all items listed here involving interaction with other students, we encourage a naturally occurring proportion of students with and without disabilities; in other words, there should be more students without disabilities than with disabilities in groups.

	STEP 1.3		STEP 1.4
Learning outcomes	Mark score	Needs work this year?	Rank up to four priorities
60. Travels to and from school (e.g., takes bus, walks, uses mobility device)	E P S ○ ○ ○	N Y ○ ○	
61. Participates in small groups (e.g., tolerates situation, takes turn, is actively involved, responds to instructions)	E P S ○ ○ ○	N Y ○ ○	
62. Participates in large groups (e.g., tolerates situation, takes turn, is actively involved, responds to instructions)	E P S ○ ○ ○	N Y ○ ○	
63. Completes tasks/assignments independently	E P S ○ ○ ○	N Y ○ ○	
64. Manages school-related belongings (e.g., backpack, materials, books, lockers, gym equipment)	E P S ○ ○ ○	N Y ○ ○	
65. Follows school procedures/routines (e.g., changing classes, following schedule, leaving class)	E P S ○ ○ ○	N Y ○ ○	
66. Does classroom or school jobs (e.g., delivers attendance/messages, gathers lunch money, runs bookstore with peers)	E P S ○ ○ ○	N Y ○ ○	
67. Uses school facilities (e.g., playground, cafeteria, library, bookstore)	E P S ○ ○ ○	N Y ○ ○	
68. Participates in extracurricular activities (e.g., clubs, sports, services groups, drama, music, volunteers)	E P S ○ ○ ○	N Y ○ ○	

Comments:

Scoring key (use scores for Step 1.3 alone or in combination):
E = Early/emerging skill (1%–25%); P = Partial skill (25%–80%); S = Skillful (80%–100%).

Community

*Complete only if **Now** was selected in Step 1.2.*

Typically for transition-age students (14–21 years).

	STEP 1.3		STEP 1.4
Learning outcomes	Mark score	Needs work this year?	Rank up to four priorities
69. Travels safely in the community (e.g., uses sidewalks/crosswalks, acts appropriately with strangers, finds destination)	E P S ○ ○ ○	N Y ○ ○	
70. Uses restaurants (e.g., orders food, finds seating, eats meal, pays bill)	E P S ○ ○ ○	N Y ○ ○	
71. Uses recreational facilities (e.g., theaters, parks, recreation centers, fitness clubs)	E P S ○ ○ ○	N Y ○ ○	
72. Makes purchases of merchandise or services (e.g., stores, salon, doctor's office, post office)	E P S ○ ○ ○	N Y ○ ○	
73. Uses vending machines	E P S ○ ○ ○	N Y ○ ○	
74. Uses banking facilities (e.g., deposits/ withdrawals, automated teller machines)	E P S ○ ○ ○	N Y ○ ○	
75. Uses public transportation	E P S ○ ○ ○	N Y ○ ○	
	E P S ○ ○ ○	N Y ○ ○	
	E P S ○ ○ ○	N Y ○ ○	

Comments:

Scoring key (use scores for Step 1.3 alone or in combination):
E = Early/emerging skill (1%–25%); P = Partial skill (25%–80%); S = Skillful (80%–100%).

Vocational

*Complete only if **Now** was selected in Step 1.2.*

For transition-age students (14–21 years) at community worksites

	STEP 1.3		STEP 1.4
Learning outcomes	Mark score	Needs work this year?	Rank up to four priorities
76. Applies for job(s) (e.g., finds potential jobs, fills out forms, interviews for jobs)	E P S ○ ○ ○	N Y ○ ○	
77. Travels to and from worksite	E P S ○ ○ ○	N Y ○ ○	
78. Uses check-in procedure (e.g., time clock, sign in)	E P S ○ ○ ○	N Y ○ ○	
79. Interacts appropriately with others based on work place norms (e.g., co-workers, customers, supervisors)	E P S ○ ○ ○	N Y ○ ○	
80. Follows worksite rules for appearance, safety, and conduct	E P S ○ ○ ○	N Y ○ ○	
81. Follows schedule of work activities	E P S ○ ○ ○	N Y ○ ○	
82. Completes assigned work	E P S ○ ○ ○	N Y ○ ○	
83. Uses worksite facilities (e.g., breakroom, cafeteria, locker room)	E P S ○ ○ ○	N Y ○ ○	
	E P S ○ ○ ○	N Y ○ ○	

Comments:

Scoring key (use scores for Step 1.3 alone or in combination):
E = Early/emerging skill (1%–25%); P = Partial skill (25%–80%); S = Skillful (80%–100%).

Other

	STEP 1.3		STEP 1.4
Learning outcomes	Mark score	Needs work this year?	Rank up to four priorities
	E P S ○ ○ ○	N Y ○ ○	
	E P S ○ ○ ○	N Y ○ ○	
	E P S ○ ○ ○	N Y ○ ○	
	E P S ○ ○ ○	N Y ○ ○	
	E P S ○ ○ ○	N Y ○ ○	
	E P S ○ ○ ○	N Y ○ ○	
	E P S ○ ○ ○	N Y ○ ○	
	E P S ○ ○ ○	N Y ○ ○	
	E P S ○ ○ ○	N Y ○ ○	

Comments:

Scoring key (use scores for Step 1.3 alone or in combination):
E = Early/emerging skill (1%–25%); P = Partial skill (25%–80%); S = Skillful (80%–100%).

Choosing Outcomes and Accommodations for Children, Third Edition.

Cross-Prioritization

COACH 3

Transfer priority learning outcomes in their ranked order from each COACH curriculum area reviewed with the family in Step 1.4.

	Communication	Socialization	Personal management	Recreation	Access academics
1					
2					
3					
4					
	Applied academics	School	Community	Vocational	Other
1					
2					
3					
4					

(continued)

Cross-Prioritization

COACH3

Rank	Overall priority learning outcomes (Word priorities to explicitly clarify what the student will be expected to learn)	Indicate which valued life outcomes the priority is meant to support						Check (✓) only one box for each priority		
		Safety/health	Home	Relationships	Control/choices	Activities	IEP goal	Additional learning outcomes	Home
1									
2									
3									
4									
5									
6									

Next step: The interviewer explains Steps 2.1, 2.2, and 3 and the relationship of the Family Interview to the next steps.

Additional Learning Outcomes from COACH

Select and mark (✓) only those additional learning outcomes to be targeted for instruction (limit to reasonable number). See manual for directions.

Date: _____ Participants: _____

_____

Communication

___ 1. Displays consistent communication mode

___ 2. Expresses continuation or "more"

___ 3. Makes selection when given options

___ 4. Makes request of others

___ 5. Signals desire/need for attention

___ 6. Expresses rejection/refusal

___ 7. Sustains communication with others

___ 8. Recognizes when misunderstood and uses another way

___ 9. Expresses greetings and farewells

___ 10. Follows instructions

___ 11. Answers questions

___ 12. Comments/describes

___ 13. Asks questions of others

Socialization

___ 14. Responds to the presence and interactions of others

___ 15. Initiates social interactions

___ 16. Sustains social interactions

___ 17. Ends social interactions

___ 18. Distinguishes and interacts differently with friends/family, acquaintances, and strangers

___ 19. Maintains safe and healthy behaviors when alone and with others

___ 20. Accepts assistance from others

___ 21. Offers assistance to others

___ 22. Makes transitions between routine activities

___ 23. Adjusts to unexpected changes in routine

___ 24. Shares with others

___ 25. Advocates for self

Personal Management

___ 26. Gives permission and/or directs others to provide personal care support

___ 27. Drinks and eats

___ 28. Feeds self

___ 29. Cares for bowel and bladder needs

___ 30. Selects appropriate clothing to wear

___ 31. Dresses/undresses

___ 32. Cares for personal hygiene

___ 33. Is mobile between locations

___ 34. Manages personal belongings

___ 35. Gives self-identification information

___ 36. Uses telephone

___ 37. Responds to emergency alarm

___ 38. Recognizes and avoids potentially dangerous situations

___ 39. Maintains safe and healthy behaviors

Recreation

___ 40. Engages in spectator events with others

___ 41. Engages in recreation activities on his or her own

___ 42. Engages in recreation activities with others

Additional Learning Outcomes from COACH

Access Academics

___ 43. Reacts to objects, activities, and/or interactions

___ 44. Directs and sustains attention to activity

___ 45. Explores surroundings and objects

___ 46. Differentiates/ discriminates between things

___ 47. Imitates skills used in daily life

___ 48. Uses objects as intended

___ 49. Understands meaning of nontext symbols

Applied Academics

___ 50. Uses computer

___ 51. Understands text has meaning

___ 52. Reads (decodes) words/phrases

___ 53. Understands what is read

___ 54. Uses writing/drawing tools

___ 55. Writes letters or words

___ 56. Counts with correspondence

___ 57. Computes numbers

___ 58. Uses money

___ 59. Uses schedule or calendar

School

___ 60. Travels to and from school

___ 61. Participates in small groups

___ 62. Participates in large groups

___ 63. Completes tasks/ assignments independently

___ 64. Manages school-related belongings

___ 65. Follows school procedures/routines

___ 66. Does classroom or school jobs

___ 67. Uses school facilities

___ 68. Participates in extracurricular activities

Community

___ 69. Travels safely in the community

___ 70. Uses restaurants

___ 71. Uses recreation facilities

___ 72. Makes purchases of merchandise or services

___ 73. Uses vending machines

___ 74. Uses banking facilities

___ 75. Uses public transportation

Vocational

___ 76. Applies for jobs(s)

___ 77. Travels to and from worksite

___ 78. Uses check-in procedure

___ 79. Interacts appropriately with others

___ 80. Follows worksite rules for appearance, safety, and conduct

___ 81. Follows schedule of work activities

___ 82. Completes assigned work

___ 83. Uses worksite facilities

Other

___ _____

___ _____

___ _____

___ _____

___ _____

___ _____

___ _____

___ _____

___ _____

___ _____

Types of Participation in the General Education Curriculum

The student may require access or instructional supports (e.g., assistive technology, AAC device, extended time, modified materials) across each of the four types of participation.

Same curriculum with supports
(same content, same level)

- Within a curriculum area class or activity (e.g., reading, math, science), the expectation for the student with a disability is that he or she will pursue and can reasonably achieve the same grade-level expectations as his or her classmates without disabilities.

- Same curriculum means same content, level, amount, and rate.

- It is expected that the student will gain access to the same curriculum in the general education classroom with supports as needed.

Multilevel curriculum
(same content, different level)

- Within a curriculum area class or activity (e.g., reading, math, science), the expectation for the student with a disability is that he or she will pursue an individually determined subset of the learning outcomes within the same curriculum area and have the same content as his or her classmates without disabilities, but at a different level.

- Multilevel curriculum means the same curriculum area and content, but at a different level, amount, and/or rate. For example, in math, most students are working on computing numbers (e.g., three digits). The student with a disability is also working on computing numbers, but at a different level (e.g., single digits), typically a lesser amount, and potentially at a slower rate.

- Multilevel curriculum is delivered within shared educational activities in a large or small group with a natural proportion of students with and without disabilities.

Multilevel curriculum
(different content, different level)

- Within a curriculum area class or activity (e.g., reading, math, science), the expectation for the student with a disability is that he or she will pursue an individually determined subset of the learning outcomes within the same curriculum area, but have different content than his or her classmates without disabilities and at a different level.

- Multilevel curriculum means the same curriculum area, but different content, at a different level, amount, and/or rate. For example, in math, most students are working on computing numbers (e.g., three digits). The student with a disability is also working on math curriculum, but is learning a different content (e.g., counting, geometric shapes), typically a lesser amount, and potentially at a slower rate.

- Multilevel curriculum is delivered within shared educational activities in a large or small group with a natural proportion of students with and without disabilities.

(continued)

Types of Participation in the General Education Curriculum

Curriculum overlapping
(different curriculum area, different level)

- Within a curriculum area class or activity (e.g., social studies, health), the expectation for the student with a disability is that he or she will pursue an individually determined subset of the learning outcomes from curriculum areas different from his or her classmates without disabilities and at a different level.

- Curriculum overlapping means different curriculum areas and different content at a different level, amount, and/or rate. For example, in social studies, most students are working on geography. The student with a disability is exposed to and involved in geography activities (e.g., a geography game with classmates), but the primary learning outcomes he or she is focusing on are from other curriculum areas (e.g., communication, socialization, access academics), such as developing a consistent pointing response, making a selection when given options, or exploring objects.

- The student with a disability may require access or instructional supports (e.g., assistive technology, AAC device, extended time, modified materials) when exploring curriculum overlapping.

- Curriculum overlapping is delivered within shared educational activities in a large or small group with a natural proportion of students with and without disabilities.

- Curriculum overlapping does not preclude also encouraging learning outcomes in the curriculum area targeted for the majority of the class.

(continued)

Additional Learning
Outcomes from General Education

General education curriculum areas (provide brief description)	Indicate primary participation option	Provide example Starting points if multilevel or curriculum overlapping
Language arts:	O Same (grade-level expectation) O Multilevel (same content) O Multilevel (different content) O Curriculum overlapping	
Math:	O Same (grade-level expectation) O Multilevel (same content) O Multilevel (different content) O Curriculum overlapping	
Science:	O Same (grade-level expectation) O Multilevel (same content) O Multilevel (different content) O Curriculum overlapping	
Social studies:	O Same (grade-level expectation) O Multilevel (same content) O Multilevel (different content) O Curriculum overlapping	

(continued)

Choosing Outcomes and Accommodations for Children, Third Edition.
Copyright © 2011 by Michael F. Giangreco. All rights reserved. Baltimore: Paul H. Brookes Publishing Co., Inc.

Step 2.2 *(continued)*

Additional Learning
Outcomes from General Education

General education curriculum areas (provide brief description)	Indicate primary participation option	Provide example Starting points if multilevel or curriculum overlapping
✓		
Physical education:	○ Same (grade-level expectation) ○ Multilevel (same content) ○ Multilevel (different content) ○ Curriculum overlapping	
Health education:	○ Same (grade-level expectation) ○ Multilevel (same content) ○ Multilevel (different content) ○ Curriculum overlapping	
Art (visual/performing):	○ Same (grade-level expectation) ○ Multilevel (same content) ○ Multilevel (different content) ○ Curriculum overlapping	
Music (vocal/instrumental):	○ Same (grade-level expectation) ○ Multilevel (same content) ○ Multilevel (different content) ○ Curriculum overlapping	

(continued)

Choosing Outcomes and Accommodations for Children, Third Edition.
Copyright © 2011 by Michael F. Giangreco. All rights reserved. Baltimore: Paul H. Brookes Publishing Co., Inc.

Step 2.2   (continued)

COACH3

Additional Learning
Outcomes from General Education

✓	General education curriculum areas (provide brief description)	Indicate primary participation option	Provide example Starting points if multilevel or curriculum overlapping
	Foreign language:	○ Same (grade-level expectation) ○ Multilevel (same content) ○ Multilevel (different content) ○ Curriculum overlapping	
	Other:	○ Same (grade-level expectation) ○ Multilevel (same content) ○ Multilevel (different content) ○ Curriculum overlapping	
	Other:	○ Same (grade-level expectation) ○ Multilevel (same content) ○ Multilevel (different content) ○ Curriculum overlapping	
	Other:	○ Same (grade-level expectation) ○ Multilevel (same content) ○ Multilevel (different content) ○ Curriculum overlapping	

(continued)

Additional Learning
Outcomes from General Education

✓	General education curriculum areas (provide brief description)	Indicate primary participation option	Provide example Starting points if multilevel or curriculum overlapping
	Other:	○ Same (grade-level expectation) ○ Multilevel (same content) ○ Multilevel (different content) ○ Curriculum overlapping	
	Other:	○ Same (grade-level expectation) ○ Multilevel (same content) ○ Multilevel (different content) ○ Curriculum overlapping	
	Other:	○ Same (grade-level expectation) ○ Multilevel (same content) ○ Multilevel (different content) ○ Curriculum overlapping	
	Other:	○ Same (grade-level expectation) ○ Multilevel (same content) ○ Multilevel (different content) ○ Curriculum overlapping	

Choosing Outcomes and Accommodations for Children, Third Edition.
Copyright © 2011 by Michael F. Giangreco. All rights reserved. Baltimore: Paul H. Brookes Publishing Co., Inc.

General Supports

Select and mark (✓) all necessary general supports. See manual for directions.

Participants: _____

Personal Needs

___ 1. Needs to be fed food and drinks
___ 2. Needs to be dressed
___ 3. Needs assistance with bowel and bladder management
___ 4. Needs assistance with personal hygiene
___ 5. Needs to be given medication
___ 6. Needs suctioning and/or postural drainage

___ _____

___ _____

___ _____

___ _____

___ _____

___ _____

___ _____

Physical Needs

___ 7. Needs to be physically repositioned at regular intervals
___ 8. Needs to have environmental barriers modified to allow access
___ 9. Needs to have physical equipment managed (e.g., wheelchair, braces, orthotics)
___ 10. Needs specialized transportation accommodations
___ 11. Needs to be moved and positioned in specialized ways
___ 12. Needs to be physically moved from place to place

___ _____

___ _____

___ _____

___ _____

___ _____

Teaching Others About the Student

___ 13. Teach staff and classmates about the student's AAC system and other communicative behaviors
___ 14. Teach staff and students how to communicate with the student
___ 15. Teach staff seizure management procedures
___ 16. Teach staff emergency procedures (e.g., medical, evacuation)
___ 17. Teach staff preventive behavior management procedures
___ 18. Teach staff behavioral crisis intervention procedures
___ 19. Teach peers and adults to ask the student to repeat or communicate in another way if not understood

___ _____

___ _____

___ _____

___ _____

(continued)

General Supports

Sensory Needs

___ 20. Needs to have hearing aids monitored (e.g., batteries, settings)

___ 21. Needs to have people use FM unit/auditory trainer

___ 22. Needs people to manually communicate (e.g., American Sign Language, gestures)

___ 23. Needs to have glasses managed (e.g., adjusted, cleaned)

___ 24. Needs tactile materials

___ 25. Needs enlarged materials

___ 26. Needs materials in braille

___ 27. Needs to be positioned to accommodate sensory needs (e.g., specified distance from source)

___ 28. Needs environmental modifications to accommodate for sensory needs (e.g., lighting, location background, volume, color)

___ _____

___ _____

___ _____

Providing Access and Opportunities

___ 29. Provide access to general education classes and activities

___ 30. Needs to have instructional accommodations to general education activities and materials prepared in advance to facilitate multilevel instruction and/or curriculum overlapping

___ 31. Provide access to community-based experiences with people without disabilities

___ 32. Provide exposure to a variety of career/work experiences

___ 33. Provide access to cocurricular activities with people without disabilities

___ 34. Provide access to materials in the student's native language

___ 35. Provide access to materials and activities associated with the student's cultural background as well as other cultures

___ 36. Provide access to nonaversive approaches to dealing with challenging behaviors

___ _____

Other General Supports (not listed elsewhere)

___ 37. Needs time limits extended or waived

___ 38. Needs class notes recorded or scribed

___ 39. Needs alternative testing modification

___ _____

___ _____

___ _____

___ _____

___ _____

___ _____

___ _____

___ _____

Blank COACH Student Record Forms for Part B: Steps 4–6

Annual Goals

Goal _____

COACH3

1. Priority learning outcome from Step 1.5: _____

2. Present level of performance based on current assessment of the priority learning outcome:
   _____

3. What are the natural, age-appropriate contexts (places and activities) in which the student will be expected to use the skill/behavior this year?_____
   _____

4. What aspect of the priority learning outcomes should be reflected in the annual goal? Check all those to be addressed this year.

   __ Decreasing extra cues/supports

   __ Respond to natural supports

   __ Generalization across settings, people, materials/cues

   __ Acquiring core skills

   __ Expand repertoire

   __ Extend or reduce duration

   __ Other

   __ Quality of performance

   __ Tempo, rate, or fluency

   __ Retention over time

   __ Other

   __ Other

5. What is the specific observable, measurable skill/behavior the team wants the student to learn this year? _____
   _____

6. Final annual goal (include contexts and skill/behavior): _____
   _____

Short-Term Objectives

Conditions	Skill/behavior	Criteria

Choosing Outcomes and Accommodations for Children, Third Edition.

Goal _____ — **Annual Goals** — COACH 3

1. Priority learning outcome from Step 1.5: _____

2. Present level of performance based on current assessment of the priority learning outcome:
   _____

3. What are the natural, age-appropriate contexts (places and activities) in which the student will be expected to use the skill/behavior this year?_____
   _____

4. What aspect of the priority learning outcomes should be reflected in the annual goal? Check all those to be addressed this year.

   __ Decreasing extra cues/supports

   __ Respond to natural supports

   __ Generalization across settings, people, materials/cues

   __ Acquiring core skills

   __ Expand repertoire

   __ Extend or reduce duration

   __ Other

   __ Quality of performance

   __ Tempo, rate, or fluency

   __ Retention over time

   __ Other

   __ Other

5. What is the specific observable, measurable skill/behavior the team wants the student to learn this year? _____
   _____

6. Final annual goal (include contexts and skill/behavior): _____
   _____

Short-Term Objectives

Conditions	Skill/behavior	Criteria

Annual Goals

Goal _____

COACH3

1. Priority learning outcome from Step 1.5: _____

2. Present level of performance based on current assessment of the priority learning outcome:

   _____

3. What are the natural, age-appropriate contexts (places and activities) in which the student will be expected to use the skill/behavior this year?_____

   _____

4. What aspect of the priority learning outcomes should be reflected in the annual goal? Check all those to be addressed this year.

   __ Decreasing extra   __ Acquiring core skills   __ Quality of performance
       cues/supports   __ Expand repertoire   __ Tempo, rate, or fluency

   __ Respond to natural supports   __ Extend or reduce duration   __ Retention over time

   __ Generalization across   __ Other   __ Other
       settings, people,
       materials/cues   __ Other

5. What is the specific observable, measurable skill/behavior the team wants the student to learn this year? _____

   _____

6. Final annual goal (include contexts and skill/behavior): _____

   _____

Short-Term Objectives

Conditions	Skill/behavior	Criteria

Goal _____   # Annual Goals   COACH3

1. Priority learning outcome from Step 1.5: _____

2. Present level of performance based on current assessment of the priority learning outcome:

    _____

3. What are the natural, age-appropriate contexts (places and activities) in which the student will be expected to use the skill/behavior this year?_____

    _____

4. What aspect of the priority learning outcomes should be reflected in the annual goal? Check all those to be addressed this year.

    __ Decreasing extra cues/supports

    __ Respond to natural supports

    __ Generalization across settings, people, materials/cues

    __ Acquiring core skills

    __ Expand repertoire

    __ Extend or reduce duration

    __ Other

    __ Quality of performance

    __ Tempo, rate, or fluency

    __ Retention over time

    __ Other

    __ Other

5. What is the specific observable, measurable skill/behavior the team wants the student to learn this year? _____

    _____

6. Final annual goal (include contexts and skill/behavior): _____

    _____

Short-Term Objectives

Conditions	Skill/behavior	Criteria

Goal _____	**Annual Goals**	COACH3

1. Priority learning outcome from Step 1.5: _____

2. Present level of performance based on current assessment of the priority learning outcome:

   _____

3. What are the natural, age-appropriate contexts (places and activities) in which the student will be expected to use the skill/behavior this year?_____

   _____

4. What aspect of the priority learning outcomes should be reflected in the annual goal? Check all those to be addressed this year.

   __ Decreasing extra cues/supports   __ Acquiring core skills   __ Quality of performance

   __ Respond to natural supports   __ Expand repertoire   __ Tempo, rate, or fluency

   __ Generalization across settings, people, materials/cues   __ Extend or reduce duration   __ Retention over time

       __ Other   __ Other

       __ Other

5. What is the specific observable, measurable skill/behavior the team wants the student to learn this year? _____

   _____

6. Final annual goal (include contexts and skill/behavior): _____

   _____

Short-Term Objectives

Conditions	Skill/behavior	Criteria

Goal ____	**Annual Goals**	COACH 3

1. Priority learning outcome from Step 1.5: _____

2. Present level of performance based on current assessment of the priority learning outcome:
   _____

3. What are the natural, age-appropriate contexts (places and activities) in which the student will be expected to use the skill/behavior this year?_____
   _____

4. What aspect of the priority learning outcomes should be reflected in the annual goal? Check all those to be addressed this year.

   __ Decreasing extra cues/supports

   __ Respond to natural supports

   __ Generalization across settings, people, materials/cues

   __ Acquiring core skills

   __ Expand repertoire

   __ Extend or reduce duration

   __ Other

   __ Quality of performance

   __ Tempo, rate, or fluency

   __ Retention over time

   __ Other

   __ Other

5. What is the specific observable, measurable skill/behavior the team wants the student to learn this year? _____
   _____

6. Final annual goal (include contexts and skill/behavior): _____
   _____

Short-Term Objectives

Conditions	Skill/behavior	Criteria

Choosing Outcomes and Accommodations for Children, Third Edition.
Copyright © 2011 by Michael F. Giangreco. All rights reserved. Baltimore: Paul H. Brookes Publishing Co., Inc.

Program-at-a-Glance

Student's name: _____ Date: _____

List education program components: 1) highest priorities from Family Interview to be included in IEP; 2) Additional Learning Outcomes from COACH by curriculum area; 3) Additional Learning Outcomes from General Education (Step 2.2) by curriculum area, also indicate primary type of participation and example "starting point" learning outcomes; and 4) general supports by category and items.

(continued)

Program-at-a-Glance

Appendix D

Additional Blank Forms for Section IV

SCHEDULING MATRIX INFORMATION

All too often, team members expend significant effort developing an individualized education program (IEP) that is not reflected in the daily schedule of activities for a student. Students may be welcomed and included in general education activities, but not pursuing the individualized learning outcomes selected as their priorities or other targets of instruction.

A scheduling matrix is designed to address the aforementioned problems by explicitly comparing a student's goals and additional learning outcomes to a list of class activities (e.g., arrival routine, opening routine, language arts, science, physical education). The scheduling matrix is a divergent activity in which team members consider the possibilities for working on a student's learning outcomes (goals and objectives) within the various class activities. This process is aided by the information gathered in Step 2.2 (Additional Learning Outcomes from General Education), which documents the nature of a student's participation in general class (e.g., multilevel, curriculum overlapping). Of course, the scheduling matrix only can be used effectively when team members are familiar with both the student and the general education curriculum and context.

The second part of the scheduling process—developing a student schedule—is a convergent activity in which decisions are made about the possibilities generated using the scheduling matrix, and an appropriate number of goals and additional learning outcomes to be addressed in each class/activity are chosen. Deciding which goals will be addressed in which daily classes or activities requires team members to consider and balance a variety of issues based on generated criteria.

- Are there sufficient opportunities for the student to work on identified learning priorities/goals?

- Are there sufficient opportunities that pertain to the student's identified additional learning outcomes?

- Does the student's schedule follow the class routine as much as possible?

- Are learning outcomes and general supports addressed at the most naturally occurring times?

- Does the student have the same opportunities for breaks as students without disabilities so they have time to just be a kid?

- Does the student have the same opportunities for small- and large-group instruction as students without disabilities?

Your answers to these and other questions that arise as a result of scheduling may lead your team to rethink the range of the additional learning outcomes in the student's program, as well as how instruction occurs. Developing a student schedule provides a way to document which educational program components are addressed across all classes and activities. For example, for one student, the team decides that using a rubber stamp to write his name, greeting others, participating in groups, and making choices are learning outcomes to be addressed across all classes and activities. Other learning outcomes are addressed during specific classes or activities. When a schedule is completed, it provides clarity for a student's participation throughout the school day. By looking at the schedule, a teacher or paraprofessional knows what the instructional focus is for a student when he or she is in math, language arts, or any other class. The physical education, art, and music teachers have a clear understanding of their role with the child; of course, they should be involved in making such decisions. The schedule is adjusted as the student progresses through the school year and as team members learn more about the student.

Helpful Hints

1. Keep in mind that a student may participate in general education class activities with his or her classmates who do not have disabilities even if his or her learning outcomes are different from the rest of the class. This can be accomplished using multilevel curriculum and instruction and/or curriculum overlapping as discussed in the introduction to COACH.

2. Keep in mind the options available to students without disabilities in your school. For example, students in high school generally have more options for the types of courses they will take—use that flexibility to your student's advantage.

3. Limit the number of students with disabilities participating in any single activity to a natural proportion with students without disabilities. For example, in a whole-class activity of 25 students, you would expect to see about 3 students with disabilities, and only one of those with intensive educational needs. There is a danger that some schools or classes get targeted as the "inclusion classes" and end up with a disproportionately high number of students with disabilities.

Scheduling Matrix Directions

Purpose

To explore scheduling possibilities by comparing a student's educational program components with general class activities

Directions

1. List the student's name and grade in the spaces provided.

2. List general class activities or subjects (e.g., arrival routine, circle time, language arts, math, social studies, industrial arts, library, lunch, recess, music, science) across the top of the matrix.

3. List the typical amount of time devoted to that class or activity under each general class activity or subject. This refers to the amount of time, not the time of day.

4. List abbreviations of each annual goal (e.g., makes requests, makes choices, offers assistance to others) in the spaces provided on the left side of the matrix.

5. List the additional learning outcome categories from the student's Program-at-a-Glance (e.g., communication/language arts; socialization/health; selected academics/math) in the spaces provided on the left side of the matrix. Specific learning outcomes can be found on the student's Program-at-a-Glance.

6. For each item listed under IEP annual goals and additional learning outcome categories, work horizontally across the page to consider whether there are opportunities for the student to have learning experiences related to the entry being considered, or you can work vertically within a class. Put a mark to indicate a possibility in the intersecting box. Use whatever marking system makes sense to you, including 1) simple checkmarks, 2) numbers corresponding to the Program-at-a-Glance, 3) a designation regarding the type of participation (e.g., ML for multilevel; CO for curriculum overlapping), 4) a designation indicating whether the possibility is available currently (C) or could be with some adaptation (A), or 5) any unique codes that you design to fit your own situation.

7. Once the matrix is completed, go back to consider the learning outcomes under each general class activity. This is the convergent phase in which the team selects which learning outcomes make the most sense to address within the activity. Consider the time allotted to the activity as well as the ease of providing instruction on the targeted learning outcome and the materials and adaptations that will be needed. The information you generate with the scheduling matrix is used to develop the actual schedule in whatever format makes sense in your situation.

Helpful Hints

1. Using the matrix is a divergent step; therefore, explore the possibilities of "what is" as well as "what could be."

2. Involve the classroom teachers in making decisions about what will be addressed in their respective classes. Your team has a head start with the information generated in Step 2.2.

3. The completed matrix can sometimes highlight the fact that there is insufficient time available to work on certain learning outcomes. This might mean that new opportunities must be created so the student has sufficient learning opportunities. It may also mean that the number of additional learning outcomes may be too extensive and the team may need to reconsider the size. Alternatively, some of the additional learning outcomes may be considered consecutively, rather than addressing all of them simultaneously. For example, you could designate some of the additional learning outcomes for work during the first semester and others during the second semester.

Scheduling Matrix

COACH 3

Directions: List the IEP Annual Goals (Step 4), Additional Learning Outcomes categories (Steps 2.1 and 2.2), and class activities in the spaces provided. Use the intersections of the learning outcomes and class activities to note instructional possibilities to assist in scheduling.

Note: General supports will need to be considered when planning a schedule.

Student name: _____

Grade: _____

Minutes: _____

Class activities

IEP Annual Goals										
Additional Learning Outcome categories										

Planning and Adapting Instruction

COACH 3

Student: _____

Class activity/lesson: _____

Short-term objective: _____

Materials needed: _____

Planned by: _____   Implemented by: _____

Describe the sequence of what the instructor will do	Describe what the student will do (in observable terms)	Describe the consequences of correct and incorrect student responses	Describe how student progress will be measured and documented

Learning Style Inventory for Students with Complex and Challenging Disabilities

Timothy J. Fox and Virginia S. Iverson

Student name: _____ Date: _____

Completed by: _____

What are the student's strengths, gifts, and talents?

Interests and important relationships

Environment	Interests	Relationships
Home/neighborhood		
School		
Community settings (e.g., child care, dance class, recreational soccer, karate) 1. 2. 3. 4.		

(continued)

(continued)

Learning Style Inventory for Students with Complex and Challenging Disabilities

Influencing characteristics of the student's disabilities

Characteristic	Strengths	Challenges
Communication		
Social		
Sensory (e.g., hearing, vision, touch, taste, smell, balance)		
Physical (e.g., movement, mobility, manipulation, seating)		
Cognitive		
Health/medical		

(continued)

Learning Style Inventory for Students with Complex and Challenging Disabilities

Multiple intelligences	Strength rating	Target for instruction/practice
Picture smart (visual, spatial)	❏ Yes ❏ Somewhat ❏ No	
Body smart (bodily, kinesthetic)	❏ Yes ❏ Somewhat ❏ No	
Music smart (musical)	❏ Yes ❏ Somewhat ❏ No	
People smart (interpersonal)	❏ Yes ❏ Somewhat ❏ No	
Self-smart (intrapersonal)	❏ Yes ❏ Somewhat ❏ No	
Word smart (linguistic)	❏ Yes ❏ Somewhat ❏ No	
Logic smart (logical, mathematical)	❏ Yes ❏ Somewhat ❏ No	
Nature smart (naturalist)	❏ Yes ❏ Somewhat ❏ No	

Comments:

(continued)

(continued)

Learning Style Inventory for Students with Complex and Challenging Disabilities

Arrangements	Can do without adaptations	Can do with adaptations	Target for instruction	Skip for now
Large group				
Small group; teacher directed				
Small group; student directed				
Cooperative group				
Independent				
One to one in a small-group context				
Other				

Comments:

(continued)

(continued)

Learning Style Inventory for Students with Complex and Challenging Disabilities

Teaching methods	Great for this student	Okay for this student	Not beneficial for this student
Visual learner: learns by seeing/watching (e.g., visual organizers, demonstrations, modeling)			
Auditory learner: learns by listening (e.g., lecture, verbal directions, verbal models, discussions, questioning)			
Kinesthetic learner: learns by doing (e.g., coaching, hands-on activities, manipulatives, games)			
Drill and practice			
Computer-aided instruction			
Reflection and processing (e.g., one to one, group)			
Applied behavior analysis (e.g., shaping, fading, time delay)			
Other			

Comments:

(continued)

(continued)

Learning Style Inventory for Students with Complex and Challenging Disabilities 				
Student responses	Can do without adaptations	Can do with adaptations	Target for instruction	Skip for now
Look at				
Touch				
Pick up				
Point at				
Mark choice				
Say/sign/point to short answers				
Read aloud				
Express thoughts and feelings by:				
Make formal presentations using:				
Artistic (e.g., sing, dance, draw, recite, act)				
Other				
Comments:				

Choosing Outcomes and Accommodations for Children, Third Edition.
Copyright © 2011 by Michael F. Giangreco. All rights reserved. Baltimore: Paul H. Brookes Publishing Co., Inc.

(continued)

(continued)

Learning Style Inventory
for Students with Complex
and Challenging Disabilities

Materials	Can use without adaptations	Can use with adaptations	Target for instruction	Skip for now
Real items/objects (e.g., cup, spoon, ball, hat, gloves)				
Miniature objects (e.g., toy cars and animals, counting bears)				
Photographs				
Line drawings/symbols				
Words/numbers				
Graphic organizers				
Workbooks/worksheets				
Picture books				
Textbooks				
Paper and pencil				
Audio/visual (movies, slides, music, PowerPoint)				
Manipulatives (e.g., math counters, dice, game pieces)				
Concrete experiences				
Games (e.g., board games, cards, bingo)				
Other				
Comments:				

Activity Analysis

Virginia S. Iverson and Timothy J. Fox

Student name: _____ Date: _____

Completed by: _____

Instructional activity: _____ Days/times: _____

Setting/location:

Team members completing analysis:

Analysis of access to the environment

Environmental factors affecting access	Can access as is	Needs individualized adaptations	Possible types of individualized adaptations				
			Materials/ devices	Personal assistance	Sequence	Rules	Social/ attitudes
Temperature							
Lighting							
Complexity							
Acoustics/noise							
Time of day							
Arrangement (e.g., seating, furniture, location of materials)							
Equipment, tools							
Other factors							
Comments:							

(continued)

(continued)

Activity Analysis

Analysis of access to instruction

Instructional factors	Can access as is	Needs individualized adaptations	Possible types of individualized adaptations				
			Materials/ devices	Personal assistance	Sequence	Rules	Social/ attitudes

Arrangements/groupings typically used:
    Large group
    Small group
    Cooperative group
    Independent work
    Other							

Materials typically used:							
Knowledge and performance outcomes (e.g., write a paper, give a class presentation, take turns, share):							
Instructional strategies/activities (e.g., teacher presentation, class meeting, partner work, coaching):							
Evaluation strategies (e.g., performance rubric, tests, self-assessment):							
Other							

(continued)

(continued)

Activity Analysis

Analysis of activity and student participation

Activity steps/subroutines (what classmates are doing)	Can access as is	Needs individualized adaptations	Possible types of individualized adaptations				
			Materials/devices	Personal assistance	Sequence	Rules	Social/attitudes

(continued)

(continued)

Activity Analysis

	Individualized adaptations
Step/subroutine	Ideas for access and participation*

*Circle ideas to be implemented and keep others for future reference.

(continued)

(continued)

Activity Analysis

Planning for learning outcomes

Steps/subroutines	Ideas for learning*	
	From general education curriculum	From IEP

*Circle ideas to be implemented and keep others for future reference.

Evaluating Impact for Learning Outcomes

Student name: _____ Date of team meeting: _____

Team members participating in discussion: _____

_____

> 1. Annual goal or additional learning outcome(s) being discussed: _____
>
>   _____
>
> 2. Valued life outcome(s) being pursued through the learning outcome(s): _____
>
>   _____

3. When was the last time this learning outcome was discussed by the team?

   Date: _____

4. How frequently does the student have opportunities to work on this learning outcome? Are the number and types of opportunities sufficient? _____

   _____

5. What interventions or strategies have been used to teach the student this learning outcome since it was last discussed? _____

   _____

6. What progress has the student made on the learning outcome? _____

   _____

   _____

7. What changes, if any, has the student experienced on the corresponding valued life outcome(s)?

   _____

   _____

8. What changes, if any, need to be made in the educational program to enhance progress or facilitate the corresponding valued life outcome(s)? _____

   _____

   _____

Evaluating Impact for General Supports

Student name: _____ Date of team meeting: _____

Team members participating in discussion: _____

_____

1. General supports being discussed: _____

   Items: _____

2. Valued life outcome(s) being facilitated through the general supports: _____

   _____

   _____

3. When was the last time these general supports were discussed by the team?

   Date: _____

4. What has been done since then related to these general supports? _____

   _____

   _____

5. What is the current status of these general supports? _____

   _____

   _____

6. What changes, if any, has the student experienced on the corresponding valued life outcome(s)
   as a result of having these general supports provided? _____

   _____

   _____

7. What changes, if any, need to be made in the educational program regarding these general supports to facilitate the corresponding valued life outcome(s)? _____

   _____

   _____

COACH and Alternate Assessments: How Are They Related?

Harold L. Kleinert and Jacqui F. Kearns

In considering the relationship of COACH to alternate assessment for students with significant cognitive disabilities, we must first acknowledge the context of such a discussion. Alternate assessments based on alternate achievement standards are part of the educational accountability systems in the United States as mandated by the Individuals with Disabilities Education Act Amendments (IDEA) of 1997 (PL 105-17), Individuals with Disabilities Education Improvement Act of 2004 (PL 108-446), and No Child Left Behind (NCLB) Act of 2001 (PL 107-110). Alternate assessments for students with significant cognitive disabilities, in the context of these national laws, were designed to ensure that all students are included in school, district, and state measures of educational accountability (Kleinert, Quenemoen, & Thurlow, 2010) and the educational outcomes of students with significant disabilities are given equal weight to the educational results of all other students under the rubric of comprehensive school reform within this country.

A HISTORICAL PERSPECTIVE

When we developed the nation's first alternate assessment for students with significant cognitive disabilities in 1992 (Kleinert, Kearns, & Kennedy, 1997), there was no mandate for alternate assessment or even for access to the general curriculum within IDEA. It was apparent to us, however, as we were training teachers on the COACH process, that the essential elements of COACH were integral to elements of alternate assessment; namely, 1) the educational outcomes identified as important for all students also applied to students with significant cognitive disabilities, 2) the development of communicative competence was an essential foundation for all learning, 3) the domains or content of that learning occurred across multiple contexts (e.g., school, community), and 4) it embraced a broad perspective of what education means. Based on our initial work with alternate assessment for students with significant cognitive disabilities, we knew such assessment would have to measure priority skills of importance to both educators and families, and COACH provided such a framework. We thus saw COACH and alternate assessment as complementary tools to promote best practices for students with significant disabilities.

IDEA 1997 included the first requirements for alternate assessment and access to the general curriculum for students with significant cognitive disabilities. NCLB and IDEA 2004 included more explicit linkages between alternate assessment and grade-level content standards. This appendix explores the relationship between COACH and alternate assessment, especially as our understanding of alternate assessment has evolved over time.

As noted in the introduction to this volume, COACH is appropriate for students with significant cognitive disabilities who participate in their state's alternate assessment on alternate achievement standards (AA-AAS). Although COACH is also appropriate for other students with disabilities with intensive special education needs, the fact remains that many of these students (at least within the United States) will participate in their state's AA-AAS. As such, the primary purpose of this appendix is to highlight the relationship of COACH to best practices in alternate assessment and to briefly outline how using COACH can improve students' access to the general curriculum, their academic achievement within that curriculum, and thus enhance their performance on their state's AA-AAS. The second purpose of this appendix is to note the differences between alternate assessment and COACH; specifically, the scope of what they are intended to address. We will illustrate how COACH addresses valued life outcomes in their most complete sense (and, thus, a broad vision for the student's individualized education program [IEP]), whereas alternate assessments (as they are presently conceived) are designed with a narrower focus in mind (i.e., to measure academic performance linked to grade-level content standards set in place for all students).

RELATIONSHIP OF COACH PRINCIPLES TO BEST PRACTICES IN ALTERNATE ASSESSMENT

We first examine the relationship between the six guiding principles of COACH with what we believe are the essential elements of alternate assessment (Kleinert, Quenemoen, et al., 2010). We will consider each of the guiding principles of COACH and note its relationship to best practices in alternate assessment.

COACH Principle 1: All Students Are Capable of Learning and Deserve a Meaningful Curriculum

Alternate assessment is conceptualized as the tool through which even students with the most significant disabilities can participate in their state's respective educational assessment and accountability system. Even students with the most severe and multiple disabilities are to be included. Our alternate assessments research across nearly 13,000 students in 7 states (Kearns, Towles-Reeves, Kleinert, Kleinert, & Thomas, in press) documents that students who are at a presymbolic level of communication (e.g., students without any formal communication system) and who have other disabilities as well (e.g., motor, sensory, health) do participate in state alternate assessments. Of course, developing a formal communication system is a fundamental educational outcome for all students, and communication lies at the heart of curricular access for all students. Indeed, one of the powerful aspects of COACH is its focus on the domain of communication as an essential element in creating access to a meaningful curriculum for all students.

COACH Principle 2: Quality Instruction Requires Ongoing Access to Inclusive Environments

As with COACH, alternate assessment must be directly linked to "effective instruction, including direct student engagement" (Kleinert, Quenemoen, et al., 2010, p. 16). Although access to the general curriculum is theoretically attainable in noninclusive environments, it is not reasonable to expect special education teachers working in self-contained settings to replicate the academic instruction provided in general education classrooms with typical peers by highly qualified general education teachers who have extensive training and experience in teaching core academic subjects (Jackson, Ryndak, & Wehmeyer, 2008/2009).

COACH Principle 3: Pursuing Valued Life Outcomes Informs the Selection of Curricular Content

An overarching purpose of both COACH and alternate assessment is to improve educational results and, ultimately, life outcomes for students. As we noted, "Teachers must learn to use alternate assessment not only to document what the student has learned but also to actually *enhance* and *extend* that learning" (Kleinert, Quenemoen, et al., 2010, p. 16). An essential difference between the purpose of COACH and alternate assessment lies within the breadth of focus. COACH starts with "broad strokes" related to a set of valued life outcomes (i.e., safety and health, having a home, meaningful relationships, choice and control, meaningful activities in various and valued places) and uses information gathered from families to help set the context for selecting high-priority learning outcomes. Alternate assessment considers how performance in core academic domains linked to grade-level content improves that student's life, both at present and in the future.

COACH Principle 4: Family Involvement Is a Cornerstone of Educational Planning

Family involvement is certainly vital in both COACH and alternate assessment. Without parent involvement in the IEP, including alternate assessment (Kearns & Quenemoen, 2010), it cannot really achieve what it is intended to accomplish. Although families of students with significant disabilities are generally supportive of their child's participation in alternate assessments, parents express more reservations as students reach transition age, specifically about the balance of academic and life skill objectives essential for their child's education (Roach, 2006). The curricular balance many families seek is addressed by the various planning steps embodied in COACH that explore both functional life skills (Steps 1.1–1.5, 2.1) and general education curriculum (Step 2.2).

COACH Principle 5: Collaborative Teamwork Is Essential to Quality Education

Collaborative teamwork is essential for quality alternate assessments as it is for virtually all aspects of quality education. As we stated, "Alternate assessments are a team responsibility—it is not just the role of the special educator to implement these assessments, but general educators, related service personnel, school administrators, parents, and students themselves have essential roles in the process" (Kleinert, Quenemoen, et al., 2010, p. 16). For example, only about 70% of students participating in AA-AAS have symbolic forms of communication (Kearns et al., in press); moreover, communication development is a critical element for all students in the AA-AAS. Thus, speech-language pathologists (SLPs) can be essential partners in both instruction and assessment if students are to develop communicative competence, as may other related services providers (e.g., occupational therapists, physical therapists, assistive technology specialists, deafblind specialists). Furthermore, the active engagement and participation of general educators is essential to the collaboration because it is unlikely that special educators will have the deep curricular knowledge of the core academic subjects to effectively teach those subjects (Ryndak, Moore, Orlando, & Delano, 2008/2009). Finally, the student him- or herself has an active role to play, both in choosing curricular targets in COACH and in alternate assessment and in monitoring and evaluating his or her own progress on key academic measures.

COACH Principle 6: Coordination of Services Ensures that Necessary Supports Are Appropriately Provided

Without appropriate supports, students with significant cognitive disabilities will neither achieve the learning outcomes identified through COACH, nor be able to show what they know and can do through alternate assessment. Moreover, coordinating supports and services must lead to applying authentic, generalizable skills that truly reflect important life outcomes. As we noted, "Alternate assessment must allow the student to apply what he or she has learned; skills are not evidenced in isolation but are parts of complex performances that integrate skills across developmental and academic areas" (Kleinert, Quenemoen, et al., 2010, p. 18). Of course, it is a fundamental element of COACH that the IEP goals identified in the planning process should be taught in naturally occurring contexts across school, community, and extracurricular settings and embedded throughout the student's active participation in valued activities.

COACH AS A TOOL FOR ENHANCING PERFORMANCE IN THE GENERAL CURRICULUM

This section describes how COACH can be used as an effective tool for increasing access to, and performance within, the general curriculum linked to grade-level content standards. We first consider some basic terminology.

What Are Grade-Level Content Standards?

Content standards represent the "bones" of the curriculum, describing what students should know and be able to do at each grade in reading, math, and science as required by NCLB, or other content areas (e.g., social studies) may be assessed by individual states under IDEA 2004 assessment requirements for states and districts. For example, the common core standards for third-grade reading include such items as, "Students will identify the main and supporting characters in a story, or students will identify the common features of folktales" (Council for Chief State School Officers and National Governors' Association, March 2010a, p. 9). In the common core standards for second-grade math, examples include such skills as, "Students will solve math problems that require regrouping" and "Students will identify and construct 2–3 dimensional shapes" (Council for Chief State School Officers and National Governors' Association, March 2010b, p. 18). Similarly, standards in the primary grades for science might include items such as identifying parts of a plant, identifying simple machines, or demonstrating an electrical circuit.

What Are Achievement Standards?

Achievement standards specify the quality of a student's performance that results in determining proficiency. Achievement standards necessarily include components of content standards, but the two terms do not have the same meaning and, therefore, are not interchangeable. A student participating in an AA-AAS is generally not held to the same definition of proficiency as typical peers at the same grade level.

When developing a student's IEP, it is important to know what content standards will be taught in a specific grade so that the team can plan the supports and services necessary for the student to gain access to the general curriculum and, at a minimum, attain the level of proficiency described for the alternate achievement standards. This access to the general curriculum is "value added" as well because students with significant cognitive disabilities then have access to peers who are talking about and learning similar curricular content. For example, third-grade students may discuss a problem and solution proposed by an author within chronologically age-appropriate literature. Similarly, seventh-grade students may also discuss an author's proposed problem and solution, again with chronologically age-appropriate literature. It would not be appropriate for seventh-grade students, with or without significant cognitive disabilities, to use third-grade literature. This shared curriculum promotes opportunities for shared learning activities and enhances social and communication opportunities.

How Do These Terms Relate to the COACH Process?

The relationship between the content standards and the IEP represents a fundamental understanding. The COACH planning process allows student IEP teams to consider links to grade-level content standards, thereby integrating them into the IEP. Kearns and Quenemoen (2010) and Grisham-Brown and Kearns (2001) illustrated the relationship of the content standards, the curriculum, and the IEP (see Figure 35).

Using COACH as the tool for prioritizing critical learning outcomes (Grisham-Brown & Kearns, 2001) allows the IEP team to determine the most important skills and concepts necessary for access to the content standards that form the foundation of the general curriculum, as well as the skills necessary for active school and community participation. This relationship is especially clear in Step 2.2 (Additional Learning Outcomes from General Education). For example, within the COACH process, the team can designate academic learning targets that are the same as those of all other students (that is, fully aligned to grade-level content standards) or learning targets that address the same content/same subject, but at a different level of breadth or difficulty (multilevel curriculum, same content). In either of these cases, there

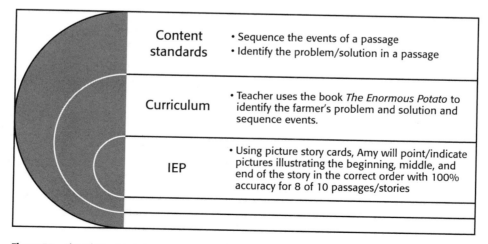

Figure 35. The relationship between content standards, the curriculum, and the IEP. (From Kearns, J.F., & Quenemoen, R. [2010]. Alternate assessments, families, and the individualized education program. In H.L. Kleinert & J.F. Kearns [Eds.], *Alternate assessment for students with significant cognitive disabilities: An educator's guide* [p. 292]. Baltimore: Paul H. Brookes Publishing Co.; reprinted by permission. *Source:* Grisham-Brown & Kearns, 2001.)

would be clear linkage to grade-level content standards. Any skill chosen for a student should be as closely linked (and even aligned) to the grade-level content standard as possible. Some state alternate assessments may actually require alignment to the grade-level content standard, so the IEP team will want to consider learning objectives that approximate as closely as possible the general education content standards. Indeed, some state alternate assessment scoring systems assign points for learning targets being closely aligned to the grade-level content standard in terms of depth and complexity.

Ensuring Student Learning

Ensuring student learning is the next step after the learning objectives have been identified for the IEP through COACH. Using research-based strategies is essential to facilitating student acquisition of the learning objectives. These strategies include 1) high levels of engagement, 2) multiple opportunities to practice across the day, 3) high levels of success, 4) systematic presentation, and 5) ongoing analysis of data (McDonnell, 1998). Some educators are concerned that the pace of the general curriculum moves too fast for students with significant cognitive disabilities. It is true that a second-grade teacher may spend less than 2 weeks on a single literary selection, such as reading and discussing the book *The Enormous Potato* (Davis, 1999), which may not be enough time for a student with significant disabilities to reach proficiency. The content standards (e.g., identifying the main characters, the author's purpose, the problem, and the proposed solution within the text), however, will be repeated through multiple literary selections across the school year, so any single reading selection serves as an exemplar to pursue a broader learning outcome. Similarly, the skills identified in the IEP for students with significant cognitive disabilities should specify objectives that can be practiced across the school year. In addition, the criterion for determining mastery should be specified in consultation with a general education teacher who has content expertise in the general education curriculum content standard.

IMPORTANT DIFFERENCES BETWEEN COACH AND ALTERNATE ASSESSMENT

This final section describes some essential differences between the intent of COACH and that of alternate assessments. We should first note that the IEP must address two clear priorities:

> (aa) meet the child's needs that result from the child's disability to enable the child to be involved in and make progress in the general education curriculum; and (bb) meet each of the child's other educational needs that result from the child's disability (IDEA, 2004, Sec. 614.[d][1][A][i][I][aa]IN)

Clearly, COACH is intended to address both sets of priorities, whereas AA-AAS are focused on measuring student performance related to the first priority; namely, access to, and progress within, the general curriculum. Most specifically, as we have noted earlier, alternate assessments must be linked to grade-level content standards (U.S. Department of Education, 2005). In this sense, alternate assessments are designed to measure the extent to which students with significant cognitive disabilities are given access to the same curricular content as students without disabilities, albeit with alternate performance standards of reduced breadth, scope, and/or complexity (U.S. Department of Education, 2004).

Within the previous statutory requirements for the content of IEPs, COACH represents a curricular planning tool that ensures that both sets of essential needs are addressed. Moreover, within the COACH process, individualized needs are grounded in the valued life outcomes of the Family Interview (Step 1), a process highly individualized to the unique circumstances of each family—this differs from the framework for alternate assessments. Although alternate assessments do allow for some degree of individualization, noting that states use differing assessments and formats, they are meant to measure a common core of content applicable to all students.

Finally, it is important to note the challenges that teachers of students with significant cognitive disabilities face in addressing both sets of IEP priorities and finding the appropriate balance between academic and life skill instruction (Flowers, Ahlgrim-Delzell, Browder, & Spooner, 2005; Towles-Reeves, Kleinert, & Muhomba, 2009)—this need not be an either/or proposition. For example, Kleinert, Collins, Wickham, Riggs, and Hager (2010) explained that instruction on life skills can be effectively embedded in core academic instruction. Yet, for teachers and other members of the school team, this is easier said than done. One of the essential elements of COACH is looking at critical life skills and the additional learning outcomes within the general curriculum and how teams might plan to embed basic and/or life skill instruction (e.g., communication, socialization, personal management) in academic and other school activities throughout the student's day. In this sense, COACH offers a map for how teachers might realize the promise of alternate assessment for their students. In other words, students with significant cognitive disabilities can learn academic content with their peers, and we can set high expectations individualized to all students, while simultaneously grounding learning in the ultimate outcomes that define a better life.

REFERENCES

Council for Chief State School Officers and National Governors' Association. (March 2010a). *Common core state standards for English language arts, and literacy in history, social studies, and science.* Retrieved April 5, 2010, from http://www.corestandards.org/Files/K12ELAStandards.pdf

Council for Chief State School Officers and National Governors' Association. (March 2010b). *Common core state standards in mathematics.* Retrieved April 5, 2010, from http://www.corestandards.org/Files/K12MathStandards.pdf

Davis, A. (1999). *The enormous potato.* Toronto: Kids Can Press.

Flowers, C., Ahlgrim-Delzell, L., Browder, D.M., & Spooner, F. (2005). Teachers' perceptions of alternate assessments. *Research and Practice for Persons with Severe Disabilities, 30,* 81–92.

Grisham-Brown, J., & Kearns, J.F. (2001). Creating standards-based individualized educational programs. In H.L. Kleinert & J.F. Kearns (Eds.), *Alternate assessment: Measuring outcomes and supports for students with disabilities* (pp. 17–28). Baltimore: Paul H. Brookes Publishing Co.

Individuals with Disabilities Education Act Amendments (IDEA) of 1997, PL 105-17, 20 U.S.C. §§ 1400 *et seq.*

Individuals with Disabilities Education Improvement Act (IDEA) of 2004, PL 108-446, 20 U.S.C. §§ 1400 *et seq.*

Jackson, L., Ryndak, D., & Wehmeyer, M. (2008/2009). The dynamic relationship between context, curriculum, and student learning: A case for inclusive education as a research-based practice. *Research and Practice in Severe Disabilities, 33/34,* 175–195.

Kearns, J.F., Towles-Reeves, E., Kleinert, H.L., Kleinert, J.O., & Thomas, M. (in press). Characteristics of and implications for students participating in alternate assessments based on alternate academic achievement standards. *Journal of Special Education.*

Kearns, J.F., & Quenemoen, R. (2010). Alternate assessments, families, and the individualized education program. In H.L. Kleinert & J.F. Kearns (Eds.), *Alternate assessment for students with significant cognitive disabilities: An educator's guide* (pp. 291–302). Baltimore: Paul H. Brookes Publishing Co.

Kleinert, H.L., Collins, C., Wickham, D., Riggs, L., & Hager, K. (2010). Embedding life skills, self-determination, and other evidence-based practices. In H.L. Kleinert & J.F. Kearns (Eds.), *Alternate assessment for students with significant cognitive disabilities: An educator's guide* (pp. 267–290). Baltimore: Paul H. Brookes Publishing Co.

Kleinert, H.L., Quenemoen, R., & Thurlow, M. (2010). An introduction to alternate assessments: Historical foundations, essential parameters, and guiding principles. In H.L. Kleinert & J.F. Kearns (Eds.), *Alternate assessment for students with significant cognitive disabilities: An educator's guide* (pp. 3–18). Baltimore: Paul H. Brookes Publishing Co.

Kleinert, H., Kearns, J., & Kennedy, S. (1997). Accountability for all students: Kentucky's alternate portfolio system for students with moderate and severe cognitive disabilities. *Journal of The Association for Persons with Severe Handicaps, 22,* 88–101.

McDonnell, J. (1998). Instruction for students with severe disabilities in general education settings. *Education and Training in Mental Retardation and Developmental Disabilities, 33,* 199–215.

No Child Left Behind Act of 2001, PL 107-110, 115 Stat. 1425, 20 U.S.C. §§ 6301 *et seq.*

Ryndak, D., Moore, M., Orlando, A., & Delano, M. (2008/2009). Access to the general curriculum: The mandate and the role of context in research-based practice for students with extensive support needs. *Research and Practice in Severe Disabilities, 33/34,* 199–213.

Towles-Reeves, E., Kleinert, H., & Muhomba, M. (2009). Alternate assessment: Have we learned anything new? *Exceptional Children, 75,* 233–252.

Roles of Team Members Supporting Students with Disabilities in Inclusive Classrooms

Michael F. Giangreco, Jesse C. Suter, and Victoria Graf

PREMISE

For decades the literature has offered descriptions of roles for paraprofessionals in special education. These descriptions have shifted from being primarily noninstructional duties to those that are increasingly instructional in nature. There has been disagreement within the field about just how far instruction-related roles of paraprofessionals should extend. In part, the premise of this appendix is that, even in situations where there is agreement about paraprofessional roles, such agreement is insufficient to pursue effective education in inclusive schools. This requires clarifying and agreeing on the roles of all team members, understanding their interrelationships, and ensuring that they are consistent with IDEA (e.g., free appropriate public education, least restrictive environment) and exemplary practice described in the professional literature. This appendix highlights key roles for team members based on available research and contemporary practices considered desirable in inclusive schools; it is not meant to be a comprehensive list of competencies. See the resources at the end of this appendix that formed the basis for the roles, along with our collective experiences in inclusion-oriented schools.

The following individuals provided editing feedback that helped shape this appendix through their involvement in the Inclusive Special Education Service Delivery Consortium as part of Project EVOLVE Plus at the University of Vermont's Center on Disability and Community Inclusion: Carolyn Dickinson, Peg Gillard, Joan Larsen, Carrie Lutz, Blythe Leonard, Allegra Miller, Walter Nardelli, Marianne Nealy, Leslie Noble, Scott Orselet, Duane Pierson, Don Schneider, Carter Smith, Susan Stewart, Barbara Tomasi-Gay, Beverly White, Lauren Wooden, and Michael Woods.

USING THIS DOCUMENT

Your team or school is encouraged to use this appendix as a starting point to consider the respective roles of team members in your own setting. You can self-assess the status of the conceptual underpinnings (see Table 3) and roles of team members in your school or start a discussion among school faculty and families. Following review and discussion within your school, you are encouraged to modify this appendix by changing the wording, adding or deleting items, rearranging the content, or otherwise editing the document so that it assists you in clarifying team members' roles. A digital version is available on the CD-ROM accompanying this edition of COACH to facilitate any modifications you find desirable. The next step is to explore ways to put these roles into action by using them as a basis for identifying staff development and support, in hiring, orientation, collaborative teamwork, and supervision.

EVERY TEAM MEMBER'S OVERLAPPING ROLES

Every team member contributes to the education of students with disabilities in inclusive schools and classrooms by:

E1 Ensuring a safe and healthy environment for learning

E2 Collaborating and communicating with other team members to develop, implement, and evaluate the individualized education programs (IEPs), access to the general education curriculum, and individually determined supports

E3 Participating in team meetings and offering ideas and input to educational program and support decisions

E4 Advancing his or her own learning to acquire or improve the attitudes and skills necessary to successfully include students with the full range of disabilities in the classroom (e.g., evidence-based practices)

E5 Advocating to ensure that students' educational and support needs are adequately addressed in ways consistent with IDEA, state standards, and evidence-based practices, as well as appropriate independence and interdependence

Table 3. Conceptual underpinning

Roles of team members **should**	Roles of team members **should not**
Be grounded in collaborative teamwork based on shared purpose and goals	Be based on disjointed approaches based on individual purposes or separate goals
Be consistent with their respective skills, knowledge, training, and certification/licensure to engage in tasks they are qualified to undertake	Include engaging in tasks for which they are inadequately qualified
Be complementary, synergistic, and based on evidence-based practices	Be contradictory, working at cross-purposes, or lack an evidence base
Result in equitable opportunities for students with disabilities (e.g., participation in class/school activities and environments, access to instruction from highly qualified teachers and special educators, access to the general education curriculum, access to appropriately modified/adapted curriculum and instruction, access to necessary supports)	Result in inequitable, though unintended, double standards (e.g., restricted involvement in class/school activities and environments, separation from classmates, inadequate access to instruction from highly qualified teachers and special educators, inadequately modified/adapted curriculum and instruction, inadequate or unnecessary supports)
Contribute to positive outcomes for students with disabilities (e.g., classroom membership, achievement of individually appropriate learning outcomes, positive peer relationships, access to increasing opportunities)	Interfere with positive outcomes by inadvertently creating barriers to membership, access to inclusive settings, achievement, peer relationships, or other opportunities available to students without disabilities

TEACHER ROLES

Teachers contribute to the education of students with disabilities in inclusive schools and classrooms and demonstrate educational ownership by:

T1   Cocreating opportunities that facilitate the valued membership of all students in the classroom (e.g., location of desk, purposeful student grouping, purposeful participation, preplanning instruction), including those with the full range of disabilities

T2   Serving as a primary adult role model for the class to demonstrate acceptance and inclusion of individuals with diverse characteristics (including disabilities) as well as problem solving when faced with unique challenges

T3   Knowing the student's learning characteristics, performance levels, and individualized learning outcomes (e.g., IEP goals, general education curriculum)

T4   Engaging students with disabilities in classroom instruction and activities in various groupings (large group, small group, individual) at a level commensurate with other students in the class who do not have disabilities

T5   Retaining a prominent role in curricular and instructional planning, adaptation, and decision making with special educators and related services personnel to adapt and modify curriculum and instruction in ways that facilitate participation of students with disabilities in typical class activities

T6   Applying differentiation, universal design, multilevel instruction, and curriculum overlapping so that students who perform at substantially different levels can pursue individually determined learning outcomes within shared class activities

T7   Facilitating interactions between peers with and without disabilities by teaching students with disabilities prosocial behaviors, applying positive behavior supports, and teaching students without disabilities how to interact with their classmates who have learning differences

T8   Codirecting (along with special educators) the work of paraprofessionals who are present in the classroom by:

- Discussing the student's characteristics, educational program, and general support needs

- Talking about the school and classroom (e.g., expectations, procedures)

- Training related to paraprofessionals roles as described in a clear job description (e.g., evidence-based literacy approaches, positive behavior supports) through a variety of options (e.g., workshops, teacher modeling, online learning)

- Planning for paraprofessional interactions and lessons with students so that they are not inappropriately expected to make pedagogical decisions

- Monitoring paraprofessional performance and communicating with them about their work in both formative and summative ways

SPECIAL EDUCATOR ROLES

Special educators contribute to the education of students with disabilities in inclusive schools and classrooms by:

S1   Cocreating opportunities that facilitate the valued membership of all students in the classroom (e.g., location of desk, purposeful student grouping, purposeful participation, preplanning instruction), including those with the full range of disabilities

S2   Serving as a primary adult role model for the class to demonstrate acceptance and inclusion of individuals with diverse characteristics (including disabilities) as well as problem solving when faced with unique challenges

S3   Maintaining a working knowledge of the general education curriculum and practices (e.g., classroom units, lesson plans, assessment practices) in order to contribute to contextually appropriate supports and maintain high expectations for student learning

S4   Providing specially designed instruction in a variety of formats, such as coteaching with the classroom teacher, teaching small mixed-ability groups, or individual tutoring, ensuring that the combination of individually determined instructional formats are implemented in concert with classroom teacher(s) and context, not merely providing instruction in the physical classroom space in ways that may be disconnected from its overall operation or resorting to primarily pull-out instruction

S5   Retaining a prominent role in curricular and instructional planning, adaptation, and decision making with classroom teachers and related services personnel to adapt and modify curriculum and instruction in ways that facilitate participation of students with disabilities in typical class activities

S6   Applying differentiation, universal design, multilevel instruction, and curriculum overlapping so that students who perform at substantially different levels can pursue individually determined learning outcomes within shared class activities

S7   Facilitating interactions between peers with and without disabilities by teaching students with disabilities prosocial behaviors, applying positive behavior supports, and teaching students without disabilities how to interact with their classmates who have learning differences

S8   Codirecting the work of paraprofessionals with classroom teachers by
   • Discussing the student's characteristics, educational program, and general support needs
   • Talking about the school and classroom (e.g., expectations, procedures)
   • Training related to paraprofessionals roles as described in a clear job description (e.g., research-based literacy approaches, positive behavior supports) through a variety of options (e.g., workshops, teacher modeling, online learning)
   • Planning for paraprofessional interactions and lessons with students so that they are not inappropriately expected to make pedagogical decisions
   • Monitoring paraprofessional performance and communicating with them about their work in both formative and summative ways

S9   Applying creative problem-solving principles to extend the power of a team's collaborative efforts

S10 Providing primary case management (e.g., facilitate team meetings and interactions, complete required paperwork such as IEP, conduct special education evaluations, serve as a key liaison with families and collaborating agencies)

PARAPROFESSIONAL ROLES[1]

Paraprofessionals contribute to the education of students with disabilities in inclusive schools and classrooms and help create opportunities for classroom teachers and special educators to spend time instructing students with disabilities and collaborating with each other by:

P1   Implementing supplemental (not primary) small-group and individual instruction (e.g., academic, functional, prosocial) and homework help for students with disabilities that has been planned by a qualified professional

P2   Engaging in classwide instructional monitoring of student work (e.g., independent or small-group work) identified and planned by teachers and special educators

P3   Collecting data on student performance and progress based on data collection systems designed by teachers or special educators

P4   Assisting students who require personal care supports (e.g., eating, using the bathroom, dressing)

P5   Facilitating peer interactions based on guidance from the teacher and special educator (e.g., teaches prosocial skills, fades presence and supports as appropriate, invites students to help each other)

P6   Engaging in noninstructional tasks (e.g., clerical tasks; group supervision such as in the cafeteria, on the playground, bus boarding, field trips) identified by teachers and special educators

P7   Responding to reassignment by school administrators as student and classroom needs change (e.g., student illness, student crisis, student success, personnel changes)

RELATED SERVICES PROVIDER ROLES

Related services providers contribute to the education of students with disabilities in inclusive schools and classrooms by:

R1   Providing supports that have been determined by a student's educational team to be educationally relevant (for IEP goals and access to general education curriculum) and educationally necessary (required to receive an appropriate education) and, therefore, are linked to one or more aspect of a student's educational program (IEP goals, general education curriculum, accommodations/supports)

R2   Providing supports that allow for student access or participation in typical school and class environments and activities

R3   Providing supports in places and ways that are contextually compatible within the classroom schedule, activities, and culture

R4   Selecting or developing adaptive equipment that allows for access, active participation, or prevents negative outcomes (e.g., regression, discomfort, pain)

---

[1]Paraprofessionals referred to here may be funded by special education, general education, or some combination. Funding streams may influence their respective roles. Because IDEA "allows for paraprofessionals who are properly trained and supervised to assist in the delivery of special education," they are present to support and supplement the work of teachers and special educators, not supplant them. Therefore, it is inappropriate and undesirable for paraprofessionals to 1) provide the bulk of instruction for a student; 2) be asked to provide support in any subjects in which they are not qualified; 3) plan or adapt curriculum, instruction, or data collection; 4) serve as the primary liaison with the family; 5) develop behavior plans; 6) make decisions about where or when a student receives instruction; or 7) function as a student's primary friend in school.

R5   Consulting with team members to transfer information and skills associated with their field to others (e.g., positioning a student for learning, programming an augmentative and alternative communication [AAC] device) that fits within inclusive educational contexts

R6   Serving as a resource or support to the family pertaining to their field of specialty

R7   Working directly with students to apply skills associated with their field to address students' educational or support needs (e.g., teaching braille, providing counseling)

R8   Working with team members to determine when supports should be continued, modified, faded, or discontinued based on relevant student data

ADMINISTRATOR ROLES

Administrators, including building or district-level special education and general education administrators (e.g., superintendents, principals, assistant principals), contribute to the education of students with disabilities in inclusive schools and classrooms and display leadership and commitment to using inclusive practices by:

A1   Communicating clear expectations about collaboration among team members and their respective roles

A2   Communicating clear expectations and encouraging inclusive attitudes among all team members about the value, shared responsibility, inclusion, and instruction of all students with and without disabilities

A3   Facilitating scheduled opportunities for collaboration among teachers, special educators, teacher assistants, and other services providers (e.g., master schedule, staff development, planning opportunities)

A4   Providing access to relevant staff development opportunities related to inclusive practice (e.g., coteaching, universal design for learning, peer supports, directing the work of paraprofessionals, assistive technology, curriculum adaptation)

A5   Ensuring constructive working conditions for personnel (e.g., staffing ratios, reducing paperwork burden, ensuring natural proportion of students with and without disabilities)

A6   Ensuring the number of paraprofessionals assigned to any one professional (e.g., teacher, special educator) allows adequate opportunities for directing paraprofessional work as well as providing professionals with guidelines and a process for directing paraprofessional work and providing them with ongoing feedback and support

A7   Making all personnel assignment decisions, supervising and evaluating all school personnel, and making arrangements to monitor any contracted personnel related to students with disabilities

A8   Providing support to faculty, staff, students, and families during student crisis situations

A9   Leading the school and/or district's annual service and school improvement planning for serving students with disabilities

STUDENT AND PARENT ROLES[2]

Students with disabilities and their parents contribute to the education of the student with a disability in the family within an inclusive school and classrooms by:

F1   Developing an understanding of the student's strengths, interests, and needs (including information about his or her disability)

F2   Offering information and insights to the team about the student that contributes to educational planning and learning (e.g., motivations, interests, disability characteristics, learning styles, talents, history)

F3   Identifying or selecting a set of the highest learning priorities for the year that become a focus for the team

F4   Making informed decisions about choices within the general education program and curriculum (e.g., elective courses, foreign language, cocurricular activities)

F4   Helping to identify supports necessary for student success

F5   Monitoring student progress and applying learned skills to nonschool settings (e.g., home, community)

F6   Communicating key information to the team about health, mental health, and community issues that may have a bearing on the student in school

F7   Playing a prominent role in long-range educational and transition planning as the only team members likely to be part of the educational team throughout the school career

RESOURCES

Carter, E.W., Cushing, L.S., & Kennedy, C.H. (2009) *Peer support strategies for improving all students' social lives and learning.* Baltimore: Paul H. Brookes Publishing Co.

Causton-Theoharis, J., Giangreco, M.F., Doyle, M.B. & Vadasy, P.F. (2007). Paraprofessionals: The "sous chefs" of literacy instruction. *TEACHING Exceptional Children, 40*(1), 57–62.

Crockett, J.B. (2002). Special education's role in preparing responsive leaders for inclusive schools. *Remedial and Special Education, 23*(3), 157–168.

DiPaola, M.F., & Walther-Thomas, C. (2003). *Principals and special education: The critical role of school leaders* (COPSSE Document No. IB-7). Gainesville: University of Florida, Center on Personnel Studies in Special Education. Retrieved January 25, 2009, from http://www.personnelcenter.org/pdf/copsse_principals.pdf

Doyle. M.B. (2008). *The paraprofessional's guide to the inclusive classroom: Working as a team* (3rd ed.). Baltimore: Paul H. Brookes Publishing Co.

Fisher, D., Frey, N., & Thousand, J. (2003). What do special educators need to know and be prepared to do for inclusive schooling to work? *Teacher Education and Special Education, 26*(1), 42–50.

Gerlach, K. (2001). *Let's team up! A checklist for paraeducators, teachers, and principals.* Washington, DC: National Education Association.

Giangreco, M.F. (2001). *Guidelines for making decisions about I.E.P. services.* Montpelier: Vermont Department of Education. Retrieved November 22, 2009, from http://education.vermont.gov/new/pdfdoc/pgm_sped/data_reports_pubs/guidelines_iep_decisions.pdf

Giangreco, M.F., Broer, S.M., & Edelman, S.W. (2001). Teacher engagement with students with disabilities: Differences between paraprofessional service delivery models. *Journal of The Association for Persons with Severe Handicaps, 26*(2), 75–86.

Giangreco, M.F., Carter, E.W., Doyle, M.B., & Suter, J.C. (2010). Supporting students with disabilities in inclusive classrooms: Personnel and peers. In R. Rose (Ed.), *Confronting obstacles to inclusion: International responses to developing inclusive schools* (pp. 247–264). London: Routledge.

Giangreco, M.F., CichoskiKelly, E., Backus, L., Edelman, S.W., Tucker, P., Broer, S., CichoskiKelly, C., & Spinney, P. (1999, March). Developing a shared understanding: Paraeducator supports for students with disabilities in general education. *TASH Newsletter, 25*(3), 21–23.

Giangreco, M.F., & Doyle, M.B. (2004). Directing paraprofessional work. In C.H. Kennedy & E.M. Horn (Eds.), *Including students with severe disabilities* (pp. 185–204), Boston: Allyn & Bacon.

Giangreco, M.F., Edelman, S., Dennis, R., Rubin, R., & Thoms, P. (1999). Vermont's guidelines for related ser-

---

[2]The balance of involvement among the student him- or herself compared with parents/guardians varies widely based on the age of the student, cultural norms of the family, and the student's ability to effectively communicate and self-advocate.

vices: Supporting the education of students with disabilities. *Physical Disabilities: Education and Related Services, 18*(1), 35–49.

Giangreco, M.F., Prelock, P.A., Reid, R.R., Dennis, R.E., & Edelman, S.W. (2000). Role of related service personnel in inclusive schools. In R.A. Villa & J.S. Thousand (Eds.), *Restructuring for caring and effective education: Piecing the puzzle together* (2nd ed., pp. 360–388). Baltimore: Paul H. Brookes Publishing Co.

Hines, J.T. (2008). Making collaboration work in inclusive high school classrooms: Recommendations for principals. *Intervention in School and Clinic, 43*(5), 277–282.

Hoover, J.J., & Patton, J.R. (2008). The role of special educators in a multitiered instructional system. *Intervention in School and Clinic, 43*(4), 195–202.

Hunt, P., Soto, G., Maier, J., & Doering, K. (2003). Collaborative teaming to support students at risk and students with severe disabilities in general education classrooms. *Exceptional Children, 69*, 315–332.

Jericho Elementary School Faculty. (2009). *Team member roles.* Jericho, VT: Author. Unpublished document.

Jorgensen, C.M., Schuh, M.C., & Nisbet, J. (2005). *The inclusion facilitator's guide.* Baltimore: Paul H. Brookes Publishing Co.

McLeskey, J., & Waldron, N.L. (2002). School change and inclusive schools: Lessons learned from practice. *Phi Delta Kappan, 84*(1), 65–72.

Olson, M.R., Chalmers, L., & Hoover, J.H. (1997). Attitudes and attributes of general education teachers identified as effective inclusionists. *Remedial and Special Education, 18*(1), 28–35.

Riehl, C.J. (2000). The principal's role in creating inclusive schools for diverse students: A review of normative, empirical, and critical literature on the practice of educational administration. *Review of Educational Research, 70*(1), 55–81.

Riggs, C.G., & Mueller, P.H. (2001). Employment and utilization of paraeducators in inclusive settings. *Journal of Special Education, 35*, 54–62.

Schnorr, R.F. (1997). From enrollment to membership: "Belonging" in middle and high school classes. *Journal of The Association for Persons with Severe Handicaps, 22*, 1–15.

Soodak, L.C., Podell, D.M., & Lehman, L.R. (1998). Teacher, student, and school attributes as predictors of teachers' responses to inclusion. *Journal of Special Education, 31*, 480–497.

Villa, R.A., Thousand, J.S., Nevin, A., & Malgeri, C. (1996). Instilling collaboration for inclusive schooling as a way of doing business in public schools. *Remedial and Special Education, 17*, 169–181.

Index

Page numbers followed by *f, t,* and *n* indicate figures, tables, and footnotes, respectively.

Notes

Notes

Notes

Notes